MANNER OF SPEAKING

OTHER BOOKS BY JOHN CIARDI

Mid-Century American Poets, 1950
From Time to Time, 1951
Dante's *Inferno* (tr. and ed.), 1954
As If, 1955
I Marry You, 1958
Thirty-Nine Poems, 1959
How Does a Poem Mean?, 1960
In the Stoneworks, 1961
Dante's *Purgatorio* (tr. and ed.), 1961
In Fact, 1962
Dialogue with an Audience, 1963
Poetry: A Closer Look, 1963
Person to Person, 1964
This Strangest Everything, 1966
Dante's *Paradiso* (tr. and ed.), 1970
Lives of X, 1971

Books for Children

The Reason for the Pelican, 1959
Scrappy the Pup, 1960
I Met a Man, 1961
The Man Who Sang the Sillies, 1961
You Read to Me, I'll Read to You, 1962
The Wish Tree, 1962
John J. Plenty and Fiddler Dan, 1963
You Know Who, 1964
The King Who Saved Himself from Being Saved, 1965
The Monster Den, or Look What Happened at My House and to It,
    1966
Alphabestiary, 1967
Someone Could Win a Polar Bear, 1970

Manner of Speaking

John Ciardi

RUTGERS UNIVERSITY PRESS
New Brunswick   New Jersey

Second Printing

Copyright © 1972 by Rutgers University, the State University of New Jersey

Library of Congress Cataloging in Publication Data

Ciardi, John, 1916–
  Manner of speaking.

  Essays reprinted from the author's column in the
Saturday review.
  I. Title.
PS3505.I27M3   814'.5'2   72–4862
ISBN 0–8135–0731–6

Manufactured in the United States of America by Quinn & Boden, Inc.,
Rahway, New Jersey

With the exception of "Goodbye," all pieces in this collection appeared
in the *Saturday Review,* copyright © 1961, 1962, 1963, 1964, 1965, 1966,
1967, 1968, 1969, 1970, 1971, 1972, by Saturday Review, Inc.

For Norman Cousins.
   Thanks for all bygones, Norman.
   And tomorrow the World.

Contents

viii

MANNER OF SPEAKING

Circles

The biographical approach to ideas—at least as the plodding literalist takes it—can be the readiest path to blindness. His is the simple splendid assumption that the life of the reverie and of the imagination must correspond directly to the factual bones of a man's biography. Keats loved Fanny Brawne. Keats wrote love poems. Therefore the love poems of John Keats are about Fanny Brawne. To the plodding literalist such a chain of reasoning is self-evident.

There is, to be sure, a firm half-truth in such a one-to-one correspondence of things. Fanny Brawne was certainly involved in whatever is happening in at least some of the love poems of Keats. It is the nature of the involvement that the literalist oversimplifies. Were the poems written as direct descriptions of Fanny Brawne as Keats thought her to be? Were they written over her head to the conceptual Fanny Brawne Keats dreamed of finding within his actual Fanny Brawne? Or were they written to the conceptual Eve that Keats wished he had instead of the makeshift Fanny Brawne he had to settle for as the best he could do under the circumstances?

I am not at all sure what started this ramble around Keats and Fanny Brawne. Perhaps it is part of my penalty for having gone back to school, if only to summer school. I have been teaching a course at the summer session of the University of Wisconsin-Milwaukee (as distinct from the University of Wisconsin-Madison) and, as ever, I have been troubled by the hunger of students to simplify the connection between one thing and another. But I also find another thought teasing my mind, and I find that, like my

3

students, I am tempted to say "because such and such happened, I am left with the thought that . . ."

The fact is I do not know what put the idea into my mind. Nor for that matter, is the idea any revolution in the history of Western thought. Yet it seems apt to our divided times, and, if only in that context, it seems worth a ramble of its own.

Simply stated, it is the idea that every man has two complete (or more or less complete) sets of emotions. The bigot is never a man completely given to hatred. He has a set of hatreds for the objects of his bigotry, but he also has a set of loves, if only for himself. No man can live by hate alone. A hatred is an outraged love.

All of us draw something like a circle within which we include all the things we are for. On the other side of that more-or-less circle lie all those things we are against. We may be against them more or less actively. Or we may be against them by excluding them from our immediate sympathies. The point is that they are excluded.

All of us, moreover, must exclude something from our immediate sympathies. We cannot—or so at least we are tempted to believe—identify with everything. Shelley, for example, was moved to draw his circle of identification wide enough to include sheep. He has left us a number of impassioned passages inveighing against the heartlessness of men who slaughter the lamb that looks at them with trusting brown eyes. Shelley had, however, the good grace and the logical coherence to be a vegetarian. Let no man understand me as advocating cruelty to lambs. It happens, however, that I am very much "for" lamb chops. Since I know of no way of getting lamb chops except from a lamb, and since it seems in every way more humane to get them from a dead lamb rather than a living one, I am in favor of slaughtering lambs. To that extent, therefore, I exclude lambs from my circle of sympathies, though I retain enough sympathy for the beasts to wish their deaths to be painless.

Am I wrong in thinking that every man has to draw his circle somewhere? Holy men of the East have made it their vocation to make the circle all-inclusive, but their one remaining possibility upon achieving such all-inclusiveness has been to starve to death, for even the grain of wheat is a living thing. The mystery locked

4

within it can make an inch of this earth beautiful, and the man who eats it destroys the possibility of that mystery. What man of the West, however, would pay such a price for the identification of his sympathies with all creation?

We are, moreover, a competitive society, and every competition is another way of drawing the circle. We put our teams in the middle of the stadium and the stands on one side of the field break into cheers when the stands on the other side groan with misery. The boys in the bombers cheered when a Japanese plane broke into flames and groaned when one of their own planes started to pour black smoke. And what man over the target of his own life and death is going to stop and think that what is burning inside either plane, whether friend or enemy, is a man like himself, a nervous system like his own, an agony to be wished upon no man in the context of our sympathies.

The bigot differs from the man of sympathies only in degree. Within his circle of identification the bigot feels as tenderly as any man can. It is not the lack of tender feelings that marks the bigot, but the nature of his exclusions. Like every man, he draws his circles protectively. What we put outside the circles of our sympathies is put there because we feel that it conflicts with what we put inside. I, for example, can feel a sympathy for the death of puppies that I cannot feel for the death of lambs, and the obvious reason is that I have been conditioned against any desire for puppy chops. Where there is no conflict no division is necessary.

I hope, however, that most of my exclusions are within the range of reason and revision, though it must be an arrogant man who dares assume that he has within him no preconditionings from sources deeper than reason and therefore beyond the revision of reason.

All of us, I must conclude, have the seeds of a possible bigotry within us. When we call another man a bigot, we mean that, in our view, his exclusions are too categorical. Most of us would call a man a bigot because he excludes for such reasons as religion, nationality, skin color, or peculiarities of pronunciation. Yet I must confess that the history of two world wars has conditioned me to a fundamental distrust of Germans, at least of German-Germans. But my wife's maiden name was Hostetter, and my own children are thereby partly German.

5

For that matter I am myself remotely German. The name "Ciardi" is not natively Italian. It's root is Lombard, and the Lombards entered Italy from Germany under Alboin in the seventh century. At the point of entry the name was Gerhardt. But ask an Italian to say "Gerhardt" and he will say "Gherardi." In time Gherardi softened to Gerardi, which passed readily to Cerardi, which in turn shortened to Ciardi. All I can add in support of my prejudice against these German goosesteppers is that my family has had 1,300 years to get over its doubtful beginnings and that it had the good sense to crossbreed with the tribal mixtures left over from the Greek colonies around Vesuvius. That admixture, plus various incidental rapes by various incidental invaders, is called a lineage at something like a racial average: the human race, that is.

I am left with no defense against the countercharges of the bigot except in the strength of my confusions. For the essence of the bigot's confusion is in his certainty. Hatred and certainty are the mother and father of this, our unloveliest child. To the extent that all of us fear something, and therefore incline to hate what we fear, there must be some trace of that fatherhood in all of us, our old Adam. But let our sympathies find their motherhood in a sense of things made supple by the grace of confessed uncertainty, and something like civil hope may yet walk on our clay feet.

August 24, 1963

Term Paper Time and No Thanks

I taught college English for most of twenty years and let me confess that the prospect of release from student maunderings and student papers was one compelling reason for giving up habit and

6

tenure to gamble as a free lance in my declining years. It is even possible that by "declining" I mean "no thanks."

I had not known, though I soon learned, that to be listed on the masthead of a magazine, even as a part-time visitor to the premises, was to live in a constant dribble of letters from students who had been given a paper to write, and who wanted me to write it for them.

At first, still conditioned by academic habit, I was tempted to help the helpless. It took me a while to learn that either compassion or water poured into cracked vessels can only leak out. No man can have his questions answered until he has thought how to ask them, and I soon learned that no question addressed to me in a letter from a student was likely to be touched by a trace of thought.

In my next phase, I was moved to answer students with an avuncular scolding about their methods and with a few notes on how to use a library. Such letters, however, if they were answered at all, only produced a cry to the effect that the local library lacked all the resources I had mentioned (the willful little liars!) and would I, therefore, define poetry, or write a page or two explaining why I was a poet, or give my impressions of William Butler Yeats (was he really a good poet?)—and so endlessly *da capo* until I became inured.

In my third phase, I took to composing snappy form letters, to be signed by my secretary, and to be left in my files as proof that I was some sort of wit. One such letter run:

Dear Sir:
Mr. Ciardi regrets that he is behind in his own homework and is, therefore, unable to undertake yours.

Sincerely,
Ima Dragon
(Sec. to J.C.)

The act of composing such letters can serve as a sort of release. The trouble with them is that they are obviously too stupid to mail. Having composed them, therefore, I always ended up by chucking them into the wastebasket.

From that point it was an easy step to the fourth phase in which

I chucked all such letters into the wastebasket to begin with. Nothing in mortal man better defines his character than his sense of which letters to chuck into the wastebasket at sight. His chuck rate of the trivial, I am prepared to assert, is a direct measure of his sense of serious purpose.

I have been in that fourth phase of my always questionable character for some time (students and teachers, please note). I am aware that, in one legend of civility, it is rudeness to throw a letter away unanswered. In an even more basic idea of civility, let me suggest that it is oafish to toss off unconsidered questions in the hope that a man with his own work to do will take time to do your thinking for you. Has no one suggested to American students that when they want favors from a stranger they are under a civil obligation to do all that is in their power to ease the work of the entreated stranger? I had assumed such an obligation to be a basic teaching. I can only report that it seems to be unknown to the young, either as courtesy or as simple shrewdness.

My character is, by now, formed and I am determined to answer no such letters. But the young, I suspect, broadcast their letters. They deal in statistical response, and I can certainly advise them on how to improve that response. To begin with, they are foolish not to inclose a stamped, self-addressed return envelope. Such an envelope is not enough in itself to assure a reply, but it will at least testify to a minimum sense of civility, and such a testimony will swing some decisions in their favor.

What is more likely to elicit a response is some indication that the student has thought his questions through to reasonable specification. "Can you tell me what inspires a poem?" is not only a stupid question, but an unmanageable one. A considered questionnaire, on the other hand, might ask (leaving spaces for brief replies): "Do your poems generally take off from a felicitous phrase? from an image? from bare idea? from a rhythm? in some other way?" Such a questionnaire might reasonably bid for an answer. For my part, I have never seen a student's letter whose questions have been specified in any such detail.

For such reasons, I thought my fourth phase was my last. I have, as a matter of fact, yet to see a student's question I have not addressed more than once in print. Why, then, should I write

8

essays for students who will not go to the library to dig out the essays I have already written?

A recent letter, however, persuades me that there is a fifth phase to go through before the wastebasket swallows all. The letter, from a student in a small town in Oregon, reads:

I have been asked to write a paper on what I would like to do for a living. I have been considering a career as a poet. Can you write me a short summary on how you became a poet, such as the educational requirements, whether or not you are satisfied with your work, where you have your works published, and approximate salary a beginner can expect.

I enter my fifth phase with the thought that no student could write so stupid a letter entirely on his own resources. Idiocy of this order could be achieved only under instruction. I clearly have a final scolding to scold, but it must obviously be addressed not to the student but to the teachers who encourage students to such acts of public idiocy. My fifth phase will consist, therefore, of a single open letter I must get off my chest, after which the wastebasket shall once more be the place of eternal rest, and this column (I hope) need never again address the mail order curriculum:

Dear Teacher:

The letter(s) I have received from your student(s) suggest that you have chosen me (probably among others) to serve as your assistant in what they call "writing a term paper," and in what I am tempted to think of as their confirmation in idiocy.

I should perhaps be grateful for your confidence in me, but my more powerful inclination is to think of your teaching methods as deficient.

I note, first, that the questions I have received are mindless in a way I do not readily associate with the young. Could it be that they are under some duress to reflect a mindlessness not their own? I hesitate to inquire further into the source of that mindlessness. I am, perhaps, naturally suspicious. Yet, let me recommend the inquiry to your own reflections.

My suspicions, I realize, may be unworthy. Yet it seems certain from the letter(s) I have received that no one has taught them how to use a library. Might not that be part of your responsibility?

Perhaps your local library facilities are limited. In that case, might it not be your duty to assign papers that can be based on existing resources? Whatever the facilities, good research method has a common base.

Have you considered that it might not be fair to students to make them base their research on letters to strangers? What happens to their grades when the stranger decides not to answer? This sort of prepubescent mail-order request for material, I suggest, leaves too much to chance. On any such measure, I have myself been the cause of hundreds of failing grades.

I will certainly deny that any student with a postage stamp may use me as part of your teaching method, if any. And I will insist that urging students to mail off ill-considered letters is a poor substitute for responsible teaching.

Your duty is to teach method of inquiry, ideas, and criteria. If you are unable to perform that duty, there is always a demand for waitresses and for charwomen. There is, that is to say, honest work available. I should think any such work might be more useful than the act of posing as a teacher only to teach infant methods to the merely juvenile.

In any case, I should like you to know that I have begun a private blacklist, and that any further letters from students in your school will be answered by my detailed private assessment of you as a teacher, with carbon copies to your superintendent of schools and to your board of education. Which is to say, I dare you.

Yours truly,
John Ogre Ciardi

April 5, 1969

Mailbag

The following two letters arrived from Minnesota in the same envelope and are here faithfully transcribed:

To John Ciardi
  John Ciardi your writing is very bad in the book I Met a Man because you do not put periods. On pages 1–2–3–4–6–9–10–11–12–14 and all the rest of the pages I do not understand because you did not put a period. On page 62 sentences 1–4 and 8, I do not understand because you put commas instead of perionds. So copy the book over please because I love it.

From Kathy K [no periond]

Sir:
  My daughter is eight years old and reads constantly.
  Please understand, in her letter she could not realize the form of the poems in your charming book, *I Met a Man*, but she is quite sensitive to the sentence structure in the majority of childrens books & could not help but notice the change.
  I do not expect you to interrupt your busy schedule with a *detailed* explanation but it is so important to her, I'm sure you understand my concern.
  Thank you again, from Kathy and:

Mrs. J.K.

Look, Kathy. Look.
See the poet.
The poet is fat.
He is fifty.

He is dull.
He is sitting at his desk writing a book.
Has he written a lot of books at his desk?
He has written twenty-five of them.

The desk is not tidy.
Make him tidy it.
It is a mess.
It is covered with all the periods he did not put in his books.
Make him put in the periods.

Where shall he put the periods?
Shall he put them after the titles of poems?
It is not necessary to put periods after the titles of poems.
Shall he put them at the end of every line?
It is not necessary to put a period at the end of every line of a
poem.
Where shall he put them?
Don't you know?
Ask Mommy.
Doesn't Mommy know?
Make him put them in anyway.

Look, Kathy. Look.
See the little girl.
She is pretty.
What is the little girl doing?
She is reading the book.
Why is she frowning?
She is frowning because she does not understand.
When the fat, dull, fifty-year-old poet does something the little
girl does not understand, the fat, dull, fifty-year-old poet is wrong.
Make him copy it over.

Look, Kathy. Look.
See the mommy.
What is the mommy doing?
She is being concerned.
She is understanding the little girl.

12

She is making sure the little girl expresses herself.

The mommy does not wish to confuse the little girl with information.

It is more important that the little girl be understood.

It is more important that the little girl express herself.

The little girl is sweet.

The mommy loves her and does not wish to confuse her.

Does the fat, dull, fifty-year-old poet love her, too?

Yes, he does, but he has children of his own to fight free of.

Does he understand his children?

He relentlessly refuses to understand them.

Does he make sure his children express themselves?

He is unable to stop them but he tries.

Does he scold his children?

Yes. Hopefully. But he is afraid it is a lost cause.

Is he going to scold the little girl?

No, he is scolding the mommy.

Why is he scolding the mommy?

He is scolding her for spoiling the little girl.

He doesn't care whether or not the little girl is entirely understood.

He says *he* has been waiting fifty years to be understood.

He says the little girl can wait.

He says the little girl has more time than he has.

He does not want to copy the book over.

He says he wrote it right the first time and he is working on another book and needs his time for that.

He says he wants the mommy to copy the book over.

He wants her to copy it over a hundred times on the blackboard.

Why must mommy copy the book over?

She must copy it over for not explaining to the little girl.

What does he want her to explain to the little girl?

He wants the mommy to explain that the poet is fat, dull, fifty, and much smarter than the little girl.

He wants the mommy to tell the little girl that the fat, dull, old poet knows a lot more about periods than the little girl does.

He wants the mommy to explain that it is only willfully cute to tell the fat, dull, old poet to copy the book over.

He wants the mommy to explain the difference between a title and a sentence.

He wants the mommy to explain the difference between a line of poetry and a sentence.

Doesn't the fat, dull, old poet care whether or not the little girl is understood?

He does care, but only within limits.

He says *he* wants to be understood.

Doesn't the fat, dull, old poet care whether or not the little girl expresses herself?

He does care, but only within limits.

He says *he* wants to express himself.

What? At fifty!

That is much too old for being understood!

That is much too old for expressing oneself!

That is ridiculous!

What a fat, dull, old poet!

What a pretty, bright-eyed, understood, self-expressing, little girl!

What a silly mommy!

Copy all of them over.

February 26, 1966

Kathy, the Bad Man, and Charlie McCarthy

My recent column in reply to Kathy's mother moved our loving readers to so many snarling letters accusing me of various degrees of assault on eight-year-old girls that I am left variously, if only partially, moved. I am moved, first, to an open disclaimer, second,

14

to a confession of recurring amazement at such storms in the mail-bag, and, third, to make my correspondents a psychic gift in acknowledgment of the pleasure I found in reading their far-ranging interpretations of my character, all of which were at least accurate, no matter how wide of any known mark.

To the first point, and as an open declaration of principle, I hereby announce that I never even think of assaulting girls until they are at least eighteen (and preferably at least thirty-eight) and that these days any such notion is purely and nostalgically conceptual.

To the second point, despite what should by now be an experienced anticipation of nonsense-by-mail, I must still confess that I have trouble understanding the premises on which most letter writers base their indignations. Could they actually believe that I was writing to Kathy? Or that I expected Kathy to turn up as a reader of my column? Perhaps the column itself is written to an eight-year-old level, but I may still rest secure in the belief that the *SR* around it is an adult preserve, and one that would invite no child to wander through looking for the gingerbread man.

Certainly it seemed clear enough to me that I was writing to Kathy's mother in a way that would be invisible to Kathy. I was, to be sure, scolding mother, though mildly enough, heaven knows. Why should I not scold mothers who thrust their cute children upon me? Nor did I ever think to deny the fact that this child was as sweet, cute, and coy as any other sweet, cute, and coy child in the act of being mother-thrust upon a stranger.

To the extent that Kathy's mother was motivated by loving motherhood, I suppose I shall have to give her my vote. But to the extent that her letter was a foolish puff, and that Kathy's questions could have been simply answered by any minimum literacy, without mother's coy fluttering for attention, I withhold my vote in the psychic election. I am myself a parent, and I have enough home-grown coyness without having to borrow more.

As I have explained before now in this column, I am not exactly against motherhood. I have even gone so far as to instigate some of it. As a matter of relative concepts, however, I think I should find motherhood to be a more intrinsically admirable condition were the prerequisites higher. It can, after all, happen to almost any girl. It is even likely to happen soonest to the most foolish.

And before the whole world is conditioned to stand and cheer at the drop of the concept, it may be as well to remember that motherhood produced, among other things, Caligula, Bluebeard, Simon Legree, Hitler, and the present defendant.

All these, as I say, are sentiments the world has forced upon me before now. And though I have found good reason to believe that motherhood can enrich and deepen a girl's life, I have yet to be convinced that it serves, *per se*, to make the bearer a wiser human being. A silly girl who becomes pregnant may go on the Hallmark register as a madonna, but she may just as readily come off it as a silly girl who has had a child.

Such were my interlinear sentiments in writing as I did, and I submit that they were suggested so far behind the lines that even had Kathy stumbled upon my column, and even had she been forced to memorize it, she could not have guessed them out in the time it takes for seven maternities. Any assault of which I am accused will have to be identified as taking place at such a distance from the victim that she could not even have felt the wind of my flailing arms. But no such question of the assaulter's distance from his victim seems to matter to the hair-trigger literalists among the letter writers, nor does it matter that the terms of the purported assault are such that they could not conceivably strike the sensibilities of the purportedly stricken child. My column pretended to be addressed to Kathy: it was, therefore, addressed to Kathy, and that's that.

Theirs is an elemental logic and one that reminds me of those simple souls of a few generations ago who once clustered around the radio to hear a ventriloquist named Edgar Bergen carry on with a dummy named Charlie McCarthy, and who then flooded the studios with mail addressed to the dummy.

Since, in this case, the dummy mail was addressed to me, I am bound to grant my letter writers one more native insight. But whose? And into what? And what is the human category of those who write to the dummy without even addressing the letter in care of the ventriloquist? The least I can do in the public interest is to recommend this sort of behavior to sociologists for a formal report to be titled "The Charlie McCarthy Syndrome."

It is with some such prospect of the public good before me, and in personal gratitude for a fine catfight of loving and indignant

16

snarling over a mouse that wasn't there in the first place, that I come to my third point and offer my correspondents the grateful gift of an ultimately insubstantial bait to claw at.

The following letter was whispered to me in a dream by the talking doll of a little girl who lives not far from me. The little girl is sweet. She has a mother. She may even grow up undistorted by that state of affairs. She does not know her doll has been whispering to me in my dreams. She does not know the bad man is getting ready to kick her sweet little doll's teeth in, if only in a dream prologue to a dream of reason.

But the readers know, don't they? The readers are Love. They will have a loving time of kicking *my* teeth in when they read my bad, bad imaginary reply to the sweet, sweet letter I never got from anyone. The readers are Love whether or not there is anyone there to be loved. I, too, am Love. My bad, bad answer (a direct quotation from at least half of my remarks to my own children) is my grateful gift to the kind of Love that loves to snarl. Nice, nice readers. Sweet, sweet letter. Bad, bad answer. Have fun, boys and girls. Have fun, readers.

Dear Mister Ciardi:
I am the little girl's doll. The little girl loves me. Do you love me? She reads your poems to me. If I were a little girl, I would become an English major, especially if I had a mother. Please tell me how to write poems, and why, and how to be an English major, and especially how to get a mother.

Your little friend,
Sweetina

Dear Sweetina:
Shut up, you conceptual brat. I'm busy.

April 16, 1966

Mailbag: Letters I Wish
I Had Mailed

Dear Miss D.:
   If you must absolutely have my philosophy of life by next Tuesday in order to get your English report written, I am afraid you will have to brace yourself for a flunk. I doubt I could produce a good one even by next Friday. I have found that it takes me at least two weeks to formulate any adequate set of life principles. Even then it becomes a rush job and is likely to leave some questions partially unanswered.

                                                          Yours regretfully,

Mrs. F.L.K.
San Diego, California

Dear Mrs. K.
   It is possible that you and I might find some points of agreement along the way but it would certainly be a mistake to begin by assuming that we will.

                                                          Yours sincerely,

Master Ronald G.
Miss Fifield's Fourth Grade
Rote School
Ad Libit, U.S.A.

Dear Ronald:
   You have me confused with Webster's Dictionary. Webster's is that book on Miss Fifield's desk. If you look inside it, you will

find words arranged in alphabetical order. That arrangement makes them easy to find, once you have learned to spell.

The words you are looking for are in bold-face type. The lighter type that follows explains where they probably came from and approximately what they mean. It is a simple and workable system and I think you would find it much easier than writing to strangers asking them to explain what is right there on Miss Fifield's desk.

Unless you have been snitching your father's stamps again, it is also five cents cheaper, and that, as you know, is a whole wad of bubble gum.

Once you have discovered how easy it is to use a dictionary, I hope you will explain it to Miss Fifield. I think it would be thoughtful, too, if you saved all that extra bubble gum you will be able to buy, and gave it to Miss Fifield. You might surprise her by sticking it on her chair after you have finished chewing it. I am sure she will be surprised to discover how much you have been able to save just by learning to use the dictionary.

Your friend,

J.C.S., Counselor at Law
Chicago, Illinois

Dear Counselor:

The document I am returning herewith has produced an interesting discussion around the office. My secretary and the girl at the desk next to her think it was intended as a letter, but most of us feel there has been one of those mixups in which you put a brief in the envelope addressed to me. If that is the case, I certainly hope you did not put your letter to me in an envelope addressed to a client.

On the other hand, if this compendium was actually written as a letter there cannot be many clients to break in on your free time.

In either case, I hope you will understand why I cannot reply to your specific points in adequate detail. The fact is I read *War and Peace* instead, being a bit rushed for time.

Yours gratefully,

Miss Katy J.
Third Grade
Loch Sitt School
Suburbia, U.S.A.

Dear Katy:
   I am sorry I cannot send you a picture of me taken while writing a poem. It takes inspiration, and inspiration is like a huge searchlight: it glows all around the poet and makes him too bright for the camera. One of the reasons poets can afford to be poor is that they can write by inspiration-light and not have an electric light bill to pay.
   Your teacher knows all about these things. She has been to college and knows how to glow. Ask her to glow for you. Don't be discouraged if she refuses at first: keep after her and tell her I said she has to show you. I am sure she will finally do it, especially if you scream and stamp your feet. Just make sure you scream loud enough and stamp hard enough. Remember that we sometimes have to work hard for the things we want in this world. In the long run she will admire you for your perseverence.

Your friend and ally,

April 17, 1965

When Do They Know Too Much?

A friend of mine, in the happy business of playing games with his bright daughter, taught her to read by the time she was four. "She snatched the words from me and they stuck with her," was his way of putting it. So it was that she entered kindergarten at least three or four years ahead of "Look, Dick, Look." And so it was that she had not been in school much more than a week before Dad was called in and scolded for having "overaccelerated her."

It used to be that teachers complained because they had to do so much of the work that should be done by the home, the church, and the social group. It also used to be an ideal of American life to build the home around reading, music, and the guidance of parents who had something to teach. Now, on the other hand, it seems parents do badly when they encourage their chicks to learn. They may even "overaccelerate" them. Which, in turn, may raise the terrifying possibility of interfering with "peer-group adjustment." There is even the danger that the bright kid (I mean "the gifted child") may come out smarter (I mean "more enriched") than the dopes (I mean "children of more average performance").

Before irate defenders of that faith we call the School System accuse me of insulting their profession and dedication, let me say I know a thankless job when I see one, and that I know and regret the practical necessities that clutter the path of the good teacher. To keep the whole truth in view, however, let me also say that I have taught teachers in many parts of the country, and that at least half of those I have met in my classrooms were so utterly of "more average performance" that it is high time to restore the good sound word "dopes" to the vocabulary. But if that truth, as I have found it, offends any foot on which the shoe pinches, let it also speak a praise of those truly "enriched" teachers in whom we must rest the greater hope, in that they must overcome not only the normal problems of teaching but the inferiority of many of their colleagues.

The one problem above all others in today's school system is, of course, overcrowding and the consequent pressure to standardize methods. What else could explain—to return to my distressed father of the bright daughter—a teacher who scolds parents for sending her a child who knows too much? Too much more than what?

There are two answers to that last question. Many teachers would incline to say "too much more than the child's group"— that peer-group that has become the fetish of the religion of "social adjustment," a religion which, in an earlier development of the tribe, was called "conformity" and as often scorned as admired.

21

There can, of course, be dangers, both real and imagined, in letting a child lose touch with others of his own age. The left-out chick may have an unhappy childhood, and such a childhood can damage both the child and the person the child grows into. On the other hand, a manageable amount of social maladjustment can be just the blessing that drives a child to introspection and even to ideas.

Nothing is certain, except perhaps that happiness will not be legislated. As Robert Frost was fond of saying, "You have to have a chance to lose." My sympathies—and gratitude—are all with the teacher who spots trouble in a child and sends out the call for psychiatric help. But they are equally with the teacher who lets the child take as many psychic lumps as he can absorb. Taking lumps is, after all, a basic conditioning for life in this universe.

I remain firmly out of sympathy with the theory that says an enshrined peer-group must determine how much it is well for a child to know at what point. I happen to have one happy slow-poke at home, the sweet oaf of my litter, and my fear for him is exactly that he is too disgustingly close to his mindless peer-group. The day I catch him being "group disoriented" (if that is the phrase for it), I mean to shower bribes upon him in the hope of buying his way to suspicion.

But if social adjustment to the group is the real good, who is to say that a really bright child, if he has been loved (which is basically to say, if he has been played with by parents who found honest pleasure in the play), cannot put down his book, reach for a football helmet, and turn into a tearing-toodlum with the dumbest, most average, and best-adjusted of them?

Very well, there may be some merit in the first answer, especially if one offers it in partial distrust. I still suspect that the second answer is the operative one: a child who knows "too much" more than his group is a child who can most readily be damaged by the enforced mass-methods of our crowded school system. Such a child might flower in the happy sun of individual attention, but he is likely to stub his toe on plain boredom when he must be held back from his normal stride in order to travel in company formation.

As far as the School System is concerned, that leaves the problem where it has always been: in the hoped-for hands of the good teacher; of the underpaid, overworked, overregulated, good teacher who cannot resist the eyes that burn toward him with a brighter light than shines from the others, and who will somehow manage to meet great need at the expense of his or her already taxed energy.

As far as the parent of the bright child is concerned, I conclude he must either find that teacher or take the teacher's place. My friend was lucky in being able to send his daughter to a private school that could offer individual attention. But having sinned against conformity in playing happy games with his daughter, he also took on the happy expiation of continuing to play with her, and thereby to teach at home. I suspect that had he not been able to afford the private school, he could still have made it his happy hobby to teach his child while teaching her to adjust, as she would have had to do, to the pace of the school system, but to keep feeding her more at the rate determined by her own happy hunger. Which is to say, Mother and Dad, you begot them, and if you are not ready to stand to the consequences of your own begetting, I am blessed if I see that you have any right to complain.

May 11, 1963

Hair Styles and Harebrains

Somewhere within our hope for civilization and our doubt that it can really work lies the school system, and within it, between hope and doubt, there comes the case of George Leonard. George lives in Attleboro, Massachusetts, and was doing well in high school there, though his time after hours was largely spent in banging a Beatlesome guitar while shaking his shoulder-length hair and emitting sounds. When so engaged, he bills himself as Georgie

23

Porgie and earns (or, in any case, is paid) money as a professional musician.

Joseph E. Joyce is principal of the Attleboro High School, a position near the top of the Attleboro School System and one apparently dedicated to a social segment that might be called American Society's Simple Earnest Souls. It seems natural for an administrator of this order to protect the mythical A.S.S.E.S. from the perils of long hair, and Mr. Joyce accordingly ordered Georgie to get a haircut or get out. Georgie, however, refused to be clipped, claiming that his hair style is essential to his professional career.

Since September, Georgie and his father have been arguing at law to protect Georgie's professional locks, and the case, having failed in Superior Court, is being appealed to the State Supreme Court with the Leonards' expressed intention to fight it to the United States Supreme Court, headline by headline, if need be.

Pending the appearance of a tattooed lady in one of our classrooms (the indelible instance), I don't know how the courts will rule on the right of students to maintain hair of a professional length, but it does occur to me that Georgie's position can be supported by general precedent within the American school system. Had he, for example, grown those locks for a part he was to take in the school play, any school would have accepted them as a temporary and self-explaining oddity, perhaps on the order of a beard raised for Frontier Day. I am suggesting that the school system doesn't really care how odd you are—it just wants to make sure you have an excuse, a written one if possible.

And still I wish the Leonards had based their case on the simple right of parents and children to work out at their own pleasure the length at which the family hair will be worn, rather than on the plea of professional, and, therefore, commercial, interest. When there are two principles to defend, always choose the higher.

Nevertheless, I am not the man to insist on purity of motive. If that long hair is good for Georgie's career, the publicity he has come by in this fight is certainly not bad for it. Let him have this addition to the cause, for whatever it may be worth, and let him fight it out on whatever grounds will win, and may he win. Man or boy, the duty to respect authority ceases when authority becomes unreasonable.

Meanwhile from Westbrook, Connecticut, comes the case of Edward T. Kores, student, and Arnold Oliver, Superintendent of Schools. Superintendent Oliver did not kick Edward out of school because of long hair. A man of nicer distinctions than are evident in Attleboro, Superintendent Oliver threw Edward out for combing his hair into bangs. As the New Haven *Register* reports the Super's explanation to Mr. and Mrs. Kores, "he wasn't suggesting that their son cut his hair but must comb it to the side while he's in school—to conform with school standards."

The Koreses, bless them, fought back but were powerless against the Super's position as supreme hair stylist of the Amalgamated School System (not to be confused with that other A.S.S.). They have, nevertheless, defended their son's right to a reasonable case of W.H.I.M. (What Humanity Is Mostly), and Edward is now in private school. May he learn there by what measure to honor parents who would rather pay up an extra tuition than bow to arbitrary stylists.

For that Super is no man to forego stylistic authority and was, according to the AP, about to "refer the matter to the circuit prosecutor for action." If Edward wouldn't comb his hair to please the Super, the Super would get the arm of the law to wield the comb. There, I submit, stands a man of purpose. Let no one tell me Americans have lost character.

On the other hand, no man need be willfully surprised when the school system displays its character at the expense of some of those tonalities some citizens associate with intelligence and civilization. I do not know how mindless we must all become before we can be fully organized for administrative purposes, but I am grateful to Mrs. Keith L. Rader of Woonsocket, Rhode Island, who writes me that she heard the principal of a Tulsa high school tick off the Georgie Porgie case on TV and summarize it by declaring that, "He must learn a lesson in conformity."

It is easy to understand that the school administrators would love to take over that lesson. Yet let me doubt that they are entirely qualified.

When I was suffering my assault by the school system (and it, mine) it seemed rather remarkably sure it knew all about how to

25

teach that lesson. We weren't, to be sure, quite as affluent then as now. A number of the kids had patches on their pants and more than a few were just plain raggedy. We couldn't have been put into tie-and-jacket uniformity for the good reason that some of the kids didn't have ties and jackets.

But if poverty left us relatively free, the propriety of the school system certainly kept the teachers nailed to a tight psyche. A schoolmarm in those days was a civic nun. It was well into the Thirties before she could "bob" her hair without disgracing herself, and even then she might lose her job for a touch of rouge, or for smoking a cigarette in her own room at Mrs. Sniff's boarding house.

It was the post-Victorian lesson in conformity, and if many of the spinsters bore it well enough, there were always a few in every school who were all but certifiably daft, and for good reason. Yet no school official, you may be sure, had any public doubt of his entire rightness in teaching his good old conformity lessons. The functionary mind is beyond the deepening of doubt.

What it has, instead, is a taste for conformity. The clear and lucid dream of all small administration is made up of identical units clicking in place. But the existence of that taste is no reason for issuing the bearer an unlimited license. Let me suggest, rather, that the schools think of themselves as agencies of a civilization, bearing in mind that one firm measure of a civilization (as distinguished from a technology) is an inclination to honor personal differences and even personal eccentricities within reasonable limits. Let the school system teach that lesson to the young, and it can count on the young to teach themselves conformity.

Nor am I arguing for anarchy. Every parent delegates a reasonable authority to the schools and is reasonably liable for its enforcement. How the young act in school is properly school business. But how they look when they leave for school (also within reasonable limits: say, at least, from the neck up)—that, I shall insist, is family business and any family may reasonably demand the right to arrange it to its own taste.

May 1, 1965

26

More Positive Expressions

When I was a boy in school (the old man said) we had bright kids, dumb kids, and what everybody thought he meant by just plain "us." We also had wild ones, tough guys, sissies, regular guys, dirty rats, sneaks, squealers, snot-noses, and teachers' pets. Our classifications were primitive and savage, but so were we, and our lines of communication were reasonably firm.

As it now turns out, we were all wrong. There are no dopes in the school system, but only "those capable of doing better." There are no brighties either, but only "more able learners." Which obviously leaves what the kids used to call "us" to go down as "able learners."

For a joyously detailed rundown of this new dispensation I am indebted to Mrs. D. H. MacMahon of Baldwin High School, Milledgeville, Georgia, who sent me a pamphlet called "Conference Time," prepared by the National School–Public Relations Association of the National Education Association of the United States (1201 16th Street N.W., Washington 6, D.C.), from which the pamphlet may be ordered at 60 cents a copy (plus 10 per cent discount on orders of two to nine, 20 per cent on orders of ten or more).

One part of the pamphlet, entitled "Watch Your Language," cautions teachers against expressions that may leave "a negative impression" and then tabulates the following "Negative Expressions" which are paired with the following "More Positive Expressions" (the parentheses are mine):

Must: Should.
Lazy: Can do more when he tries.
Trouble Maker: Disturbs class.

27

Uncooperative: Should learn to work with others.
Cheats: Depends on others to do his work. (!!)
Stupid: Can do better work with help.
Never does the right thing: Can learn to do the right thing.
Below average: Working at his own level. (!)
Truant: Absent without permission.
Impertinent: Discourteous.
Steal: Without permission. (?)
Unclean: Poor habits.
Dumbbell: Capable of doing better.
Help: Cooperation.
Poor: Handicapped.
Calamity: Lost opportunity. (?)
Disinterested: Complacent, not challenged. (Teacher flunks for misusing "disinterested" for "lack of interest.")
Expense: Investment.
Contribute to: Invest in.
Stubborn: Insists on having his own way.
Insolent: Outspoken. (I think teacher flunks again.)
Liar: Tendency to stretch the truth.
Wastes time: Could make better use of time.
Sloppy: Could do neater work.
Incurred failure: Failed to meet requirements. (Oh, my God!)
Mean: Difficulty in getting along with others.
Time and again: Usually.
Dubious: Uncertain.
Poor grade of work: Below his usual standard. (!!)
Clumsy: Not physically well coordinated.
Profane: Uses unbecoming language. (I'll bet teacher doesn't know how to distinguish "profanity," "blasphemy," and "obscenity.")
Selfish: Seldom shares with others.
Rude: Inconsiderate of others.
Bashful: Reserved.
Show-off: Tries to get attention.
Will fail him: Has a chance of passing, if (!!)

The tabulation concludes brightly, "And now it's conference time!"

I hope I know a good thing when I see one, but why stop with the comparatively positive when the golden superlative is only a step beyond? Both as a guide to parents who were brought up speaking only American English, and toward the perfection of this world's emphases, I hereby offer some samples from a projected guide to "Even More Positive Expressions," each followed by "Most Positive" substitutions:

Energetic: A Hell-raiser.
Temperamental: A stinker.
Working up to average competence: A dope.
Has not performed up to our highest expectations: Hopeless.
Does not always respond to behavioral guidance: Is a young hood.
Reading achievement not in the upper percentiles: Is illiterate.
We believe him capable of cooperating more effectively with
    others: Is a spoiled brat.

The NSPRA of the NEA of the U.S. is not exactly a pioneer in these psychic territories, but more nearly one of the settlers (nesters? squatters? sheepherders?) who are bringing their own substance and stability to the conquest of the golden land, whatever they, in their happily uplifting circumlocutions, imagine that golden land to be.

Some time ago I found myself browsing a similar sort of guidance offered to teachers in (as I recall) the New York school system. I have forgotten most of the details, but none, I shall believe, of the tone. One piece of advice to publicly-relating teachers was to avoid saying "slums" and to say instead "older, more densely populated areas of the city."

Then, in the course of more such, I came on one that stuck tight. Instead of "underprivileged child," teachers were to say "a child whose experiences have been limited to his immediate environment."

Public relations aside, I must treasure that one as zeroing in on the exact responsibility of the school system. And this responsibility still remains: to bring the child not out of but through his immediate environment into the environment of the mind of man; into (if only at long and hoped-for last) that conceptual neighborhood where Aristotle, Sophocles, Dante, Shakespeare, Praxiteles,

29

Copernicus, Michelangelo, Newton, and—make your own list—the great imaginations live to great experiences.

I beg the NSPRA of Etc. to believe me when I say I am joshing its PR guide only mildly. At worst, it can be said to work at its own level. I must certainly sympathize with a disinterested (as distinguished from "uninterested") search for a diplomatic language in dealing with anything as unpredictable as parents. With every such educational agency I know we are building classrooms faster than we can put good teachers into them. By sadly evident mathematics, therefore, some of those classrooms must be profaned (though, I hope, with neither blasphemy nor obscenity) by mere clerks. A clerk is different from (not "than") a teacher, as the rote mind is different from imagination. And to the rote mind one must speak rote. Fair enough: go ahead and program those second-class filing systems that cannot take anything more significant than second-class programming.

But I cannot fail to find a certain dreariness of tone in those "Negatives" and "More Positives." And I must believe that tone to be exactly the one most likely to deafen a child to the language of that conceptual neighborhood to which he must move if he is to hear anything like the resonance of mortal ideas made immortally vibrant.

April 27, 1963

To Be Sure

These are confusing times and in them nothing seems to be as universally manifest as the desire to be sure. Americans seem to live in a rage for the downright certainty. Never mind the eggheaded doubletalk, no ifs, ands, or buts, answer yes or no.

Is it our frontier legend, our formerly traditional isolationism, and our self-claimed championship in nuts-and-bolts that has made us so passionate for the downright and so certain that we know what it is? I shall not pretend to know. I am left with the impression, however, that "Let's give him a fair trial before we hang him" is a more native sound from the American mind than, say, "Perhaps, but on the other hand." Americans still tend to believe that it takes a hard-driving, square-shooting, downright, no-frills, dead-certain man to make the wheels turn, and since, by God, this is a no-fooling wheel-turning country, let's get to it with no highbrow, foreign nonsense about it.

One such champion of no-nonsense turns up in the mailbag on a letterhead that reads "Counsellor at Law"—a suspiciously fancy import for good old American "Lawyer," I should think. Public-relations window-dressing aside, however, he leaves no doubt that he is a man for no frills. "Now," he writes, "who is our greatest living poet? We hope you give a (single) name—not a debate." (Is an answer called for? I doubt it.)

Another main-line express highballing it all out for Downright Junction is Dr. Max Rafferty, newly elected philosopher in charge of California's public education, and hard at the job with nothing like a body of knowledge to encumber his philosophizing. Here are some of the sounds of the Raffertian mind on various subjects covered in a Los Angeles *Times* report for February 14:

POETRY—"One poet won a Nobel Prize for writing without punctuation or capital letters. Another was put in the booby hatch."

SCULPTURE—"Virtually all modern sculpture looks like [sic] it was left on the stove too long and melted out of shape."

ARCHITECTURE—"When I look at a new church these days, I often wonder if it was designed as a house of worship or for a takeoff from Cape Canaveral."

DRAMA AND THE NOVEL—"This is the first generation that has allowed its writers and actors to wallow in filth."

Given these specimen sounds from the Raffertian mind, no reader is likely to be surprised by Dr. Rafferty's conclusions, for they are

31

simply an extension of the same noise. "I think it is time," he concludes, "to blow the whistle on this sickening philosophy. It's not
going to be the philosophy of California education for the next
four years."

One might add that the sound Dr. Rafferty makes is not likely
to provide a "philosophy" for education, any where, at any time.
But why argue with the doctor? He is not the disease, but only a
symptom. He campaigned for his office by offering the people of
California exactly this sort of sound, and they have chosen it as
the sound they think the American mind should make. How can
one fail to suspect that their endorsement of such jingoism is part
of their rage to be sure? Truth, after all, is simple enough, if you
do not confuse it by letting in either information or reflection:
just stand up and say it foursquare and that's all there is to it—to
be sure.

Nor is California alone in this. Almost any daily newspaper will
report on some citizen's group that has been making the same
sounds, usually in an effort to keep education "in the good, God-
fearing, decent American way." Several Wisconsin papers (I am
indebted to a reader for a fat file of clippings on the matter) have
recently reported a typical action in Edgerton, Wisconsin, in
which a telephone campaign by unidentified parents drew five
hundred people to a meeting called to protest the reading lists and
the discussion topics in use in the public schools. Whereupon the
school board, all but inevitably, instructed school administrators
to "avoid discussion of objectionable material."

But objectionable to whom and on what grounds? Springfield,
New Jersey (Newark *Evening News* report, January 27), has just
organized a three-member committee to halt the distribution of
"smut" among juveniles. Is there any need to give examples of
how the committee's statements sound? Any newspaperman could
improvise them, all but word for word, from the last story on the
same sort of thing. But the three-member committee knows
exactly what smut is and what its effect on any given psyche will
be—you may be sure.

There may even be a case to be made for these assured persons,
or for some of them. Yet there is an appalling sort of mindlessness
about their public declarations—the sort of mindlessness one must
suspect will be with us for as long as children grow up ignorant,

32

stay ignorant, and beget in their own image and ignorance. Even when there is something to be said for the positions they assume, there is a dead sound to what they say. Nor do I know of any way to discuss with them the deadness and wrongness of that sound.

Let me offer instead, and only to such as can hear the difference, a few examples of the sound a mind may make in the resonance of ponderable idea. Let me assume in this that the specific issue has been put aside. The one point of these samplings is to explore what sort of sounds a mind does give off, and to compare these sounds with the sounds of the Raffertian certainties.

The laws of conscience, which we pretend to be derived from nature proceed from custom.—Montaigne.

I have labored carefully not to mock, lament, or execrate, but to understand human actions; and to this end I have looked upon passions . . . not as vices of human nature but as properties just as pertinent to it as are heat, cold, storm, thunder and the like to the nature of the atmosphere.—Spinoza (with my thanks to Harrison M. Schlee of Carnegie Tech for sending me this quotation).

In most of the world it is much easier to come by sexual experience than to gain accurate information about sex.—Phyllis and Eberhard Kronhausen, "Sex Education," *Phi Delta Kappan*, December, 1961.

The honest man must be a perpetual renegade, the life of an honest man a perpetual infidelity. For the man who wishes to remain faithful to truth must make himself perpetually unfaithful to all the continual, successive, indefatigable, renascent errors.— Charles Pierre Péguy.

The artist's contribution to religion must in the nature of things be heretical.—Karl Shapiro.

April 13, 1963

Mr. Chairman, Fellow Citizens

Not long ago your local correspondent was visiting friends in a nearby city and interrupted the drinking to accompany the man of the house to a session of the City Council, an adventure later entered on the expense account as "Local Color." Among the speakers of the evening, the most colorful was easily our national friend, Mr. Richard Roe. Your correspondent does not certify that what follows is a verbatim transcript of Mr. Roe's remarks. He does certify, however, that it was set down with a hot psychic pencil immediately on his return from the council meeting, and that wherever the letter may err, it does so only that the spirit may triumph.

Mr. Chairman, Fellow Citizens:

I say it is high time we put our shoulder to the wheel of concrete action and get this program off the ground. The mushrooming pressures of our population curve have created a whole battery of problems we must brace ourselves to implement face to face.

We are in the maze, I say, and there are no two ways about it. City Hall is approaching the abyss of it, and unless the road beyond is clearly charted, our children will reap the whirlwind of our jerry-built failures. Our educational system has become a veritable Gorgon's knot, and unless we can find the key to it, we can look forward to salvaging nothing from the wreck.

I am saying that the ineptitude of this administration has woven a noose around our children's heads and that unless we put a foundation of dramatic action under them—*now*—we shall soon be forced to sink or swim.

Now, I say. The architects of our present policy have left us an

34

unweeded garden whose course is headed for certain disaster unless we man the pumps and set our house in order. Rest assured that once the problem has become insoluble it will be too late for patchwork remedies. It is up to us—*now*—to lay the groundwork of the map of the future.

I am not here to accuse. Let us close our eyes to blame and take a hard look at the record. I could say we are in a mess of our own making, but it will do no good to look back in anger while the house burns down. That will never get us off the horns of this dilemma. I say instead that we are all in this population explosion together and that it is time to come to grips with it. These are the facts:

In percentage terms, the number of classrooms in this city has shrunk to one for every fifty-six students. Twenty years ago it stood at a percentage of one to every thirty-one students. We have been losing ground at an average rate of 1.25 students a year. Figure in our foreseeable expansion over the next twenty years and we shall soon be at the vanishing point.

At the present rate, our population bulge has already engulfed us. We are becoming not a city but a sea of uncharted humanity. No wonder we are on split sessions.

Half our children are in school by 7 A.M., while half of them are free till noon, at which time half come home, while half go to school until 6 P.M. During these short winter days some of them never get to see daylight except through a classroom window.

And despite these exhausting dawn-to-dark sessions, no child is getting more than five hours of schooling a day. How can we hope to prepare them for the somber responsibilities of the bright future we want them all to have? I say we stand at the crossroads and that it is time to fish or cut bait.

It might not be so bad if we had enough teachers to keep the ratio of students at a percentage of twenty-eight to one in each session. But what are the facts? Our present budget allows us to put only four-fifths of our teachers into the classrooms they occupy; one-fifth of them stand idle in each of the split sessions. In other words we are using the plant at far above capacity while leaving one-fifth of it idle. Here is another crossroads at which we stand, and I say it is time—now—to get on the escalator or give up the ship.

35

We all know what has to be done. What we don't seem to realize is that we are going to lose our shirts unless we get our hands out of our pockets—*now*. The future will not wait. Endless delay will turn out to be a short road once we have bogged down in it. I tell you, Mr. Chairman and Fellow Citizens, that we may already have traveled very close to the disastrous end of that road.

I repeat that I have no wish to narrow the broad view by pointing the finger of blame at any man on this council, or by discussing the council's idiotic policies in any but a spirit of cooperative understanding. The council for that matter can only go as far as we hold it to. Where we go next lies, finally, with us.

It is up to us to dig down to the sacrifices we must make. Shall we forever be terrified when the word "millage" rears its head? Let us be terrified, rather—if you will excuse the expression—that we are not hanging a millage-stone around our children's necks!

There is only one question: Is the future of our children worth what it will cost? I for one refuse to be found wanting when my conscience accuses me of having neglected my responsibility. I know in my heart that every parent hears this still small voice in his heart as a clarion call to duty.

In the same stillness of our hearts we know there has been too much talk. What shall it profit a man that he keep down his real-estate taxes only to have the ground cut from under his feet by the avalanche our children will inherit?

For, Mr. Chairman, my Fellow Citizens, make no mistake: the avalanche of our continued inactivity is already rising to meet us, and the next time it comes around may be too late. By then, millage alone will not be enough to keep us afloat. To keep our heads above water then, we shall have to plunge ourselves into a bond issue that will go far toward drying up our civic wells.

We shall be in over our heads then. And what man among us will be able to face his children with a dry eye, knowing, as he must know, that he has buried his child's talent in the ground he has cut out from under him?

Mr. Chairman, my Fellow Citizens, I say again that there has been too much talk. The future can no longer be delayed. The time is—*now!* (Applause.)

April 24, 1965

36

On Lighting Candles. And on Blowing Them Out

Now and then I have visited the first three or four grades of a local school, and I have invariably come away thinking that nothing could match the immediacy with which young readers respond to the power of words and forms. It is the good luck of our school system to take into itself annually one of the best imaginable audiences for poetry. Blessed are the beginners. Theirs is a purity and intensity of illusion all of us can hunger back to.

The books we read at that stage may have been tawdry, but to read was to have happen. Come the hour when we had to be scolded to bed, Horatio Alger's hero had yet to fight his way free of the rich villain's slander of his good name, Tom Swift's submarine was filling with smoke, and Yale was trailing by three runs in the fourth while Frank Merriwell was still struggling to loosen the knots with which the gamblers had tied him to the post in an abandoned warehouse. Who could think of sleep? We read on by flashlight under the covers until our mothers caught on to that trick, too. And as we read, our hearts pounded, our fears drove us, our loyalties burned. There was no distance between us and the page.

Must we lose our marvelous immediacy forever? I can recall only twice in the last twenty years when I put down the book because I was short of breath, my heart pounding with excitement, my senses carried away by the power of the illusion. The first happened as I was rereading *Crime and Punishment* after many years. I came to the scene in which Raskolnikov, in bed and asleep, dreams that a dark figure is standing at the foot of his bed,

37

and in an imperceptible shift from sleep to waking, discovers that the figure is really there. By whatever magic makes us, his terror and mine became one, and I had to let the book sag from me for lack of strength to hold it. Let me cite the second in due tribute to Norman Mailer, about whom I have felt less than whole admiration at times. The book was *The Naked and the Dead*, and the scene was the one in which the squad of GI's is negotiating a narrow ledge across the face of a mountain. Turned back after they have had to leap across a crevice from one narrow foothold to another, they have to make the leap again. One after another the GI's make it across. Then, almost inevitably, one of them misses and plunges away into the abyss. And at that point, as I can still recall with a flush of emotion, I was suffering from such acrophobia that I had an actual sensation of plunging with the doomed man, my nerves cramped with the strain.

And that second time was the last. I have never again experienced such direct physical capture by a piece of writing.

Once marvelous and easy, then rare and marvelous—and when ever again will the power of the word take such possession? There have, of course, been other joys. I still remember the glow with which "Prufrock" first came off the page, and Auden's "In Memory of W. B. Yeats," and Frost's "America is Hard to See."

And so for many other poems. It can still happen. It happens sometimes even at this workaday desk, even among the inanities spilled out of the mailbag. Suddenly, after basketsful of coyly tickling nonsense, a poem declares itself with that instant lift of recognition, with the joy of hearing a language that seems to awaken all its own speaking ghosts.

I suppose that calm of joy is a richer and a better thing than the first physical immediacy of the child's and the adolescent's reading. Yet what a pity it is that we must lose one in order to find another. Or is it possible to keep both, and must I learn that I am one of the unlucky ones in having lost a power of reading that better readers keep through their lives?

If the loss is particular to me, I have no choice but to blame my too many years of reading as a teacher and as an editor. William Dean Howells would have known what I mean. As editor of *The Atlantic Monthly* he paid Mark Twain the compliment of reporting that he was so carried away by one of Twain's books (was it

Huckleberry Finn?—I hope it was) that he forgot to read it as an editor and let himself be swept along as if he were only a reader. Perhaps the price of learning to watch the page for the sources of the illusion is that the illusion itself must lose immediacy, whereby one admires, if at all, more wisely but with a less physical reaction.

But why must the young be made to lose not only immediacy but awareness as well? A few years back I found myself reading to a bright third grade class a poem called "The Stranger in the Pumpkin." Everyone in that class was able to identify that stranger instantly. I asked for his first name and the class chorused, "Jack." I asked for his last name and the class chorused, "O'Lantern." The poem itself is simple enough despite such obscure allusions. Perhaps it is about the school system:

THE STRANGER IN THE PUMPKIN

> The stranger in the pumpkin said:
> "It's all dark inside your head!
> What a dull one you must be!
> Without light, how can you see?
> Don't you know that heads should shine
> From deep inside themselves—like mine?
> Well, don't stand there in a pout
> With that dark dome sticking out—
> It makes me sick to look at it!
> Go and get your candle lit!"
>   —From *The Man Who Sang the Sillies*,
>   J. B. Lippincott Co., copyright 1961.

As it happened, I found myself speaking to some high school students a few days after I had read this poem to their brighter relations back there in the third grade. For the fun of it, I decided to try the same poem on them. But when I asked them to identify the stranger in the pumpkin, they went blank.

"Is that symbolism?" one of them managed to ask in the voice of the higher criticism, with a slightly yokel accent.

And how could I possibly tell them that yes, it is symbolism of a sort, but that, in context, the question is the wrong one? If Gina Lollobrigida happens to walk by, I suggested, they would certainly miss the point if they have to ask, "Is that a girl?" "If you have to ask that question," to cite Louis Armstrong's famous answer, "you'll never know."

Those high school students were not the best I have met—the best manage to keep their reading eyes alive despite the fog-colored glasses most of their teachers pass out. But neither were they the worst. They were more nearly dead-on-the-average, their souls confused by being told they should recognize signs of life—of their own lives—in Washington Irving, in the tintinnabulation of Poe's everlastingly mindless bells, and in the emotional sarcophagi of *Silas Marner;* their minds confused by the insistence of their parents and teachers that they have *something* ready to say on whatever questions the college entrance exams came up with—"and watch out for symbolism: that question has come up in each of the last three years."

It is the good luck of our school system to take into itself annually one of the best imaginable audiences for poetry. It can only be the system's bad practice that sends out of itself annually a graduating class of semi-literate dolts stripped of the emotional excitement with which they began reading, and unstored by the insights that might lure them on to recognition.

June 18, 1966

Hatred

Our local high school's graduation ceremonies were scheduled for the football stadium with the high school gym as a rain site.

Graduation day built up to a soggy swelter. My daughter was to graduate, en route to Swarthmore in September, and all day long she and her classmates were running in and out of the house, dripping excitement, plans, and sweat.

40

The graduating class planned the symbolic release of two white doves during the ceremony, and the doves had to be visited and admired. One group had decided to wear armbands sporting a white dove. Another announced it would distribute small American flags to pin on the shoulder of their academic gowns. The intent of the flag-distributors was clearly to distinguish between patriotic Americans and peace doves, and the doves had to meet and discuss this affront to their motives—which they solved by deciding to wear both insignia.

There were other momentous decisions. Mom had to be asked which ribbon looked best on the graduation dress that would in any case be covered by the blue imitation-academic gown. There would be many parties that night, and itineraries had to be discussed if not planned. If they drew and donned their regalia early, Dad would have a chance to snap away with the Polaroid, and that, of course, had to be planned in frivolous detail. There was more excitement than purpose in the discussions. Having decided weeks ago exactly how they would plan things, they had to reconvene every half-hour to discuss all the plans again.

At 5:00, with the interminables set for 6:30, the swelter turned into a spurt of showers, the showers fading to a steady drizzle that managed to cool nothing while raising the humidity. We were in for it. The gym was an airless box with too few windows too high in one wall, and, as it turned out, the slant of the drizzle was such that even those inadequate vents had to be closed. Add about three hundred graduates and more than a thousand parents and friends, and we were in for a Black Hole of Calcutta painted an institutional beige.

A psychic year and two quarts of sweat later the class had death-marched its way to its places, the band had ground out its approximate and endless tonalities, the choir had piped distantly with that aggressive indifference to human suffering that motivates all music teachers given a chance to "offer their program," and after some blessedly brief and unrhetorical remarks by the class president, the salutatorian came on, an earnest young man with a carefully compiled list of the issues of all our lives.

He began by condemning the school system for the endless flow of busy work it had handed out to him in place of a questing education, and he made firm points, though just a bit overfirmly.

I found him to be honorable, refreshing, and relentless. Having just discovered the world, he had yet to discover any doubts about his discovery. Yet he was asking hard questions and asking them well. Some freshman instructor, I found myself thinking, would find in this lad his recompense for the illiterate year. Once softened by a reasonable uncertainty, this would be an intellect. At the moment, however, he had won his honors by what he called "an unthinking docility," and he was in a mood to savor them.

Having categorized the school system, he moved on to the war in Asia, to the race issue, to pollution, to the lack of confidence in the federal government, to the military-industrial complex, to unrest, to the dedication of the socially committed young. He had, as I recall, just mourned the deaths at Kent State as a sign of police repression when a voice from the audience called: "Is this a graduation or a rally?"

There were anger and hatred in that voice, and it was instantly joined by a chorus of jeers that seemed to have been waiting only for a signal. There was more than a physical swelter in the room. For a moment there seemed even to be the possibility of violence. Certainly there was a pent rancor against anyone who would question, who declared a difference, who dared "rock the boat." I thought of the hardhats invading Wall Street, righteous and truculent—except, alas, that these were neighbors and parents, and they were disrupting their own children's chosen spokesman.

As noted, the boy was a bit gauche in his sense of certainty. But it was not his rhetoric that had moved this hatred. The jeerers would have sat patiently through any number of round, smooth platitudes. His offense had been to question established values, and the answer to such questioning had become a brawl of catcalls and red-faced shouts. Nor were the hecklers in a mood to quit. It took both the superintendent of schools and the president of the board of education, speaking in turn, to assert the boy's right to speak, and to restore a grumbling sort of order. The president's remarks on freedom of speech provided a countercue to those who identified with the boy, and a handful of parents and friends—perhaps as many as 3 per cent—stood up to applaud.

Then it happened. The few who stood in the audience to applaud passed on one of those indefinable crowd signals to the graduating class, and the class responded by standing to applaud.

Perhaps as many as 60 or 70 per cent of the graduates rose—certainly well over half of them. For an instant then that sweat box contained an epiphany of the generation gap.

On both sides, of course, there were dissenters, as there were those who would not get involved, as there were, I suppose, a few sheep who rose because those around them were rising.

Yet the difference in proportion was overwhelming: among the parents perhaps as many as 3 per cent declaring themselves, among the graduates a clear majority—one side and another of a mood, of a commitment, and of a climate of ideas; one side and another of a community's image of itself.

It will do me for a pictogram. The line between the age groups has seldom been more clearly drawn. If I confess that what little is left of my hope rides with the young, the difference would be as visible to one with opposite views, so long as he is willing to open his eyes to a view. We are divided, the picture says, and I see small hope of a kindly tolerance across that division.

Yet, as nearly as I can sense the mood of a crowd—and I speak as an old manipulator of audiences—the flow of hatred was all from the old to the young. The graduates rose not against but for, not in hatred of their parents and neighbors but in affirmation of their classmate's right to speak.

It is a mad world in which the young must be tolerant of the intolerant old, in which the young must accept the hatred of their elders and return not hatred but dissent.

Think, neighbors; for God's sake think. It may be righteously self-satisfying to ask—I have heard you ask it—"Why do they hate us?" It will be more useful to ask, "Why do we hate them?" You know why of course. They tell all of us that we have given our lives in tawdry faith to tin gods. They dismiss our sacrifices and our hypocrisies as pointless. They cancel us. And we hate them for it. Even though they are probably right. Especially because they are probably right.

August 1, 1970

Unsolicited Opening Day Address by Prexy

Ladies and gentlemen, welcome—and welcome back—to Diehard University. I shall start the academic year by describing the contract you have entered into by the act of enrolling in this university. That contract is clearly set forth in the university catalogue, but since literacy is no longer prerequisite to admission, let me lipread the essential points of our agreement. As you emerge from this convocation you will be handed a digest of these remarks in attractively prepared comic-book form with all dialogue limited to basic English and with the drawings carefully designed to help you over any grammatical difficulties. Those of you, moreover, for whom the requirements of Sub-Literacy One have been waived, may dial AV for Audio Visual, followed by 0016, and a dramatized explication will appear on your TV sets.

Diehard, as you know, is no longer dedicated to excellence. The trustees, the administration, the faculty, and the federal government—not necessarily in that order—have concurred that excellence has been outnumbered. The restated policy of Diehard University is simply to salvage what it can from what little it gets from the too much being thrust upon it.

We recognize that the achievement of any given intellectual standard is no longer prerequisite to a Bachelor's degree. The insistence of any educational institution is defined by its minimum standards, and Diehard no longer has any. As a contractual agreement, the faculty undertakes to confer a Bachelor's degree upon you in acknowledgment of four years of attendance.

If you are willing to settle for that degree, I suggest you do not waste money on textbooks. The presence of a textbook may tempt you to open it. The psychological consequences are obvious: if you must actually open a textbook in order to meet nonexistent minimum standards, how will you ever be sure you are not a moron? Your whole future career could be warped, in such a case, by guilt and uncertainty. Our educational activities, let me say, are so organized that any member of the in- or out-group of the affluent society can stroll through them in the intervals between political rallies, draft-card burnings, love-ins, water fights, sit-ins, sit-outs, strikes, sympathy marches, student elections, anti-raids and generalized adolescent glandular upheavals. These programs have been carefully constructed to assist your social development as students. I urge them upon you as the social duty of every minimalist. Diehard would serve no purpose were it to allow an intemperate emphasis on learning to deflect its minimalists from the fullness of their undergraduate social development and thus, indirectly, from future computerization.

To further that social development, Diehard imposes no rules of extra-curricular behavior. We shall not act *in loco parentis*. With a mild shudder of revulsion, we return that function to your legal parents. We have problems enough with our own failures and cannot accept as ours the genetic failures of others.

This university has eliminated dormitories. Where you live, with whom you live, and what you do off campus are matters between you and your parents, or between you and the police, as the case may be.

You are free to demonstrate on all matters of conviction, or, simply, on all matters. For your convenience we have set aside a fireproof, waterproof, open-occupancy convention center called Hyde Park Hall. You are free to occupy it and to harangue in or from it at your pleasure. You have full license for all non-criminal acts that occur in Hyde Park Hall. Any criminal actions you may engage in there will be, of course, between you and the police.

Should you choose to act unlawfully in any of the otherwise assigned buildings of the university, you will be warned once that your actions are unlawful, and the police will then be summoned to take normal action against a breach of the peace.

The university will seek your advice on all matters of student organization, social development of the university, and community relations. We shall seek that advice temperately and with as much open-mindedness as we can achieve in our senility. In seeking it, however, we do not pledge ourselves to be bound by it. Where your views seem to be reasoned, they will be honored in reason; where they seem intemperate or shortsighted, they will be rejected in reason. A faculty-student board will be elected to study all grievances.

In no case, however, will that board, or any body of this university, consider a general amnesty as a condition for ending a demonstration that violates lawful procedure.

Diehard will not consider any request made by a minimalist for changes in the curriculum, faculty, or academic qualification. On these matters we ask nothing from you and we will hear nothing.

We do confess to a vestigial nostalgia for the long-honored and now outmoded idea of the university as a bookish community of learning. While most of you are pursuing your social development, therefore, the faculty will direct such students as are inclined to volunteer for it, in a course of study leading to the degree of Laureate in Arts or in Science. We shall continue to grant the Bachelor's degree in Arts or in Science without requirement, though to assist your social development we do invite you to attend various discussion groups to be held at carefully spaced intervals.

With those who elect the Laureate program, the university insists on a different contract. It insists that in the act of electing such a program, the student will have submitted himself to the faculty as candidate for a degree to be conferred at the discretion of the faculty. The faculty, having already thrown away minimums, must insist on reserving to itself the right to formulate maximums for those who are willing to reach for them. It is the student's business to qualify, or to revert (without prejudice), to the social development program leading to the degree of Bachelor.

I ask all those who are interested in a course of study to return tomorrow to start our further discussions. The rest of you may now return to your pads to drop out, turn on, and tune in. If you are arrested between now and your graduation, the university will credit the time up to your conviction toward your attendance and will do its best to readmit you upon completion of your sentence. By decision of the board of trustees, days of attendance completed while out on bail pending an appeal will be counted toward a degree.

If the police, that is, are willing to let you out of jail, and if you are willing to check in on the roster, we are willing to keep the attendance records and to grant appropriate degrees upon satisfaction of the requirement.

We are not willing to have our reading and discussion time interrupted by protest, no matter how passionate, that breaks the law. Nor are we willing to police the law. Criminality is the proper concern of the police; ours, we believe, is reasoned discussion. When the discussion goes beyond reason and to the point of interfering with the curriculum of those who have chosen one, we reserve the right to suspend or to expel you from the hazy premises of our failing venture into education for those few who are interested in the unlikely.

Hello. Goodbye. And may your standardization be your fulfillment.

September 28, 1968

Who Writes the Contract?

The college year is once more on its way and the faculty and the students are once more engaged in the contest to decide what a college is for. There will be shadings of the issues—there will always be good boys siding with the faculty and faculty mavericks siding with the students—but in the nature of things the two groups will inevitably tug in opposite directions.

College, as some students are sure to argue year after year, is an important social experience for which they are paying. They aren't, of course, or they are paying no more than a sliver of the whole budgetary pie, but the college budget is not likely to mean

47

anything to an undergraduate. He has it in his head that his (or Dad's) money is running the place, and why, therefore, should he not be free to decide what he gets for his cash? His is the simple and simple-minded argument that the customer is always right (and what right has the faculty to decide what courses a man should take, or to make all those rules about how he shall behave even outside the classroom?).

I am, of course, talking about liberal arts students. Or perhaps I am only talking about non-students who are in the liberal arts college to dodge the draft or to get a social degree on the way to becoming advertising salesmen or to taking over the family insurance agency. Engineers, medical students, law students, and all such technical and professional candidates come to school prepared for a hard scrubbing because they know that the faculty is their one chance of establishing professional or technical competence. The same freshman who will argue a dangling construction with his English section-man will keep his mouth respectfully shut when his calculus instructor cites him for error.

In part, let it be noted, the confusion of the liberal arts student is inseparable from the confusing but essential fact that the liberal arts college has no real notion of what it is supposed to be or of what it is supposed to accomplish. The faculty can, at times, summon some fine rhetoric toward a definition of its purpose. Always, however, the rhetoric turns out to be a paraphrase of the idea that an educated man should "see life steadily and see it whole." Nor is anyone justified in holding that idea in contempt. The trouble is that students are thinking about *their* lives in what they like to believe are specific and real terms (they never are), whereas the faculty is thinking about the life of *man* as a continuing experience. It is thinking that the college is one of the central memory banks of that continuity, and that a man can be educated (as distinguished from being "trained") only as he takes into himself some significant part of that memory.

And the faculty is, of course, right. But with the proliferation of the curriculum into hundreds, and even into thousands, of new courses, it does become harder for the faculty, as for the students, to see what paths run where through the thickets. The students are left to take some of the faculty's total purpose on faith, but between them and full faith lies a barrier of suspicion: the students are not at all sure the faculty is in touch with any reality they can accept as persuasive.

During most of the Eisenhower years, for example, I was trying to teach undergraduates some sense of the American-English usage appropriate to formal writing as exemplified by that puberty ritual called "the weekly theme." I was, therefore, required to red-line many a construction that was obviously acceptable to the President but not to me. Several students made a regular thing of bringing in newspaper transcripts of the President's latest stylistic flourishes as proof that I was an incompetent. And given his choice between the authority of the President of the United States and that of an unknown pedant, what student will fail to have his own sense of rightness and his own endorsement of illiteracy?

I am suggesting, as a further difficulty, that our society (though it is beginning to pay passing tribute to the liberal arts) is not really much interested in the liberalness of the liberal arts. If the American father is willing enough to work his son's way through college, that father is certainly not "making sacrifices" because he is eager to have his boy study poetry, Plato, or the history of art. What the old man wants at the degree-end of the four years is a solidly employed son signed on to a pension plan that can certify a marina in Florida for the sunshine years. And though the hope of this world may finally lie in the resilience with which each generation manages to escape from its parents, the boys, often enough, see it as Dad does. The professors are sad prunes wizened from every memory of the juice of life, and if Prune Hall won't submit to (student) reality, let Prune Hall be picketed. It's a free country, isn't it?

Among those who do not think the country—or at least the campus—is quite as free as some students would like it to be is President Wilson H. Elkins of the University of Maryland, who, according to the Washington *Daily News*, greeted the parents of incoming students with a warning that Maryland would not welcome students who meant to "take matters in [let me believe he meant "into"] their own inexperienced hands."

Since the *Daily News* did not give the full context of President Elkins's remarks, I am not sure what he had in mind. If he was thinking of such things as student picketing for social causes, I could wish his statement had been softened a bit. If he was thinking that he was not going to put up with the sort of foolishness that used to go into panty raids, I could wish the statement had been stronger. But if he was thinking that the faculty and the administration determine the curriculum and academic standards, and that it is up to the students to meet those standards or to get out, then I can wish for nothing but prolonged applause for Prexy.

For before the students get around to deciding for themselves what will constitute their education, let them be reminded that on entering college they submit themselves as candidates for a degree the requirements of which are at the discretion of the faculty, and the grant of which is faculty certification that the student has met not his but its requirements. Even if the liberal arts college cannot define all of its own purposes (primarily because it has too many), it still has as firm a duty as has the school of medicine or of engineering to establish the terms of the contract under which its degrees will be granted.

The terms of that contract are set forth in the college catalogue. In it, every incoming student is free to read them for himself. If he does not like the contract as offered (denominational colleges, for example, have a right to impose doctrinal and moral restrictions that might be intolerable in a public institution), he is not required to sign. He is free to contract with another school if he can, or to go on about his own business. He is not free, however, to violate a contract to which he has committed himself.

I do not mean, and I cannot believe that President Elkins means, that our colleges will welcome only an intellectually stunted generation of conformists. Troglodytes there may be in the strata of tenure, but it simply is not the nature of a liberal arts faculty to hate open discussion or to ban self-expression, so long as the discussion and the expression remain within the disciplines of the given course. In the good undergraduate colleges the faculty is there in the hope of eliciting ideas from students.

But to have idea there must be the discipline of idea. Nor does the faculty use the word "discipline" in the same sense the Army does. Academic discipline is not a matter of indoctrinated obedience but of the responsible application of tested criteria. The

50

faculty is there to establish and to transmit those criteria; the student is there to apply them to the faculty's satisfaction.

That, gentlemen of the entering class, is the nature of the contract, and let there be no nonsense about whose opinion is as good as anyone else's in a free country. The freedom of the classroom is the freedom to grow within the measure of sound intellectual standards. Take those standards into your head before you try taking the curriculum into your hands. Or get out of school and be as free as you like—and as ignorant. If only until the draft board catches up with you and submits you to another set of notions.

October 23, 1965

To the Damnation of Deans
(*A Prejudice*)

I leaned on my first lectern in January of 1940 as a new-minted instructor at the University of Kansas City. After a shade under four years with the Army Air Corps, beginning in 1942, I taught for seven years at Harvard as an instructor and then for eight years more at Rutgers, ending up as a full-chicken professor of English, a post and tenure I resigned last June.

These are not notes for a *curriculum vitae* but credentials in faith, as testimony that I have served a fair stint of campus time, and that if I cannot assemble facts and figures to do my lying for me, I have at least invested a lot of years in the prejudices I take away from the ivy.

Nothing has fueled my prejudices as richly as has the discovery that the college at which I dreamed of teaching does not, to my knowledge, exist. Harvard is the one possible exception I know of,

51

and if it shines both by comparison and its own merit, its splendor is yet marked to some extent by the fungi of that administrative blight that has marked the face of all American colleges, a blight whose simple disaster is the fact that college policy has passed almost entirely from the hands of the faculty into those of the administration.

I make no effort to be impartial on this point. Education is too important a business to be left to deans. The deanly condition is the condition of ignorance camouflaged by secretaries, charts, IBM cards, and statistics, but ignorance none the less. That ignorance is occupational. Let a good man be trapped into a dean's swivel chair and his inhumane ignorance grows upon him as a condition of his employment. The only real difference between the arrogant and the apologetic deans is that the apologetic ones know to what extent their work drains them of mentality. How can one leave educational decision to men who lack the time to read a book?

My nostalgic notion of the true college was of an absolute and self-determining body of scholar-teachers. They are the faculty. They are appointed for their distinction and responsibility. And they, by discussion and vote, set the college policy, which is then passed on as formulated to a variety of clerk known as a dean. The duty of such clerks is to count the paper clips and add up the totals as instructed, leaving the faculty free for the important business of gathering information, of thinking about it, and of transmitting the information, the thought, and the method of thinking to students.

But if that is the ideal college, the ideal world is a cloud. Far from being clerks, those deans, sub-deans, overdeans (and the janitors) have become executives who outrank the faculty in pay, power, and persuasion. I have known distinguished professors to go into a reasonable approximation of a tizzy when a dean raised his voice. I have known a dean to walk into a departmental meeting called to elect a new chairman, and to announce to the department that no matter how they voted, only so-and-so would be acceptable to the administration. I have known presidents to convene the full faculty for a discussion of academic policy, receive the clear vote of the faculty, and within a few days announce a policy exactly opposite that voted by the faculty.

52

Now and then a professor has rebelled, but professors are poor rebels. They have, in fact, largely abdicated their responsibilities as members of the ideal faculty, probably for the same shabbily genteel reasons that have made them shy away from anything so sordid as the discussion of pay and working conditions. They have shown less professional character in making themselves respected than have plumbers and steamfitters.

There are times, in fact, when my then profession made me ashamed for it. As a former president of the National College English Association, I attended a number of meetings between teachers of liberal arts and corporation executives. I happen to believe, let me say more than parenthetically, that most academics begin by making a central decision about money and the competitive life. I myself made such a decision until I found that planned poverty among sheep bored me. It can be a good decision. In essence, a faculty member decides to live on about one-third the life income (if that much) that he might have earned in business. He is buying time for the life of the mind. His decision is both honorable and self-dignifying. Or so I thought, with occasional lapses into doubt, until that meeting.

The meeting took place at Corning and a number of high-ticketed executives took the floor to say the liberal arts colleges were important to them, that they sought liberal arts graduates for employment, and that they would continue to support the colleges as a sound investment so long as the colleges turned out men they could use. In fact they loved us.

The last gold-plated executive was hardly seated when my colleagues were up all over the floor begging to know what they could do to turn out a better-suited product. The sheep! Had they elected the life of the mind only to nibble at the feet of the first golden tower they came upon? It was a pleasure to tell them they had disgraced themselves and to remind them that they had no duty to provide raw material for Republic Steel or Standard of New Jersey; that their one function was to lead students to the disciplined life of the mind for its own sake; that if corporations could then make use of men so humanized, let that fact be to the credit of the corporations; but that the faculty destroyed all it stood for when it thought of mechanizing students for readier passage through the employment office.

53

That abdication of responsibility, whether to corporate lures or to front office directive, has gone too far, and it has done so needlessly. An unreasonable dean can always be put in his place by a responsible faculty member.

Some years ago I received a reasonably standard nasty letter from a dean. "You will explain at once," it began. And it then went on to say that "to not keep adequate records is a grave matter."

I sent the letter back with a note saying its tone was unacceptable, that his request for information would have to be rewritten in a form acceptable to the consensus of a full faculty meeting, and that while he was rewriting, I should prefer that he not split infinitives.

The point was not bravado. I have had to write several such letters in my time and they were always written conscientiously. The point is that the dean always becomes a dear good fellow when he writes again. He is always sure that I must have misunderstood his intention, that certainly there is no need to burden the agenda of the faculty meeting, and that he is, of course, delighted to extend all due apologies.

And the point behind the point is the fact that our faculties, in all but the most depraved institutions, still have the power—if they will demand it and exercise it. Our colleges will be measurably better the day deans become the clerical servants of the faculty. A faculty incapable of self-determination is incapable of governing a classroom dedicated to the discipline of mind in good order.

March 24, 1962

More Deans, More Deaneries

In my remarks a while back about college administrators I was not, as various letter writers would have it, courageous (thanks for the medals), nor striking-a-blow-for (I have no worlds to save), nor probing to the core of the problem (has it a core?). Neither was I, as others would have had me be, exhaustive, omniscient, nor dispassionate. Neither was I entirely fair. Why waste fairness on deans? I was simply enough—and as labeled—declaring a prejudice. To state a simple fact, deans have, in general, grown to be officers of higher rank than the faculty, and I see no good in that fact.

That it is a fact is beyond dispute. Two years ago I lectured at the Air Force Academy (Sky Blue U or Aluminum U, as the boys call it), and there the matter of relative rank was left in no doubt: the classroom teachers hold various ranks up to Light Colonel, department heads are Full Chicken Colonels, the dean I saw listed was a Brigadier, and what corresponds to the university president is (or was then) a Two-Star Splendor.

What the Air Force has made dog-plain in its table of organization is not left in much doubt in the civilian colleges. The deans have become higher brass, the faculty is at best made up of field-grade subalterns, and the books, I suppose, are rapidly reaching the point where they can be scanned by IBM machines with no real need to distract the G.I. student-body from its extracurricular patrols.

Yes—to reply to some of the busier letter writers—I happen to know some civilized deans. I even know a few who are learned men, or who were on their way to being learned men before their careers in intellect were interrupted by their careers in administration. And yes, I think I know a few administrative people I should guess to be superior to anybody on their faculties. The fact remains that deans as a whole are an overbusy lot much too far from the bookshelves and not to be entrusted with educational policy. Let them take care of building and maintenance, of the details of classroom utilization, of student discipline, of the parking problem and dormitory assignments, of medical care, record-keeping, food-services, alumni relations, and admissions—the last under careful directives from the faculty. But if our colleges are to be colleges and not social clubs or employment offices, only the faculty can be trusted to decide curriculum and degree requirements, admissions policy (as distinct from the clerical procedures of admission), scholastic standards, and the academic goals of the college.

Such policies cannot be determined by inferior officers. In taking over the province of academic decision the administration has made itself the higher brass. Certainly the deans can offer good reasons for their way of going: there are always good reasons. Perhaps by Judgment Day it will have become clear that every man-made catastrophe began in the good reasons of some committee, congress, praesidium, or board of directors.

Since literally dozens of deans have written in to demand equal time in which to state their side of things, let their side be stated. The following is a report by Dave Morris, Staff Writer of the Albany *Times-Union*, under the headline "College Officials Outline Policies." I append all of the direct substance of his report, omitting only a further list of panelists not quoted. The parentheses are mine:

While college and university professors should have a voice in determining the policy of the institutions at which they teach (that's generous of you, boys), it is the administrative heads who are rightly (hear! hear!) responsible for those policies.

This, in effect, was the opinion of the heads of various area educational (?) institutions and organizations, who met yesterday at Rensselaer Polytechnic Institute to discuss how much participation faculty members should be allowed (by gracious permission?) in university government. The meeting was called by the Rens-

56

salaer chapter of the American Association of University Professors.

Addressing the group of area educators, Dr. Bertram Davis, one of the panelists and editor of the AAUP Bulletin, Washington, D.C., said, "Faculty participation helps to insure that the purposes of a college are adequately fulfilled." (I knew there was some reason for having that faculty around.)

Dr. Davis said, however, that the purposes of the educational institution could not be fulfilled by the faculty alone. "It needs deans as well," he said. Dr. Davis added that professors "should know what is happening at their respective schools (the deans will tell them, I assume), but that they must put their faith (Faith, say you? As in, for example, the Trinity?) in the administration."

Dr. Edward A. Fox, a member of the faculty at RPI, pointed out that the principal job of professors was teaching and research. He said trustees and administrators have problems enough keeping the plant running. (That parking problem again.) "The faculty does not have this problem of running the plant," Dr. Fox contended, "and can thus view the goals of the university more clearly." (I think I'm with Dr. Fox, but I can't tell from this report which side he is on.)

There follows a list of other panel members, including Dr. Evan R. Collins, president of Albany State University College, and Dr. Richard G. Folsom, president of RPI, who are then quoted as follows:

Dr. Collins said that while faculty members were involved "in the day-to-day problems of the university (books, for example?), it was the job of the board of trustees to develop long-range plans" (while sitting around the luncheon table, for example?).

Dr. Folsom pointed out that deans become secretaries (assuming they know how to type) when they must listen to the dictates of the faculty (nasty word). He emphasized the importance of the dean's work, and said that the effectiveness of his office depends on the responsibility of the people in charge (a state of affairs that could not, of course, apply to the responsibility of the faculty in charge).

57

Even a good reporter—and I take Mr. Morris to be a good one—may in some part miss the particular emphasis a speaker intended. It may be that any one of the gentlemen here quoted would want to amend or expand the remarks by which he is represented. But, in general, no man can miss the fact that this is the official sound of the deanly mind. "We have this plant to run," it says, "and, of course, we are going to let you people in the faculty stay around to watch us run it, but making education work is really our job you know, and if you don't know, we're telling you, so pipe down and have faith in us, because we know all about how it has to be done, and if we had to listen to you we'd become mere secretaries."

. . . Something like that. Followed, of course, by reasons; a lot of them, and all of them good.

Followed by the final debauchery of our educational system into a diploma-mill in which the mere matter of ideas is relegated to faculty clerks, while the decisions are made by chart-riding administrative brass in the golden swivel chairs.

May 19, 1962

Ruminants and Factitioners

There are some deans I do talk to and one of them is James E. Gates of the College of Business Administration of the University of Georgia. Dean Gates is, in fact, one of my favorite intellectual ruminants, if I may so call him without evoking the picture of a bovine and green-flecked chin, but rather of a peaceful and successful life-form given to the green of this earth, from which it extracts, stores, and reworks life's succulent grasses.

A combine, if I may myself wander to one side (as a ruminant

58

might stray off to crop an inviting daisy), is as near as a machine can come to being a ruminant, but misses the mark by all daisies. For the ruminant picks and chooses quietly at its own pace and pleasure, happily ready to stop and chew the contemplative cud on no notice whatever. A combine, on the other hand, is a noisily compelled machine for devouring and spitting out all that lies before it without either selectivity or storage, and certainly without pause for meditative cud-chewing.

The combine enters into this vagary because the green I refer to is of the mind, and because our universities draw to themselves both ruminants and mechanical monsters. The mechanical monsters are the data-gulping, card-filing, and indexing minds that chew straight swathes through the library toward a mental granary of hard information. They are sometimes awesome men, but there is no pause in them. They are awesome as a computer is awesome. They are the "factitioners" of intellect. But only upon the true ruminant may one bestow the title "humanist."

"*Weile doch!*" cried Goethe—"Linger awhile!" And, in less literary language, Walt Whitman spoke his joy when he said, "I loaf and invite my soul." The difference between a combine and a ruminant is that no combine has heard such invitation, whereas every ruminant lives within it the instant he can escape compulsion.

I hope I haven't made any sort of monument of Dean Gates, for I rather suspect that he does nothing (at least by natural inclination) that any factitioner would think of as Important. I hope he doesn't. My own faith on that score can be summarized in my long-standing motto: "Never Write Important Poems."

What Dean Gates does do is much more congenial than Important. He browses through his reading at what I hope is happy random, and periodically compiles a little mimeographed newsletter which he mails out to other ruminants, suspected ruminants, and potentially (or at least hopefully) salvageable factitioners. Myself a ruminant (though only part-time, alas), I would not dream of laying a wax wreath at his feet; no true ruminant can stomach wax. My present purpose is to thank him for good grass and for daisies among the grass and to say my thanks as I savor a daisy or two he has led me to crop.

Among the notes in his last newsletter I found one (a purest daisy) on the results of psychological tests given to two groups of children, the first ranking high in I.Q., the second in "creativity" (I don't know how measured). The two groups were asked to rank in order "the qualities in which they would like to be outstanding." The results ran as follows:

High I.Q. Group	Creative Group
character	emotional stability
emotional stability	sense of humor
goal directedness	character
creativity	wide range of interests
wide range of interests	goal directedness
high marks	creativity
I.Q.	high marks
sense of humor	I.Q.

Let me pass over such jargon as "goal directedness," which is a factitioner's translation of the English word "purposefulness." In this particular field of fact the daisy that must draw all true ruminants to their meditations is the relative ranking of "sense of humor" by these two orders of mind.

The ruminant vote cannot fail to go to the second group—partly in terror of any group of children that would rank a sense of humor as the least of desirable traits. It is in defense of mankind that one must be appalled by a humorless I.Q.

And at once I find myself trying to summon back what Professor Gordon Allport of Harvard wrote about "adulthood" in his *The Nature of Personality*. It is at least ten years since I browsed that book, and I shall answer to no factitioner for scrupulous accuracy. What we all know is that adulthood is no matter of mere chronological age; every man's world contains more than enough children between the ages of twenty-one and ninety-plus. Adulthood is a state of constantly developing (as opposed to arrested) personality, and among its central qualities (as I recall) Professor Allport placed, as about equally important, *a sense of perspective, the ability to feel oneself into the situation of another,* and *a sense of humor.* (Professor Allport, needless to say, is not responsible for the way I report his ideas, nor for the way I rephrase them: were I a factitioner I should stop to check, but I am

60

a ruminant out for daisies. Any daisy is daisy enough. Let some-one else—say, those quiz kids who place character first in the scale of things—count the petals.)

And having sniffed and cropped my daisy, I find myself chew-ing it over and wondering if perhaps "sense of humor" might not usefully be rephrased as "the ability to chuckle." For there are many orders of humor from the belly laugh to the wry and rue-ful chuckle at oneself, and not all of them become a man. I suspect, in fact, that the belly laugh was invented by the ape as an explosion of his own sense of superiority the day he knocked down another ape and felt good about it. It is the ape's self-vaunt-ing declaration of how ridiculous he has made the other ape look. And it is still that when the barracks ape slips the hotfoot to one of his brothers and then roars out his belly laugh at the poor fool who dances around holding one foot in his hands.

But what ape has ever looked at himself, recognized that he is himself mildly ridiculous, and realized at the same time that what is ridiculous in him is not his own invention but something rooted in the nature of being? Between the belly laugh and the chuckle lies the whole range of primate evolution. For only a man can chuckle the true chuckle. And among men, only the true rumi-nant—the seemingly unpurposeful man loose in the green of this world, easy in the knowledge that daisies may be come upon by any indirection and that any mouthful may include the flower, recognition.

Dew on your daisies, Dean Gates, and thanks for what mean-ders.

June 15, 1963

A Praise of Good Teachers

Commencement time has come and gone again. The boys and girls in their caps and gowns have mugged handsomely into the cameras of their proud parents and for their own handsome images of themselves. Off they go now, out of their caps and gowns, to whatever they are going to, if any man can guess what that might be. It is over again, and the faculty can rest for a while. Whatever the teachers could do has been done.

And of course, has just begun. The boys and girls have yet to learn how the good teachers keep working in them, how the ideas keep marching from the good minds long after the last class. The boys and girls are in a hurry. June is no time to sit still and look back for long to praise good teachers one has just left. The age, moreover, lacks a vocabulary for praise. Let them go.

But I am in no hurry. I have that advantage over them. And the further advantage of a foolish willingness to fumble at that missing vocabulary. Let me use my advantages for their good as well as my own, to think back to all good teachers—theirs and mine—and to praise for all good teachers the two I must praise most. What better commencement exercise can there be than to thank deservingly? The last commencement speaker having peered farther into the future than human eye can see, I take the occasion to look back, if only as a counterbalance to the overgeneralized and overforeseen world.

So must I thank particularly, and too backwardly, John Holmes of Tufts. Tufts, now a university, was a college when I got there in the Thirties, and Holmes, now a professor, was a young English instructor. Then as now, Tufts was one of those truly good schools that gem New England. I found many good teachers there. Professor Miller, now retired, taught me Municipal Government and has stayed with me every time I have walked into City Hall. Professor Neil taught biology and dazzled me by his demonstration of how a disciplined mind goes about asking a question. English was my major, and everywhere within the English Department good teachers opened doors for me. But if they were an expansion—and they were—John Holmes was an explosion. He was not only a great teacher but just the teacher one insane adolescent had been starved for.

It is hunger that goes to the best feast. I had the hunger, but how can I really say what feast Holmes was? He cared. But caring only begins a teacher's work. Holmes *knew*. And what he knew was exactly what I needed. My other teachers were scholars. They loved literature but their essential training was in history. John Holmes was and is a poet, and a good one. What he knew about was the *insides* of a poem. What he lived was the happy excitement of each living poem as he found it. And he knew how to transmit that excitement and make it real.

I lived on Holmes's shoulder while I was at Tufts. Since I lived in town, he wasn't even rid of me during the summer. I would bring him six, eight, a dozen screaming poems a week, and he would read them, talk about them, tug at them. There were no rules about it. Each poem was its own thing. One would give him a chance to show me something about rhyme, another something about rhythm, another something about imagery, and so on. It was a good twenty years later that I came on a sentence by Wallace Stegner that summarized Holmes's body of knowledge. "A writer," wrote Stegner (as nearly as I can recall), "learns his craft through a million particulars." Holmes had no poetic edicts. What he had was a sure sense of those millions of particulars.

Praise knowledge then. But whenever has knowledge been enough for a teacher? There must be generosity, the gift of articulation, and the power to elicit enthusiasm. These are the gifts of the great teacher, and John Holmes has these gifts greatly. Thank you, John. And for those thousand cups of coffee. And for all the books I borrowed and hope I always returned. And for every time I get back to Medford to find you there. I have turned out to be a rotten letter writer—so bad that I have discouraged even your letters, which are always great ones. Bear with that as you have borne with so much more. But accept this praise that I have not yet entirely learned how to say.

When I left Holmes, I went to the University of Michigan, and there, as my second great master of the million particulars, I met Professor Roy Cowden, now emeritus. I am not sure I can describe Professor Cowden's teaching method. I hope he will forgive me if I confess that his weekly seminar was a torture to me. In love, I could not bring myself to cut it; in nature, I could not keep myself awake in it as he droned over manuscript revisions in Hardy. But once a week, too, came the feast of those individual conferences when I sat beside him and he held in his hand the manuscript I had given him to read.

I cannot recall as much as one word he ever said. What I can see yet is his finger. He would hold the manuscript, we would both look at it, and then his finger would begin to weave, hovering over the page in slow figure-eights, slowly, slowly—and then pouncing down. And by whatever magic he worked, I always knew where it was going to land before it landed, and why it was going to land there! Don't ask me how: I don't know. But it was teaching. It was great teaching.

Thank you, Professor Cowden, for that dowsing finger. I want you to know I still see it come down on the page at times. Let me hope it comes down as truly now as it did then. And let me hope this year's young will find such teachers to remember, once they have stopped hurrying and made their real commencement.

July 8, 1961

64

Mass Miseducation

The student uprising at Berkeley seems to have passed at least its first pitch of intensity, but the campus clearly remains aware of contested issues, and there can be no doubt that faculty, administration, and students—whatever the individual casualties and inconveniences—are the better for their continuing confrontation.

A great university is always a cumbersome administrative rite at whose mechanical altar the IBM machines hum and the punchcards click and flutter. In the vestry rooms behind that altar, committees meet and ponder their instructions from and to the machines. There is no need to doubt the sincerity and the qualifications of the committee members, but it will not do to ignore the influence of their environment. The walls are thin where they meet and the hum, click, and flutter of the electronic machines is a perpetual presence. Like the tiny but persistent clatter of prayer wheels, the sound runs on forever to remind the hearer that the shrine is dedicated to the millionage of merit, the individual prayer-click being as nothing within the overhum of the All. It is easy, therefore, for those men to think in terms of mass output and to arrive at principles and regulations that might govern a vast traffic of units, rather than at policies that emphasize the individual.

But a great university must also be the echoing vault and resonator of the individual. At whatever cost in hum-click efficiency, the student must be allowed his personal contact with his chosen disciplines, and within those disciplines he must be granted expression, some degree of intimate contact with his mentors, and the right to commit himself to his view of world problems. An extraordinary mind may survive machine education, but the average output of the machine will not be good enough to justify the expediencies of mass administration.

The issue at Berkeley is complex but its core is the student's demand that he be received into education as an individual, and that his reasonable right to think about world issues and to act upon them as an individual be recognized. Because that demand is inseparable from the ideal function of any free university, there can be no doubt that the university will hear and heed. The students have reminded Berkeley that it has not yet learned to be what it must become, and in time Berkeley will be grateful for that reminder.

But if Berkeley brought the problem into the headlines, it did not bring it into being. Our great university centers have taken to mass education in about the way the officers' clubs of pre-World War II took to the arrival of the draftees. In camp, the yardbirds were assembled and told they were in the army. They were then sent to the supply sergeant, assigned to barracks, and turned over to drill sergeants. On campus, the freshmen are exhorted by the president (if he happens to be on campus) or a dean. They are given room assignments, sent to the bookstore for supplies, and then turned over to teaching fellows. The teaching fellows, needless to say, are busy and they didn't really want to teach undergraduates in the first place. They have enough to do in meeting their doctoral requirements and if it is a choice between satisfying a full professor's curiosity or a freshman's, the freshman will just have to wait. The chances are that the freshman will still be waiting by the time he has become a senior. There is a better than fair chance that he will complete his four years on campus without having spent as much as four hours in direct conversation with the tenured faculty.

Like the teaching fellows, of course, the professors are busy. When a university goes from 10,000 to 30,000 students the committee work goes up by some more than arithmetical progression, and those committee meetings must be gone to. More urgently, the faculty member has his research projects to get on with. No one, you may be sure, ever made a scholarly reputation by sitting around to talk things over with confused undergraduates. The only real pay-off is in bibliography. So the professor takes to his

66

cubicle in the library stacks and if the student manages to track it down he finds a sign on the door that announces:

THIS IS NOT AN OFFICE

And if the student then hunts down the professor's office he finds a sign announcing:

OFFICE HOURS: MON. 2:00–3:00
AND BY APPOINTMENT

And on Monday it turns out that 2:00–3:00 is the hour just before the professor's seminar in Lesser Romantics, that he is busy shuffling his notes, and that he is leaving after the seminar for a lecture at the University of Hawaii.

This case history may border on caricature but at no point does it actually violate the frontier. Not only have many university faculties become primarily graduate faculties in a concerted withdrawal from undergraduate teaching, but they have bred into the brightest of their new Ph.D.s a contempt for teaching. A man who just squeaks through the doctoral requirement may have to drift off to Hoopoe State College. Hoopoe, to be sure, is bidding in a seller's market and has to go to $14,000 and an associate professorship to get any sort of authentic eighteenth-century man from the main factory. And his grindmates will nod to him when they meet at the annual convention and slave auction (at which nothing but teaching fellows and assistant professors really come up for bidding). But the fact is quietly registered that the man is a dropout from glory. He has lost status.

Nor is the true measure of status to be found in the age and dignity of the college to which a man is summoned. A Columbia appointment, to be sure, would have been one up on Hoopoe. But the true measure of status has become freedom from teaching. The graduate-club dream now begins at $18,000 a year on an appointment as research professor with the understanding that no true scholar can be expected to teach more than one gradaute seminar every other semester.

Nor does it matter that this dream is not for every man to waken to. Let a man establish a reputation as a hot bibliography

67

and the dream is within reach. Large numbers of bright young men have picked off just such appointments, and the existence of those appointments has registered on the academic factories that turn out maximum-prestige doctorates. A man may still be forced out into the world, and there he may be forced to teach a full schedule, but his regular presence in the classroom is the proof of his professional failure. The really good ones, he knows, are not required to be there.

So mass education drifts higher and higher, perhaps even to the point of anoxia. And so it is that if the Berkeley students have forced their administration to squint down the educational log and to wonder whatever happened to Mark Hopkins, they will have performed a service to all education in America. What has to be achieved is a teacher-student relationship and that relationship cannot begin to develop until our graduate centers take on the responsibility of turning out teachers—go-to-class, hang-around, talk-to-students teachers.

March 27, 1965

Dead Geraniums

Every teacher sooner or later winds up with a private collection of weird examination answers, and having myself darkened enough classrooms to have caught the basic occupational diseases, I have culled a fair collection of my own. Inevitably, that means a story coming on. But fear not. My present purpose is not to start an academic joke book. What I really have in mind is one more sneaky way of leaving a lot of mail unanswered. But first the story.

Back in 1940 I taught a summer school course in modern poetry at the University of Kansas City and, as it ever must, examination time came on. A standard examination device in such courses is a series of "spot passages," unidentified specimen quotations from the poets studied in the course. In that section of the examination the student is instructed to identify the author of each passage and to give reasons for each identification.

Ideally, such passages should be taken from poems not specifically assigned as part of the course reading. The idea is to test not the student's memory, but his ear for the qualities of each poet's speaking voice.

As such, it is a fair minimum test. Many students who seem to be hopeless at assembling a critical reasoning process do nonetheless have a sound ear. Given a previously unknown passage, they can recognize it as being in the manner of one poet or another. When they are able to do that much, even when they seem to have no summonable critical discourse, I am tempted to believe that a minimum recognition has taken place and—all else permitting—to let it go for a low pass.

This summer school class, however, was made up of school teachers. I am reporting no more than simple fact—and sadly—when I say that the work done in our college summer sessions, when the teachers come flooding in to pick up their advancement credits, falls a whacking cut below the standards required of undergraduates in the regular school year, low as those standards too often are. Although that summer session was my first experience teaching teachers, I had discovered long before final-exam time that I could not insist on normal undergraduate standards unless I was prepared to flunk 90 per cent of the class.

I was neither as old nor as mean then as I am now and I was not so prepared. I not only took my spot passages from poems that had been specifically assigned, but from poems that had been discussed at some length in class.

One passage was from Eliot's "Rhapsody on a Windy Night." I hoped the teachers would identify it not only as Eliot's but as an example of his "shock" style, of the sort of passage that begins with a smoothly standard "poetic" diction, tone, and rhythm, but then shifts abruptly into a tonal discord, a hard rhythm, and a clashingly "unpoetic" image. One such passage is the opening of "Prufrock." The first two lines set off as languidly as the early Yeats:

> Let us go then, you and I,
> When the evening is spread out against the sky,

Then they are followed by the abruptly shifting third line:

> Like a patient etherized upon a table.

The passage I selected was another such (as, in fact, we had discussed in class), the first line all languid flowing; the second, socko:

> Midnight shakes the memory
> As a madman shakes a dead geranium.

One of my teachers had a bad time with that passage. First she wrote "T. S. Eliot." Then she crossed that out and wrote "Hart Crane," only to cross that out and write again "T. S. Eliot." Then back to Crane, and back again to Eliot, and so on through a dozen vacillations till she crossed out the last "T. S. Eliot" with one great bold stroke and wrote in firm block letters, adding an outsize exclamation point as her monument to mind: "HART CRANE!"

Her choice so made, it was time to add some reasons for it. Her comment—unforgettable word for word—ran: "At first I thought this was by T. S. Eliot. But Eliot is more of a negativist. And Hart Crane is more of a positivist. And a madman may be doing a silly thing shaking a dead geranium, but at least he's trying!"

This prairie flower of my first academic summer has popped in and out of my mind any number of times since. In my private mythology, in fact, she is the nymph Inflexa, the patroness of Rigor Mortis, whose special ritual is the Absolute Category. The gift of her mind is to be forever immune to the arts.

Give such a dutiful categorizer a series of firm labels along with any amount of itemization under each label and you may reasonably expect that all will be memorized to be spilled back on demand. But talk about the general sense of things, of the feel of ideas, of the impurity of ideas and motives, or of the essential multiplicity of the language of the arts, and the categorizer is lost: the flunked end of all summer. For what conversation can any man hope to enter into with such a mind?

I returned from this later summer's end to find the mail stacked twelve-weeks high. Having finally sorted it, I find myself in possession of one file folder in which there are twenty-two letters, all bludgeoning away at one or another of the poems published in *SR*, and all asking in what must have been meant as scorn: "Do you call *that* a poem?"

I could answer that I obviously do call it a poem, some sort of poem, or I should not have accepted it for publication. It is easier, of course, to toss the whole file into the wastebasket. And that, as a matter of fact, is just where it is going. Why should any man use up the hours of his life explaining to people what they have already shown themselves to be unwilling to understand?

For certainly they are categorizers all. They have locked onto the idea "poem" as an absolute category. They could no more set sensitively conceived limits to that category than could my prairie flower of twenty-two summers gone to her idea of "positive" and "negative." The categories so conceived are stony blanks. They leave about as much room for discussion as would a boulder rolling downhill.

Let it roll. But forgive me for stepping aside. Even a madman would stop shaking his dead geraniums long enough to get out of the way of that one.

And where *is* that wastebasket?

October 26, 1963

Library Science and "These People"

The obviously sleepy towns of Orange and East Orange, New Jersey, have had more than their share of rude awakenings of late. There has, in fact, been hell to pay among the split levels of that particular twin buckle in the suburban belt. Oddly enough, the bells that rang so rudely seem to have been set off in the East Orange Public Library.

A library, as I hope some good souls will agree, is no place for alarm bells. It is, rather, a quiet storage place, and what it stores is the memory of the human race. It is a place for the soft rustle of pages and the quiet stir of thoughts over the reading tables. Ideally, there should be a long slanting fall of light from tall windows as the afternoon goes. If there can be a fluff of elms and maples at the windows, so much the better. If, now and then, a lady in a smock gum-shoes busily by with an armful of books, her slight distraction is of the nature of the place and does not matter. But, please, no whispering: no book can be heard properly over a mindless buzz-buzz from the next table. And above all, no alarm bells!

Yet alarm bells there were, and, as one more thing for the library's memory bank to record, the story goes so: Last February, as some readers may recall, the embattled librarian of East Orange (which is to say, the guardian of those memory banks) braved the wrath of the barbarian hordes and rose to the defense of his plundered shelves. Overdue books had not been returned! The holy pillars of the printed word were obviously tottering. Something had to be done. And it was done, all in one slap-happy night when the local constabulary went raiding through the wee hours and hauled fifteen criminals from their warm beds to the cold calaboose. Their crime: all fifteen had failed to return overdue books.

Who knows what they teach at Library School these days? But certainly the curriculum must be changing. A man might reasonably hope that one course to be required of all librarians would deal with the problems of getting the right books stolen. The function of a library, after all, is to get people to read those books, to get the memory-bank into their own heads. If you have to let them be stolen in order to get them read, for heaven's sake let them be stolen. Since when has the orderliness of the library records been more important than the basic act of reading one good book avidly? Even an overdue book. Even a stolen one. In reason, let an exception be made for rare books whose market value might induce theft-for-greed. But let every theft of the gifts of mind be cherished and encouraged.

That course, however, seems to have been dropped from the librarian's curriculum in favor of some doubtful innovations. East Orange's library theory seems all too clearly to reflect the growing influence of such intellectual fads as Night Stick Inventory. Even the Dewey Decimal System is in danger of being supplanted by the Mug File of Suspected Readers. The first thing you know, a man will have to submit to fingerprinting and be cleared by the House Un-American Activities Committee before he may ask for a library book.

A man might wonder, too, if Library Science, East Orange style, has really thought this thing through. It was hard enough to get the kids into the library on sunny days. If East Orange persists in this sort of thing there will be no kids showing up even on rainy ones. Not even when Mother station-wagons them right up to the front door. Assuming that Mother is of that breed of intellectual tigress that will send them forth to brave the police state between them and "Black Beauty."

There seems nothing to foresee in this direction but a spotless vault of a library with every book in its place, with every card in the file accounted for, and without so much as a single book over-due. In fact, without so much as a customer in the place and with no books at all in circulation. It is a bookkeeper's dream, though not exactly a bookman's.

Even better, after a few years of this perfect state of things, the librarian, in his antiseptic isolation, will finally be able to stamp himself "Canceled," lock the front door of his dream house, and walk quietly into his particular sunset, leaving behind him no least disorder resembling intellect in process, nor any least trace in all the Oranges of an absent-minded man with ashes on his vest, a gleam in his eyes, and an overdue book in his hands.

That happy and sterile end, however, is not yet in sight. There still remains some distance between Heaven and the split levels. Meanwhile, the Night Stick Inventory so brilliantly applied to East Orange's library problems has spread to neighboring Orange, where last month that other eager constabulary rode from 2 to 7 A.M. hauling startled and still-sleepy wretches to the local police headquarters, Magistrate Ovid Colalillo presiding. There the culprits were ordered to put up $10 bail or to spend the night in the clink. Their crime was less literate than that of their East Orange neighbors: they had failed to pay $1 fines on overtime parking tickets.

As if to underline the effects of gross guilt on the human soul, one of the accused who had had the bad grace to be ill, collapsed before the dreadful bar of Magistrate Colalillo and had to be taken to Memorial Hospital. At that point Hizzoner, having imposed fines on five of the guilty, stayed the even hand of justice and suspended the hearings of the rest.

Top honors of the evening, however, must certainly go to Police Lieutenant Louis Aronchick. "If these people," Lieutenant Aronchick declared, "had paid attention to the summonses originally, they wouldn't have been awakened." An impeccable piece of logic, Orange style.

Lieutenant Aronchick's way of referring to "these people" is especially to the point and leads directly back to the Library System. He must have grown up in the days when the local library was glad to have its books read. Had he taken advantage of that old-style willingness, he might easily have found in the library a book called a dictionary, and therein he might once have found the word "citizen," which, in its plural form, might have provided him with a much-to-be-preferred synonym for "these people." Had he looked further, he might have found "citizen" defined as "a member of a state or nation, especially one with a republican form of government, who owes allegiance to it by birth or naturalization, and is entitled to full civil rights." Then, had Lieutenant Aronchick-to-be underlined the last seven words of that definition, at least on the page but preferably in his mind, he might conceivably have begun an escape in that instant from the sort of contempt that has since deformed his vocabulary to the point where he says "these people" when referring to "citizens." I am less certain what Magistrate Colalillo forgot to underline in his boyhood reading and in his law books, but something certainly, and that something an essence.

Had that essence had time to penetrate the Police Department and the Magistrate's Court, whatever passes for mind in the

74

Oranges would have given off a better sound in the course of two mad nights last month. And who can doubt that the libraries of the Oranges would then have rested on firmer foundations?

August 26, 1961

Bookkeepers and Keepers of Books

In a recent column I suggested that sending the police to haul people out of bed and into the clink at 4 A.M. (East Orange, N.J.-style) is not a happy way of getting overdue books back to the library. I should have thought that proposition was self-evident, as I believe it will yet seem to a keeper of books, which is to say, to a true librarian, which is to say in turn, to a librarian who lets his books into his life as well as into his clerical procedures. It is only to bookkeepers, which is to say, to the fussy-minded literalists in the ranks of the librarians, that such a proposition can seem offensive. A functionary has no mind.

A functionary can, however, write a letter on library stationery and claim to be speaking as a librarian, and I enter in evidence a fat file of such letters accusing me of—among other things—(1) anarchy, (2) encouraging the plundering of library shelves, (3) failure to keep faith with the oppressed librarians of this world, (4) gross cynicism, and (5) a general assortment of deficiencies ranging largely from paranoia to schizophrenia and back again by way of communistic irresponsibility.

Three such bookkeepers, in fact, write me to announce that they are having their revenge by taking my own books off their offended shelves. (I am not quite sure how that works. Keyes Metcalf once told me that it costs the Widener Library something more than $3 to go through the clerical steps of discarding a book.

One bookkeeper announces that she is dumping eight of my books. Does she charge more-or-less $24 to public funds, or does she stay late and do the deed on her own time? Or does she simply lock me up with the illustrated books on anatomy and other items listed as Special Collections? Or does she misfile me with "Who's Who in South-Central Tasmania"?)

I seem to be headed for The Dark Shelf, but before I go I hope the keepers of books will allow me to say that I have no real intention of burning down the libraries. I can even, and happily, endorse the ideal of efficient library records tidily kept. But I must still make the point, in defense of us all, that a man guilty of a misdemeanor is not a felon and has not surrendered his rights and dignities as a citizen. Whatever my psychiatrist may uncover when I get around to one, I do not generally encourage lawlessness. Reasonable respect for the law, however, requires no man to respect unreasonable police action, and on that point I mean to stand to all opposition.

That opposition does not exclude an awareness of the librarian's problems. Any man who serves the public has problems. But a man who lacks the grace to handle such problems humanely is in the wrong calling. The head of a department of the Los Angeles Public Library writes me:

In this dustless, inhuman globule of a place you describe as a "library" apparently no one asks "What do you mean the book isn't in?"—or dashes to the shelves with an eager enthusiasm that fades to perplexed dismay at a shelf virtually devoid of Hemingway—or patiently asks to wait his turn for a volume and comes in after three months to find it is still not returned. In the lunatic West Coast atmosphere where I work, this is an hourly occurrence. It not only plays havoc with the emotions and the blood pressure, it means that I sit patiently year after year ordering ten more copies of a Hemingway title or wondering if the budget will permit replacement of the two sets—at ten dollars a throw—of "Remembrance of Things Past" that some lover of literature took out very legally on his card but never returned. (This same character also in the course of his borrowing "read" some forty volumes of modern poetry that were unreturned and unreturning

76

when he left for an unknown address—this might even cause you to turn a hair.)

Without implying any endorsement of this "character," I can report no turned hairs, though I am a bit confused as to how many books a man is allowed to take out at one time on one card. However sad the "character," he is a foreseeable vexation of any librarian's lot. Let him be restrained, but let the restraint be from reason. He constitutes no justification for the kind of police night-riding made infamous by the Gestapo.

This bookkeeper's real problem is that he just doesn't like people and, thereby, cannot much like his job. My suggestion is that he find more congenial employment in a more isolated place.

May I say to him (and to some dozens of others who asked the question more or less indignantly) that what the East Orange Librarian should have done, had he thought as much of the rights of his neighbors as he did of the condition of his shelves, is obvious enough. He should, after adequate warning, have filed a civil suit for recovery of damages to the library. There can be no doubt that the court would have found for him and that it would have assessed all costs against the defendant if found liable. The rate at which court costs can mount would have been more than enough to scare other laggards into returning their overdue books.

By all means guard those shelves, dear friends. But the minute you believe that orderly accounting is more important than the rights of even your negligent neighbors, in that minute you become no keepers of books but bookkeepers.

If there is time still left me before I am hauled to that Dark Shelf, I must certainly use it to reply to another California bookkeeper, this one in Burbank. "If in order to protect the rights of the great majority of library users," he writes, "the public librarian stubs the toes of the irresponsible few, this is a sacrifice well worth making."

I have no peace to make with this man's mind. I find him all too eager to sacrifice others to his own notion of the good. Whoever appointed a public librarian as anybody's toe-stubber? And to whom is this sacrifice so well worth making? To Joe Doakes pulled out of his bed at 4 A.M. to be dropped shivering into the local clink? Sure, Joe is no pillar of the community. He may even be a negligent slob. But he hasn't gone in for armed robbery yet.

If this bookkeeper finds heart's comfort in knocking them down that happily, I remain unpersuaded that the keepers of books will share his love of the big stick. The true librarian will keep not only his books but the idea of his library. The problems of accounting, clerical frustrations, budgetary pressures, bad pay, and all the annoyances that come to any man in the service of the public will fret him, but he will not grow surly and sadistic. Who keeps an idea keeps a mercy, and we all have need of one another's mercies. Even when we have been negligent. Even when we have been warned. Even when the librarian has problems. And especially when local police decide to get funny.

September 30, 1961

Homily

When it began life in its first Greek combination of roots, *homilia* meant simply "a moral discourse or sermon delivered to a substantial gathering of people." As any man's introspection will tell him, it is not possible to sermonize at congregations for any length of time without becoming tiresome about it, and so our word "homily" has come to mean any sort of tedious sermonizing. The idea of sermonizing to a crowd does remain buried in the roots of the word, but in another sense the crowd may be no more than one busy child. Homilies, for example, are what parents talk to their children, laboring through hopeful tedium to point the way. And never more so than when the parent in question finds himself addressing a local public school.

He is there in the first place because the schools go on having what they call "assemblies" and because *someone* has to be roped in to say *something*. He is there in the second place because he cannot talk his way out of every invitation to be banal in the public service. And he is there in the third place as a sort of extended parent, hopefully trying to persuade not one child and not his own, but a whole assembly hall full of other people's children to. . . . And there his reasons break down. What does one hopefully persuade the young to do?

The student charged with making the introduction (which is always a mangled misreading of the *Who's Who* entry with the book titles always garbled) concludes by saying that the day's speaker will now bring his message. And what message is there?

I am grateful to Dr. Reuben L. Kahn for one such. If it is a homily, it is so in the first Greek sense, without the accrual of tedium. And it has the added merit of arising from a man's reflections on his own great career.

Dr. Kahn, professor emeritus at the University of Michigan, where he still continues his researches, is a distinguished serologist, now at work for the Atomic Energy Commission on the effects of radiation upon the body's immunizing mechanisms. He is perhaps most widely known for the Kahn test for syphilis, which has universally replaced the earlier Wasserman test, offering a faster, less cumbersome, and more certain method of diagnosis. He is perhaps least widely known as my good friend, that being a matter of my luck rather than his. Now a spry and still searching seventy-eight, Dr. Kahn has published an article titled "The Inspiration of Research" in the *Michigan Quarterly Review*, and it is from his article that I excerpted the one homily I could offer the young with no need to confess deceit to my own subsequent self-inquiry.

Here, with my thanks for it, is Dr. Kahn's preachment as he looks back over his own far from finished career:

Many students believe that brilliance is absolutely necessary for research. Students have frequently told me that they were not brilliant enough to turn to research, but I think that they most likely lacked not the brilliance but the interest and the dedication. I, for one, was far from a brilliant student at college. There were a number of far more brilliant students than I who accomplished relatively little in their careers.

I am one of those who believes that brilliance in a given field can in a large measure be acquired. It is well known that in our daily work we hardly ever exhaust our mental powers, just as we rarely achieve the highest physical development of which we are capable. Physiologists are well aware of the inherent capacity of the organs of the body to increase greatly their functional ability. If a lung or a kidney is removed, the remaining one will perform the work formerly done by the two. Body cells possess an inherent capacity for far greater functional activity than they are called upon to perform in daily life. The same applies to brain cells. No university student can foretell how brilliant he might become in his chosen field unless he gives himself a thorough trial, and the only way he can give himself such a trial is by solid effort.

Dr. Kahn is both a brilliant and a wise man, but let me suspect (continues the visiting homilist, gripping his lectern) that he yields too much to modesty. I value his homily, and I hope the young of all ages may be instructed by it. But my uneasy parenthood leaves me uncertain. Dr. Kahn makes a fascinating physiological case for the argument that particular kinds of brilliance can, in large part, be acquired. My first thought is to wonder if they are not acquired by those who have an initial charge of brilliance and who then work at it. Certainly there are brilliant starters who let go because they do not care enough. And everyone knows that brilliance plus hard work is the established formula of great genius.

But Dr. Kahn is putting forth the more unusual proposition that almost any man—brilliant or not—who will really extend himself, stands a chance of stretching his ordinary capacity to the point of achieving brilliance. He is suggesting that a one-horsepower mind can turn out two horsepowers of work, that the two-horsepower mind so achieved can turn out four, and so on.

There must be some limit to that progression, to be sure. And, just as surely, Dr. Kahn is not implying that a mentally deficient person can become brilliant through hard work. But may it not be that mental deficiency is precisely the inability to work hard?

I am sure that is the case with writers. The difference between a working writer and a would-be writer is basically in the fact that the working writer works. He works not only when he is feeling well but when he is off his feed, and the quantity of his work is measured to some extent by what is published, but even more by the far larger part that goes into the wastebasket. And he works because he has found what he wants to work at.

At the risk of twisting Dr. Kahn's homily out of his mouth in order to make my own—and I hope I am not guilty of having done so—I want to argue for brilliance as the appetite for work not as drudgery but as joy, as what Robert Frost called "the pleasure of taking pains."

I am emboldened to read that sense into Dr. Kahn's argument because his own life and presence breathes forth nothing more certainly than the joy of his absorption into his work. Let that example be my final homily to the school system.

All the boys and at least some of the girls seem to be thinking in terms of making a living, and I want to use Dr. Kahn to remind them that it is better to find the work that will make a life rather than a living, and then to work at it with an absorption that is both devoted and joyous.

Forgive me, Reuben, if on the surface of things I seem to have used your homily only to put forth my own. I dare do so only because I am certain that we are agreed in depth. And thank you for arming me for my encounter with the terrifying young. I should have been much more at ease with your kind of youth. Let me hope for a chance to share more of it soon.

December 11, 1965

Confessions of a Circuit Rider

I am on the lecture trail and tonight's lecture is over. It is long after midnight and I must be up before six to make my airline connection to the next place. I am tired but the hotel room is too hot when I close the window and too drafty when I open it and the bed swelters around me when I try to sleep. There is, of course, nothing wrong with the room or the weather or the bed. The room, in fact, is luxurious beyond the dream of most of this world. There are people sleeping soundly on straw somewhere and finding the straw a luxury. All that is wrong with the weather, the temperature, or the bed is inside me. I am having an attack of insomnia, and insomnia distorts every thought that passes through it.

As part of that distortion, I keep thinking of the beagle-faced student who stuck to me for an hour after the talk. He had his soul out to affirm and he had decided that I was his affirmation. Something big had happened to him within the insomniac distortion of his own life in some small town that had been blown open by his visits to the library. Or not really blown open but just cracked and crazed. With every good intention he was charging me with being important.

How does one deny that charge to the hot eyes of an insomniac who insists on staying up for his dreams? What he was accusing me of was nothing I had done. He was charging me with his own mystique of importance, with his hot and, God knows, human need to find Significance. The need was in him and I had come along, booked by my agent, with advance puffs in the local papers, and with all the trimmings that prepare a small college for the appearance of a lecturer from Outside.

How could I deny his need without accusing him of having squinted all his life through a local knothole into a nonexistent universe? Insomniac to insomniac, I sit up smoking and thinking of things I might have said to him.

"Son," I might have said, and do in fact try to say to him, "until now you exist only in the mercy all of us owe one another, but without having begun to imagine a language for it."

It sounds, alas, like something out of an arty novel. Or like something out of a TV script imitating something out of an arty novel. But I still see his eyes and they have to be told something, somehow. Poor beagle. All his fervor was sniffing around in search of nothing but a master. It is discomforting to be mistaken for a half-god, even by a beagle.

"Look, beagle," I try to tell him, "I was paid well over $1,000 for coming here tonight to give a spiel not much different from

82

the spiel I gave in another town last night and from the one I shall give in still another town tomorrow night and so on until by the end of the week I am left with checks for several times more than the estate my father left. Somehow that suggests some measure of a man's life but I don't know what measure it is, so let it pass. The fact is I never get up on a platform except for cash, and then only when I am overpaid. I am not worth it, and the world is insane to pay these prices, but there are some of the world's insanities I am careful not to argue with. Now please go home poor and let me get to sleep rich. But for God's sake take those beagle eyes to a good book and try formulating from it something like a perception that has no dog eyes attached to it."

But that sounds wrong, too. I had spoken to the students about poetry and I had spoken as honestly as I should have spoken to any of my own classes had I still been on the faculty. I am, to be sure, a bit of a ham by now. Every good teacher is to begin with, and by now I have been riding the circuit a long time and I am good at it.

What I am good at is the art, or the craft, of sensing an audience. I could, if I wanted to, take my audience craftily, keep it laughing with just the right touch of dissembling candor, make sure the pace does not slacken, and come through high and hard at the end. All it takes is skill and by now I have that. Nor is there anything wrong with skill. It takes a man to be skillful.

But not all of a man. What takes all of a man is something like a sense of honesty. At least of self-honesty. It may not be exactly that, but honesty is a name that will do for whatever it is. And there is—confess it—something about the idea of honesty that does not mix well with the idea of being easily skillful. But why? Am I about to become a beagle, too? Must every honesty be a clumsy mortal sweat? Yes, where it touches mortal issues. But there are no mortal issues involved in riding the lecture circuit. I am doing what I am good at and I am trying to make an open and honest communication of it.

Not that there is any way of being entirely honest to any audience. An audience is not a person but a collective beast. That beast must be engaged by certain formalities. There is also the fact—a fact known to everyone who has learned to sense an audience—that at times one's mind loses a connection, especially

83

when the talk is not canned, and I loathe canned talk. So a man drops a stitch now and then. Or mixes the metaphor as I am doing now. That is the point at which the skill-man takes over, faking the chords until the theme comes back to him. The one theme I can honestly pursue, of course, is never to fake an idea. Nor will I, if I can help it. But can I always help it? I talk too much, and inevitably I find myself worrying for fear that I have faked what must not be faked. All one can do then is confess his worry to the members of his audience, apologizing to each.

And then, from his uncertainty to mine comes—sooner or later but always comes—the beagle with eyes that leak worship. Nothing, alas, warns beagle not to love uncritically. A beagle is a life-long insomnia.

The best I can do now is to use my insomnia to teach me what to say to the next beagle. In four more days this two weeks will be over. I shall be able to sit at my desk for months in the most unimportant way, and all the world's miles from tonight's beagle and last night's and tomorrow night's. The good of exorbitant fees is that it takes only a few of them to meet the mortgage payments and to have an extra steak to toss to the wolf at the door. The damnation of it is that the wolf is so much easier to handle than that beagle. I have the wolf skinned by now, to mix another metaphor, but the beagle stays alive to terrify me.

In this churn of insomnia I could almost let myself into the romantic fraud of self-accusation. I could roll around on this bed of neuroses and relish every itch as the fabric of my twentieth-century hairshirt. But guilt is a luxury I cannot afford.

I told the beagle, with such gentleness as I could master, that his eyes were wrong for any world I know how to look at. And that was all of it. Except that I came small and tired and that I shall leave sleepless and more tired. But any lie that was told was told by his own insomnia, not by mine.

In four days I shall lose him again for months to come. And, blessedly, I shall have my own bed to sleep in. But what I wish right now is that he would get his beagle eyes out of this night's insomnia and let me get one snatch of this night's sleep.

November 7, 1964

84

The Courage of His Confusions

It is easy enough to praise men for the courage of their convictions. I wish I could teach the sad young of this mealy generation the courage of their confusions.

Perhaps there was a world once in which conviction was a sufficient base for humane perception. I think I know a bit about that world. Both my parents came off an Italian mountain, from an ancient, ritualistic society whose pattern had been set and locked as far back as crones could mythologize or scholars guess. On those mountains things were as they had been and would be, and why ask questions?

The immigrant parents clung hard to their convictions here in America, in a world made to another pattern. But what the parents told their children described no world the children met outside the house. The enormous emotional dislocation of the children of immigrants—especially of the children of immigrant peasants—centers in the conflict so many children felt, of needing to respect their parents at the same time they knew their parents were talking intense nonsense when they tried to describe the rules of the world outside. Convinced ignorance describes no world.

But if the conflict between immigrant parents and their children is an extreme case, it is only the extreme of a conflict that may exist between all parents and all children. We labor to teach the young rules of conduct that amount to convictions, yet which of us is really sure of the convictions we peddle to our cubs?

May it not be that we have made too much of conviction as an ultimate goal? Show me a man who is not confused and I will show you a man who has not been thinking. He will be a man who has not asked enough questions.

He will, in fact, incline to think that the reason for asking questions is to answer them. Is it? May it not be the greater merit of questions that they lead not to answers but to new questions, and the new questions to others, and they to others yet?

There will always be more questions than thoughtful men can answer, though the unreflective, to be sure, will always have their fast answers ready. The essence of intellect is in the engagement of proliferating confusion. And if that proliferation is the real subject matter of intellect, then it must follow that conviction can be achieved only by turning away from the inquiry; by refusing to face things in their visible complexity.

Conviction, I am arguing, is possible only in a world more primitive than ours can be perceived to be. A man can achieve a simple gnomic conviction only by ignoring the radical describers of his environment, or by hating them as convinced men have hated, say, Darwin and Freud as agents of some devil.

It is by the failures of the self-convinced that I find myself with little to say in final praise of the simple virtues. I have spent enough of my life among them. The American farm belt—at least in its dream-image—is the biblical desert of those uninquiring virtues. Honesty, hard work, forthrightness and downrightness, piety and patriotism (and add the distrust of strangers) are the rural virtues of which our editorialists have created the myth of the farm-to-market heaven.

But let it be said also of these good simple folk—and they are good only insofar as they are simple—that they have more answers to their lives than they have questions of them.

I, for one, do not know how to live without more questions than I shall ever have answers for. And to the extent that I can believe my questions have encompassed all the answers of those simple folk, and gone beyond them to questions those simple folk have not come upon—to that extent I am bound to believe I have outtraveled them, and that my life has been better experienced than theirs. How could I think it less than a human disaster to throw away my questions in order to come to rest in nothing more than their answers?

Yes, I am confused, but I will prefer the larger confusion to the smaller certainty. The true force of education is nothing if it does

86

not drive a man into more and more meaningful confusions. What man of recent times has been better confused than, say, Einstein? His engagement of the confusing universe was his act of mind, positive and creative and of life. What sane man can let himself despair of his mind's life-force?

Let that be my plea to the young. The chances are they have already been taught more convictions than they will be able to live with unless they shut their minds. But let them be told at least once that the courage of one's convictions may in reality turn out to be the cowardice of one's mind, the retreat into easy and self-binding certainty. Where mind is the measure there must be the courage to face one's confusions whole.

For conviction may too readily be no more than the rejection of painful possibility. I once appeared on a Religious Week panel at a New Jersey College, speaking, by request, on "Images of Man in Literature." As one part of my talk I tried to describe the universe of such naturalistic writers as Zola, Hardy, and their followers. What, I asked, if the universe turns out to be vast and indifferent in just the way science seems to have described it to the naturalists? What if it is no more than a physical condition of basic indifference, but one that is essentially dangerous to creatures racially conditioned to a particular atmosphere and able to survive only within a relatively narrow range of temperature and pressure?

When I sat down one of my fellow panelists raised his distinguished head to the rafters, spread his arms dramatically, and cried with an impressive resonance, "Whence cometh my aid?" Whereupon he allowed for a dramatic silence and turned to me as if to say, "refute that if you can!"

How does one refute an emotion? Certainly every man has known the emotion of that question. But what do those words say if not, "I need to believe the Universe is watching me!" Perhaps we all need to believe that. But what if it isn't? Was not my colleague really crying, "The Universe owes me a meaning satisfactory to my emotions"? What the young might better consider is the formulation: "The Universe is worth being confused about." It takes courage to engage that confusion deeply. It is at least a ponderable proposition that the courage to engage it is a better, because a more humane, act of mind than is that order of conviction that can survive only by refusing to consider seriously those questions an inquiring mind must find unavoidable.

June 2, 1962

Confessions of a Circuit Rider — Epilogue with Some Static

My spring lecture tour began in March and continued with some furloughs through May. Eight days before I was to start it, I received a phone call from one of the campuses I was to visit. My caller identified himself as a lawyer working for the Civil Liberties Union and recited some serious charges against the college.

It had, he told me, refused to allow Negro leaders to speak on campus. It actively supported the activities of what he called "a Birch-like group." And it had threatened to expel students who had tried to contact me.

The charges were both disturbing and nebulous. On questioning, my caller confessed he knew of no specific refusal to allow a Negro to speak, but rather that "the way things are it would not be possible for a good Negro leader to speak on this campus." Had any Negroes spoken on campus? Well, yes, there had been two Negro speakers this year, but none who were "activist enough."

A number of turns in his way of phrasing himself made me think he was a student rather than a lawyer. I asked him who was "activist enough" to his way of thinking. He thought, well, maybe Rap Brown. Had the students asked Rap Brown? I was asked what good that would do—"they" would never allow him to speak.

I tried questioning my caller about the "Birch-like group." It

88

turned out to be a little hard to describe, but I was told some of the faculty were definitely members.

I turned to his third charge. I told him I did not understand how students could be expelled for trying to get in touch with me.

The students, he told me, had announced in the college newspaper that they would attempt to get in touch with me, and one of the deans had replied in strong disagreement, and threatened expulsion.

Threatening to expel students if they tried to write to me?

Expulsion was certainly implied.

Could he send me a copy of the paper?

He certainly would. (And never did.)

By that point, I was sure my caller was a student. I asked him to spell his name so that I might write it down accurately. He gave me the name of the president of the college. I asked him about his law practice. He didn't exactly practice anymore, he said, but sort of worked for the American Civil Liberties Union. I asked which branch of the Civil Liberties Union he worked with. He said it wasn't exactly the CLU but a committee interested in that sort of work. A student committee? Well, yes it was. And was he himself a student? Well, yes he was. And not in fact a lawyer? Well, no he wasn't.

I asked if he had any doubts about the ethics of misrepresenting himself to me. He said, well, he was sorry, but that the "mess on campus" was so bad the committee thought a little deception was justified in a good cause.

I asked how many students were on his committee, and he told me it was very popular. Did he know, roughly, how many? Well, there were quite a lot.

I told him I had a lot of questions to ask and reminded him he was running up a phone bill: Would he like me to call him back so we could talk on my time? He told me that wasn't necessary because he had a job in one of the deans' offices and was using a college phone.

I passed over a few ethical questions on that point and went back to "quite a lot." Did that mean, say, a hundred? He didn't think there were quite that many. Well, five then. Oh, there were more than five. Were there ten? I asked. He said he saw no point in playing a numbers game and that the principles of the committee would be important even if only one man could be found to defend them.

I could agree that principle matters more than numbers, and I told him so. Did it matter more than facts, or would he agree that principle is based on and arises from the facts of any given case?

He argued that when a principle is really important a few minor details don't really matter. The "mess on campus" was bad and anything was justified to make things better.

Would I, therefore, cancel my appearance and send him a letter he could circulate denouncing the "restrictive policies" of the administration? Or if I could not cancel, would I keep the lecture date, but skip my talk about poetry and use my time to attack the administration's policies?

I had had enough weary circles around nothing. I pointed out that I had a legally enforceable contract with the school, and that while a cancellation for cause was not out of the question, he was left with an obligation to give me detailed and documented evidence. Under no circumstances, of course, could I take the school's fee for a talk on poetry and use the occasion to blast the school's policies.

He said he agreed and promised me full documentation by special delivery.

Eight days later, having heard nothing, I began the tour. Thirty-seven days later—two days before I was to appear at the school—I received from my agent a letter on school stationery signed by a Professor X. The letter repeated the same charges in the name of a faculty committee and asked that I cancel my appearance or use the occasion to enter a strong protest against "restrictive policies."

Such a protest I must certainly enter. When I had read the letter, I phoned the school, asked for Professor X, and was told there was no such man on the faculty. It had already occurred to me that the same civil-libertarian who could latch on to the dean's phone could latch on to a school letterhead. Nor later, when I arrived on campus, could my questioning of students and faculty turn up evidence of any "mess on campus."

Let me enter a protest anyway. I enter it against the restrictive policies of students (I am convinced mine was no prankster) so utterly convinced of their rightness that it justifies any deception, impersonation, cheat, lie, evasion, or distortion of fact; who think nothing of asking others to break legal contracts without good cause or to betray the agreement by accepting a fee and using the occasion to abuse the payer; who seem to have no notion that intellectual honesty is itself a principle and that honored agreements are the one basis of civilized dealing; and who are sure that the piddlings of their own standardless emotions make them the custodians of all banners.

I suppose it is folly to have lived beyond thirty, but it is a folly time imposes. We the senile can see that we are about to drown in the rising tide of the puerile. There is still time for a damnation.

Here come the monstrous young lurching through the arches like the barbarians, and here sit the senile, like Roman senators. Be damned to you, axe swingers. You will be busy destroyers till your destroyers come. Get on with the destruction. We will not budge. And take what you can: We give you nothing but our damnation.

Nor am I sure I mean all of that.

But damn you anyway. Without a damnation there is no way of holding to what must be held.

October 26, 1968

Mailbag (*A Letter to Would-Be Summer Editors*)

Dear Miss Doe:

I am happy to know you are an honors English major. Your project for a senior thesis next year sounds admirably ambitious, though I suspect you may find that "Romantic Love in English Poetry" is a bit too panoramic for a single year's work, and even perhaps more than enough for a lifetime of dusty files. Mightn't you do well to set yourself a smaller but more manageable project —perhaps no more than the idea of romantic love in one or two English poets?

Certainly your experience as editor of your college literary magazine will stand you in good stead in whatever writing you do, and I must say I am impressed by the number of sonnets you have published in it in the last two years. You are right, too, in thinking it is virtually impossible to support yourself through creative writing, especially the writing of poetry. It is only prudent, therefore, to think of some sort of paying work, and certainly an editorial career can be an exciting one when it isn't being dull.

As far as I know, however, *SR* has no editorial openings for the summer. You can see that it would not make good sense to hire an editor who has to be replaced in three months.

Summer aside, I am bound to say I know of no publisher who is hiring editors or junior editors straight out of the commencement procession. Most of the editors I know began as relatives of the firm, as book salesmen, as newspaper people, as authors who had made some reputation of their own, or as secretaries to an editor. I gather you are not related to a publisher, have not sold books, do not want newspaper work, and have not established a literary reputation beyond your own campus. The most likely entrance into an editorial office, therefore, is with pad in hand. A good secretary can always find work. Let me urge you to learn shorthand and typing.

I know that night courses in a business college may seem a long way from romantic love in English poetry, or from one masthead to another. Nevertheless, there is reason in learning to be a secretary. If you have editorial ability, you will find it a lot easier to demonstrate from inside the office than from the outside. You will be working for an editor and you will be in one of the best possible situations for learning what an editor does.

If you are a good book reviewer, moreover, it would be a simple matter to run up a few reviews on your own. Unless you make a nuisance of yourself, the boss will be glad to have a look at them, and delighted to find something he can use. Or if your work is hopeful but not quite ready, it would still be natural for him to keep you in mind for possible future assignments as you develop.

Similarly, if you have good editorial sense, you will certainly find a chance to demonstrate it. If you lack talent, there is, of course, nowhere to go. But if you have talent, the big step may well be the step that puts you inside the office.

While I'm pontificating, let me add another thought. Your letter is all about you and what you plan to do. May all your boughs bear. But I find nothing in your letter about what you might offer an employer in return for the pay he is to give you at fixed intervals. Is it carping to suggest that an employer might reasonably be more interested in what you can do for him than in what he can do for you? Or at least as much interested in the one as in the other?

Please understand that I am trying to describe the world without necessarily implying total approval. As part of that attempted description, I submit that your teachers have been hired sympathies, bless them. As dedicated men and women they have made it their vocation to be interested in you and your development. I doubt that you will find many employers similarly dedicated. They will be men and women with a job to get done, and their professional interest will be in whether or not you can deliver what they need for the job. There is no question of their being willfully cold about it. Some will be, to be sure, but as a rule their simple interest will be in whether or not you can forward the work in hand, whereby you are in if you can and out if you can't. It is a mistake in any known world to expect of them the sort of sympathy you are used to from your teachers.

Your letter, I am getting ready to say, is girlish, and charming, and starry-eyed but suggests nothing a prudent man would be eager to put on his payroll. You could guess, too, I suppose, that this is the time of the year in which many such letters show up on every publisher's and editor's desk. What is sad about those letters is their altitude from reality. Their writers are always eager, bright, willing, shyly captivating, or romantically ablaze with the hope of a great career, and always as unemployable as the high noumenon at Klein's.

It seems never to have occurred to the writers of those letters that an editorial decision is not always an exercise in the perception of pure beauty, and that it is always one in which a certain amount of stockholder's cash must be invested.

I am not suggesting that all publishers are howling money-grubbers. I am astonished by the number of literate and even learned men I know among them. They must be businessmen, to be sure, but they are often willing to be unbusinesslike when their sense of merit is involved. I have known them to relish a decision that loses money but that pleases their sense of what good publishing should be.

They would be mad, however, to hire untrained young enthusiasms to make their losing decisions for them. Those are the decisions only the boss is entitled to make, and there is a long seasoning from the senior honors thesis to his desk.

Please do not understand me to be scornful of young aspiration. I am not sure but what I envy it when I am not thinking back in dread. I have to point out, however, that somewhere between aspiration and attainment you will have to answer to some of the points I have made here.

And there, worse luck, is your heavy-handed letter from the world; you send me your soul's hope and I send you to business college. But what else should I tell you? Is it my fault that you are not related to a publisher, have no literary reputation, and can offer no previous experience? I hope you have a zoom of a career. But first learn typing and shorthand. Then learn how to justify yourself to the payroll. And then ride for the stars.

Indefatigably, alas, this world's uncle,

Yours faithfully,
John Ciardi

February 20, 1965

Rejection Slips

At least half the mail on any editorial desk yearns, implicitly or explicitly, toward the unanswerable and always pleading question, "How do I become a writer?" In its most common subform the question reads: "If my writing is not publishable, will you analyze it for me and tell me how to improve it?" And often, as if flashing a credit card in payment of the check, the writer adds: "I am a subscriber."

I mean to quarrel with our subscribers only on principle and only when I must, but I must in reason if the assumption is that a subscription buys not only the magazine but the personal services of the editors. Let me believe, rather, that *SR* is bargain enough at the price, without including the editors, who are, in any case, no bargain.

Neither are they teachers. If a writer seriously wants guidance, he should enroll in a workshop at the nearest university, extension service, writers' conference, or adult education center. If there is none available to him where he lives, I know of nothing he can do except, perhaps, to move. And if the reasons against moving are more compelling than the desire to be a writer, then that man has something more important in his life than his writing, and he would be well advised to go for what is most important to him. The writer who means to write will find his guidance, whatever it costs him. Nor will any substantial part of it come from an editor—not at least until he is well advanced in his own craft. About all the editor can do for the beginning writer is done when he buys a given piece or rejects it. If he buys it, he may very well offer some suggestions. If he rejects it, he will normally do so with a rejection slip, the essence of which is "Sorry—not for us."

95

In the mercy that a day's work may hope to earn, there is little more an editor can do about unpublishable manuscripts. It is out of the question to think of providing individual criticisms, and nothing can change that fact, no matter how yearningly the question is put. Some of the other most common subquestions can, however, be answered with more or less standard information, and those I shall try to answer here.

Q. How do I go about submitting manuscripts for publication?

A. Legibly, and with a stamped self-addressed return envelope. Standard practice is to type the manuscript, double-spaced, on regular typing paper. Put your name and address on each page. Write an accompanying letter, if you like, but it will serve no purpose: the writing must sell itself. Above all, if your ego cannot stand the thought of having your writing returned with a printed rejection slip, keep the manuscript at home. The editor does not hate your soul. But he will have before him baskets full of the work of equal souls, some of whom may be better writers. His job is not to carry on a correspondence with your soul but to get through those baskets and to find in them the manuscripts that speak to his soul and, as he hopes, to the souls of his readers.

Q. Will my manuscript be read by the editor himself?

A. Yes—as far as the first cliché. No self-respecting editor will willingly buy clichés and the first one is reason enough to stop his reading. He owes at least that much to the readers of his magazine. If you want the editor to read to the end, you need only make sure that you provide him with no cliché-marked stopping places.

Q. How do I break into print?

A. More or less as everyone else does—by submitting manuscripts, collecting rejection slips, and restudying the writing in the hope of improving it until your manuscripts begin to break down the resistance an editor is hired to have. Any one editor may be wrong, but when any considerable number of them have sent back your manuscripts with plain rejection slips, that total adds up to a kind of information any reasonable man can interpret.

Q. Where can I get an agent?

A. In the future—maybe. Until you have published a few things on your own you probably have nothing to offer an agent. He lives on 10 per cent of his authors' sales and 10 per cent of nothing is no return. Go the first mile on your own, and when you are ready for an agent he will find you.

There are people who advertise as agents but they generally make their living by charging you a reading fee, not from a percentage of your sales. The code of ethics of the American Society of Authors' Representatives forbids advertising, and it is *SR* policy to accept no advertising that offers to place for sale the manuscripts of unknown authors.

In general, too, an agent is not of much use to a poet. There are too few paying markets for poetry, and their fees hardly invite agency interest. Any persevering poet can soon learn the possible outlets for poetry as thoroughly as an agent is likely to know them.

As with agents, so with publishing houses. There are vanity presses that publish at the author's expense, and all such must be approached with great caution. Their method of operation is legal enough, though it is ethically questionable when it involves flattering the writer beyond his merits in the hope of getting him to invest his money in a publication that will be ignored by all but his friends.

If you are in doubt about whether or not the agent or publisher is reputable, there is a simple test. Type out a batch of the worst possible writing you can bring yourself to commit, and send it off to what mystery-story fans call "the suspect." If he replies in nothing less than dithyrambs and panegyrics, duck: you have uncovered a pirate.

If, on the other hand, you sneak back to his letter and reread it with long rapt pauses, and then turn to the carbon of the manuscript and begin to think that maybe you outdid yourself without really knowing it at first—then, ah then, son of man, you have invented no part of the mistake the human race may turn out to be, and the universe does continue to spin around you in the same motion that includes mind and talent and the sublimities of both, but as a writer you are beyond the furthest hope of love or mercy.

And though your other virtues are as the stars in the firmament —though you honor your parents, love your children, earn your paycheck, vote thoughtfully, and do not beat your wife or husband, as the case may be—though every civil merit shines in you, and though you yourself shine in society as a personage, yet, I submit, you have no business with editors, nor have they any with you.

Your soul remains as real, and as unreal, as any other, and the editor means it no disrespect. But your papers on his desk are a daily nuisance of which he must rid himself in the simplest way, and the simplest way is the rejection slip.

You may not like the form of that slip, and your ego may find in its impersonality a rebuff to the intensity with which you recognize your own individuality. Yet the rejection slip, though necessarily vacuous, is always sweetly worded. It is meant to convey no rancor. And properly understood, it does answer your question. You wanted to know what he thought of your manuscript and he has told you, impersonally, yes, but politely enough: he doesn't like it.

And that, alas, does happen to be one of the answers of which the universe is capable.

August 21, 1965

The Editors Regret

The most common item of equipment on *SR*'s poetry desk is one that has become painfully familiar to one segment of the subscription list and is known as the rejection slip. The one I inherited nine years ago and still use, is printed in blue on an *SR* letterhead and reads as follows:

The Editors of *Saturday Review* regret that the inclosed material has not proved suitable for their current needs. They appreciate its merits and wish to thank the author for submitting it.

Let me confess that I dislike the awkward evasiveness of that phrasing. "Has not proved suitable for their current needs" is, at best, hollow. If your poem came back with a rejection slip attached, you can bet, at long odds that current or future need has nothing to do with it, and that it will never work out for any need at all. There are times when a poem the editor would like to publish is simply too long for any space that may become available in foreseeable time, and he must return it as simply beyond his resources, but in that case—if he really likes the piece— he will certainly put his regrets into a letter and hope for a look at some poems of more manageable length. What the rejection slip says in plain fact is that he has no use for the poem now or ever.

"They appreciate its merits" is, of course, another evasion. No editor tosses material into the out basket if he sees any real merit in it. To be sure, he may think of it as competent, but since when was competence good enough?

That printed slip is a special case of using words to make a social noise. One makes social noises by way of clearing his throat in preparation for saying what he really has to say. Or he makes them as a social cover-up for nothing to say when the situation seems to demand a few words whether or not they mean anything. The social noise of the rejection slip is of the second case.

What is there to say? The information any man gets from a rejection slip when he opens his return envelope is already manifest in the fact that the manuscript has been returned. And yet there seems to be some sort of social convention requiring that some sort of letter (if only an imitation of one) must accompany the self-evident, and why not a real letter? But *SR* receives somewhere between 400 and 600 poems weekly. How can any man hope to write or to dictate an individual letter with each set of rejected poems? The pallid subterfuge of the rejection slip is mathematically inevitable.

There can be no thought of liking rejection slips, and no one does. I once spent years accumulating a massive collection of them from the very best magazines and I even kept them together in a special drawer of my desk. But be sure I did not keep them to love. They were there as some sort of metaphysical hairshirt, my soul's wardrobe of prickly reminders, and a loathsome documentation of editorial stupidity.

I am on known ground, therefore, when some young man sends back his rejection slip with his own rejection of me scrawled across it. His is a motion of the living fire, and may the motion fan him to the heat of an irresistible creation.

Nor am I surprised when some virago of the bluebird sonnets writes me a snarly letter to demand why I haven't at least the good manners to acknowledge a personal communication personally—though I may wonder who let loose the premise that the act of submitting a poem for sale is a personal transaction.

Nor am I surprised when a plaintive matron writes to say she is wounded by the coldness of having her poem so treated. Not, of course, that she thought the poem was good enough for *SR* but she *did* so want me to see it personally. (Semantics, anyone?)

The core of it all, of course, is in that "personally." In any case, let me assure her, and any other reader who may care, that I do personally see all poems submitted to *SR*. There is no preliminary screening process. I look at them all. But let me note a difference between "looking" and "reading." "Reading" means all the way through and then, probably, over again. "Looking" means reading until the eye has come on a reason for rejecting the poem. The first cliché is generally reason enough. In most cases, moreover, the first cliché is likely to be the first thing in the poem. It usually has to be because the second thing in the poem is the second cliché, and the third thing the third cliché, and so on. What can one write in such cases, except a short essay on the nature of the cliché, about which any would-be writer should have known already?

But to think in that direction is to assume that most amateur poets care about the nature of poetry. They do not: they care only about releasing their own emotions. For even a bad poem is likely to be an intense act of the writer's personality. "I want to be paid attention to!" it says. And back home in everyman's ego, who doesn't?

So it is that the writer's objection to the rejection slip is not because it is inane, but because it is impersonal. Any inanity or evasion scrawled on a memo pad seems to do well enough. So long as it is "personal."

But whatever the form of it, there are only three things an editor can do with a manuscript that has been submitted to him.

He may buy it—and it is always a pleasure to find a poem one can buy with any enthusiasm. He may reject it. Or he may like it but be troubled by a number of details he wants to talk over—nondirectively, but in the hope the author will want to run them through his closest attention one more time.

It can be the editor's most valuable function to make such suggestions. I have myself been grateful to a number of good editors who led me to see things that needed reworking in a poem I had let myself hope was ready to go. Roughly a quarter of the poems published in *SR* contain changes that resulted from this sort of correspondence. And it is on such correspondence that the editor's time should be spent; not in chatty little elaborations of the self-evident. Beyond such correspondence, there can be nothing to say but "thanks, yes" or "sorry, no."

Still, of course, ego is ego, and the writer's more so. Some sort of social noise is demanded: one will be made. And if it can be made in a way that can soften the blow any ego must feel at being rejected, then let soft influences be brought to bear.

But how? Is it possible to phrase (what does not exist) a loving rejection? Obviously not. It may still be possible to phrase an acceptable one. I have tried and failed. But there, among the natural resources of the continent, is the ingenuity of our readers, and I hereby call for help at large.

No prizes. A few months ago John Fuller offered ten pounds of soda crackers to anyone who could come up with a replacement for the typewriter sentence, "The quick brown fox, *etc.*" In what is now known as the soda-cracker crisis, he finds he owes approximately 40,000 pounds of the stuff and was last seen trading in futures on the Chicago Commodities Exchange.

January 2, 1965

The Slush Pile

Souls do rise to rapture in their hour, and that rapturous impulse is surely related to the best emotions Mankind can summon from itself and summon itself to, but when the rapture emerges as a poem, and when the poem is later mailed to an editorial office, then what began as a soul's cry becomes one of many manuscripts in the "slush pile," which is to say, the editorial accumulation of unsolicited manuscripts.

No man's soul will be gladdened to learn that it took wing only to drop a manuscript into something called a slush pile. Yet even the purest cantor of immortal song, were he to achieve a moment of dispassion, might be willing to grant that any large accumulation of unsolicited manuscripts (his own, of course, excepted) is likely to run low grade in the assay.

Let souls have the comfort of knowing that editors do depend on their slush piles. With no more than a one-in-a-hundred exception, for example, all of *SR*'s poems come out of the slush pile, and I should guess that something like 15 or 20 per cent of them have been by poets whose work I did not know until I met it in the slush pile.

Nor is *SR* unique in this. I know of one large-circulation "slick" that engages an agency to read its slush pile under a contract that requires the agency to produce a specified number of publishable pages annually. I take that contract to be any writer's warrant that he will be read hopefully. The agency's readers will like nothing better than to find a piece that will help get them off the contractual hook.

There still remains the fact that most of the stuff in the slush pile is obviously bad. And there then rises the question: How long should any editor read after he is sure that there is nothing there for him?

That question is raised for me by the Reverend George L. Kress, minister of St. Mark's United Presbyterian Church of Forest Hills, Florence, Alabama. Mr. Kress had been watching Educational Television, to the current delinquency of which I contributed about a year ago when producer Lane Slate came around to shoot a film about me as part of a series grandly entitled *The Creative Person.*

I had once worked with Lane Slate at CBS and he is, let me say, good news to any conversation. The Ciardis had a great week of Slate-on-the-premises and were sorry to see him go. The kids ate breakfast on camera and then slammed off to school, all in happy good behavior. Judith fixed pancakes for them in such lounging duds and in such a hairdo as no morning of this world has known. (And can it matter that the breakfast sequence was shot at 4 P.M. and that the pancakes dripped when they came off the griddle?) Meanwhile, I recorded miles of tape, Slate's crew shot miles of film, and what came out when all those miles were snipped, edited, and then fed together strikes me as a fair enough look at whatever was being looked at.

One of the things that was being looked at was the not-so-creative editor sitting in his *SR* office rejecting poems, and it is to that sequence Mr. Kress addresses a certain indignation:

I hope not too many aspiring poets were viewing our local Educational TV channel a few evenings ago when it profiled John Ciardi. The experience might have proved discouraging.

Mr. C. was shown at his *SR* desk, which he visits once a week, examining the 600 poems submitted weekly. I know now why my stuff comes back so fast.

Fronting Mr. C. were the piles of poems. Beside him yawned a deep wire basket labeled REJECT. In less time than it takes to tell, Mr. C. picked up a mss., gave it a glance lasting fully three seconds, and tossed it to the wirewolf. [EDITOR'S NOTE: *Hooray for "wirewolf!"*]

As viewers watched him screening the mss., Mr. Ciardi's voice explained his system. "I read just the first line," it said. "It tells me all I want to know."

103

Discouragement, in appropriate doses, may be a better thing than Mr. Kress conceives it to be, but lest any contributor go off with his soul in total defeat, let me point out, since Mr. Kress neglected to, that there was in that scene another prominent basket marked HOLD and that a fair number of poems went into it, generally in no more time than it took to toss the others into the "wirewolf."

It is only at the HOLD basket that anything like a process of reading starts. I am not reading on my first run through the slush pile but only looking, and what I am looking for is as simple a thing as obvious silliness.

I have on my side of the process not only years of practice but the fact that the badness of bad poetry is immediately obvious, or at least as obvious as, say, the badness of bad violin playing. The first wry squeak will identify the novice. Up from that first sad squeak, with, perhaps, a pause in the HOLD basket, there are various levels of not-bad performance that are not good enough for national publication. The real murderers of sound, however, cannot hide the absurdity of their playing, and I suggest that it would be a confusion of the idea "soul" and of the idea "competence" to assume that an aspiring, untrained violinist could, for an instant, palm himself off as one worthy of a national audience.

But let any reader judge for himself. I do not have with me the slush pile Mr. Kress saw me run through on camera, but I have this week's, and from the current reject basket I have hauled back a sheaf of the poems that happened to be on top. All of them went into the reject basket in the first place because they were obviously silly. Here are their openings, along with some parenthetical clues for the soulful who may be charitably slow to identify silliness:

"Sun drenched sand between my toes . . ." (Are those his feet or are they a couple of starfish?) "Lying naked in the sand,/ The heat oppresses me . . ." (An odd place for the heat to be lying naked.) "When staring up at the foliage above . . ." (Yes, that's the right direction to look for "above.") "Dear Lord, please teach me how to grin . . ." ("Son," replied the thunder, "you already look silly enough.") "I wandered vainly hither and yon . . ." (Those *are* the two best places for all-purpose wandering.) "How sterile to be so moderne . . ." (Thou sayest a goodlie

104

mouthful kidde.) "Life's a funny proposition after all . . ." (You foxy old deep thinker, you.) "You make me beautiful with your eyes . . ." (Honey, you ought to see what I can do when I get all of me into the act.) "All my totality I impart . . ." (Impartially?) "Some things I just don't understand . . ." (Ah, intellectual humility!) "In dark I lie unseeing . . ." (You picked the right place for it.) "Where are my lover's lips? . . ." (Two to five they are on his face, wherever *it* is lurking.)

Those, I want Mr. Kress to know, are fair and random samples, and I confess further to every intention of discouraging any man, woman, or child from writing such specimen drivel. It already takes too much time just to toss it aside. Did I actually spend a full three seconds on each of those filmed rejects? I must have been mugging for the camera that day. I'm sure I can usually do it in two. If only I didn't have to waste time ripping away those unread covering letters that hide the top poem, I'll bet I could even get it down to about one second on the average. Among other things, you see, I need the time for *reading* those poems in the HOLD basket.

November 5, 1966

The Poetry Explosion

An everlasting question out of the mailbag runs: "Why do you publish the poems you do?" Sometimes the writer has had his own poems rejected and his question may run: "How come you turn down my poems and then publish the junk you've been running?" Sometimes he is just generally irate and the question runs: "Considering the way you have been sounding off about poetry, how do you dare publish such lousy stuff?" And sometimes he seems actually out for information: "Can you tell me on

105

what principles you select poetry for *SR?* I must confess the poems you print seem very different from week to week."

I should like to imagine a universe in which opinion is openly free-wheeling. Let the speaker be wrong if need be, so long as he has thought about what he is saying, and says it meaningfully. Opinion in good order must permit difference. It is not required, however, to surrender to such difference, or to water itself down by too many overpolite qualifications, and be damned to you, sir. Had I thought the poems were "lousy stuff" I should not have bought them. If they are "lousy stuff," then I am obviously incompetent. Prove it to me and I shall resign gratefully, for no man should waste his days on work he is not good at.

But if I must deny that the poems I have bought for *SR* are "lousy stuff," neither am I prepared to argue that any of them are the best possible poetry, or that all of them are good poems in any time-defying sense. On what could any editor found his hope of publishing nothing but time-defying poetry?

Consider a simple mathematics of fact. *SR* publishes approximately 120 poems a year. I for one have never been able to believe that 120 finally good poems are written in any one year. Had the nineteenth century, in total, produced at such a rate, one would have to read at least 12,000 poems to get a basic sense of that century's achievement. Add then 12,000 more for each of the preceding three centuries, and a man would have to be responsible for 48,000 poems to cover English poetry from John Skelton to, approximately, the late Swinburne.

Good poetry simply is not produced in such quantities. But assume that there were as many as 120 great or even almost-great poems written in any one year in the United States. By what act of monopoly could any one editor hope to get his choice of all of them? Scores of little magazines publish thousands of poems every year, and the self-supporting magazines, big and little, certainly account for at least a thousand or two more. By simple calculation, there is not the remotest chance that *SR* or any single magazine could manage first crack at all those thousands of poems. Could we contract for first crack at the total output of, say, thirty or forty of the best poets now writing, and eke out the total with "discoveries" from unsolicited manuscripts, there is no doubt that we could guarantee (subject to the imperfections of my taste)

106

to publish about the best poetry now being written. But any such monopoly would certainly be bad for poetry. American writing is better off without the literary pope that such a monopoly would tend to create.

For all these reasons, there can be no question of publishing the best poetry, but only the best available. Inevitably one must accept poems with which he disagrees in part. If a man cares for poetry, one really stunning stanza can surely justify three mediocre ones: swallow the mediocre and let the poem be published rather than lose the good of it.

The fact is that any man interested in current writing must read a great deal of poor stuff in order to find the good. Suppose one knew absolutely nothing about the nineteenth century but was a critic of great discernment, and suppose then that he were turned loose in a library containing every poem written in England in the nineteenth century, with instructions to find the good poets. Can there be any doubt that he would find himself in the situation of a man trying to extract gold from sea water?— he knows it is there, but the mortal cost of finding the few grains per ton will certainly wear him out before he has extracted the gold of John Keats from the chronological dross, and he will surely be dead before he comes within striking distance of a substance called Browning.

It is time that handles that process of extraction. And time is served by many hands. When you go to the library for an anthology of nineteenth-century poetry, hundreds of readers, critics, and editors have been through the total, have forgotten whole tons of it, and have called to one another's attention those poems they have been unable to forget. The unforgotten, which is to say (or so one hopes) the unforgettable, is the true extract.

The poetry published in *SR* cannot hope to be such an extract. Fallibly, willingly, hopefully, one reads the poems, discarding hundreds in order to find one or two. It may even be a mistake to say one reads them. Maybe the process is better described as "trying them on the dendrites." If they strike the nervous system as pieces of a poetic reality, one may not understand them, but if he cares at all about poetry, he must gamble on them. The real test is not in any one issue, nor in any one year, nor even in any one decade. Perhaps twenty years later one may survey the whole volume of selections to see how many have made it into the first step of time. And who would not be satisfied to find that twenty years and 2,000-plus poems later, he has managed to pick as many as fifty that seem to have bored their way into the memories of some of those who care about poetry.

The hope is as slim as that, and I must believe the final measure is exactly as subjective as those dendrites, but one may still hope he is operating on some sort of principles, and that those principles will reveal themselves, if only in part, to his own introspection, and to a careful survey of the poems he selected. What sort of poem have I inclined to? Why did I pick that one? What is the principle of selection? Will Shirley forgive Herman Wouk and return to him? These mysteries time will tell when all present editors and irate readers are gone beyond all deadlines and indignations.

May 20, 1961

Trial of a Poet

The scene is a holiday in the imagination and is, of course, carefully rigged by the Poet-as-Answerer. The Questioner is Anyman (you, for instance) suffering from the disadvantage of having fallen into another man's reverie. The Poet, even the poet posing as an editor, is entitled to say it at least once in his own way without caring whether or not the reader understands. He does, of course, hope that the reader will.

The way this imagination is rigged, the questioning has been going on for some time as the curtain rises, perhaps never really to fall again. In fact, certainly not to fall again. Because the Poet is shameless about taking every advantage, he has placed himself facing the audience and, by placing the Questioner with his back to it, has left him faceless.

Q. Of all the people who go swimming in mirages, how many, will you certify, actually get wet?

A. The race is capable of every imagination.

Q. Avoid generalization, if you please. How many get wet?

A. Some always. Of the poets—the good ones—all. And of those few, some inevitably and specifically drown.

Q. Is it your intention to bear witness to miracle?

A. Please define the word "miracle."

Q. Let the record show that "miracle" is hereby defined as the occurrence of the unoccurable, as phenomenon without cause, and/or as the unforeseeable foreseen.

A. So defined, I accept miracle as my intention.

Q. Do you thereby deny the rational intellect?

A. Please define "rational intellect."

Q. Let the record show that "rational intellect" is hereby defined as the process of inference from phenomena to cause and/or category, and/or of deduction from category and/or cause to phenomena.

A. Wow!

Q. Please confine yourself to direct answers.

A. I do not deny the rational intellect.

Q. But what else can follow from your stated affirmation of the miraculous?

A. To answer directly, and to list the consequences in the order of their probable importance: (1) the perception of possibility, (2) the revision of theory, (3) the mechanization of possibility, (4) the creation of corporations—or the revision of existing corporations—to mass-produce the newly mechanized possibility, (5) the exploitation of a market place, and (6) the installation of the resulting commonplace.

This economic cycle, however, describes only what some rationalists call "progress." When the miracle involves inwardness rather than mechanics (i.e., an idea as opposed to a TV set or a micro-frequency egg-candler), the perception of miraculous possibility and its installation as one more miraculous commonplace occur simultaneously.

Q. Be pleased to define "progress."

A. "Progress" is the acceleration of stationary choices. It is always conceived as linear motion and it results always and only in rotation. Within the miraculous commonplace it is best thought of as the multiplication of chairs in a cell for solitary confinement. Within itself, it dreams of a carousel with infinite horses for merely plural riders, but always with the same calliope playing the same tune.

Q. Be pleased to define "miraculous commonplace."

A. It is the state of being that seeks to engage the difference between a day containing twenty-four hours and one containing twenty-seven. Or between one containing three minutes and one containing three years. It is the idea of registering that measurement to which clocks cannot reach their hands, and on which perception forever stubs its toe.

Examples of the miraculous commonplace are: birds, clouds, and mountains, to name a few. If the instance be mountains, for example, their miraculous commonplace is in the way they flicker and disappear into their distances, flicker and reappear from them. Sometimes, that is to say, there are no mountains. And sometimes they are always there. I am, of course, quoting. From, of course, myself.

Q. The attribution of quotations is irrelevant. So you propose that it is of the nature of this miraculous commonplace to climb a mountain that is not there?

A. Immediately at the next change of weather, or the next. Any returning mountain may instantly be climbed.

Q. And if the mountain were to disappear while it is being climbed?

A. One need only imagine a better suited mountain and continue the climb under more exacting conditions.

Q. And when one has reached the top of the mountain?

A. Must I assume that it has a top?

Q. Let the record show that such an assumption is directed.

A. Cancel all mountains at the top and start another imagination.

Q. What, then, will you say of reality?

A. Please define "reality."

110

Q. Let the record show that "reality" is hereby defined as "that which exists as a primary and underivable fact dependent upon no other."

A. As, for example, the corpse of a man drowned in a mirage?

Q. Be pleased to answer the question, which is: "What, then, will you say of reality?"

A. Whose reality?

Q. Do you propose to defend the existence of multiple realities?

A. Of infinite realities.

Q. Let the record show that "reality," as defined, is a universal. The question, therefore, is asked of everyone's reality.

A. I don't know everyone.

Q. You imply, therefore, that you will speak only for your own reality?

A. For my own realities.

Q. Do you propose to defend the existence of multiple realities within yourself?

A. Infinite realities.

Q. And you refuse to go on record concerning any reality but your own?

A. I do.

Q. Then answer in terms of your own reality as you understand it.

A. As I understand it, it exists. And only as I understand it can it exist. That much to answer your question as put. I must insist, however, that it be put as "What, then, of your realities?"

Q. Let it be so put.

A. They exist exactly in the sequence in which I imagine them.

Q. And in no other?

A. What other?

October 20, 1962

111

The Purportedly Sad Aardvark
and the Queen Ant

I

I have this from the Aardvark who
first gave it tongue:
     "Once, in Peru,
when anthood in its gleaming hordes
had colonized for yards and yards
the virgin land, there lived a Queen
named Antennìa, the High Serene
Mother of Mothers, Potentess
of 70 billion (more or less)
red warriors and as many drones.
Powers, Principalities, and Thrones
knelt to her throne. At her command
great towering twigs, huge grains of sand,
were felled and shaped to build her towers
inch above soaring inch. Such were her powers.

So high she built her royal hill
that some of it is standing still,
and still from that wind-ruined mound
one sees, for feet and yards around,
her endless pastures, view on view—
the purple vistas of Peru.

Such were her powers. And chief the power
of sovereign intellect. In her great hour

112

her courtiers and her scholars were the flower
of universal learning: arts,
science, wit. The noblest hearts
from her own lands and foreign parts
far as Antillia and Aphidia,
thronged her court at Formicidia.
While from the reaches of the world,
from far as the Great Brooklet curled
between the earth and the unknown,
baled caravans trudged to her throne
with gram on gram and mil on mil
of treasure in an endless spill.

Such was the court on which I came"
—the ancient Aardvark said—"her fame,
her grace, her power, her glittering hill
might have endured a year, might still
have gemmed the earth: in fact, had I
but had my lunch," I heard him sigh,
"before I chanced to pass that way,
she might have spread her royal sway
a whole ell further by today.

Yet though all things must pass away,
let this praise of her live in rhyme:
I have not eaten better in my time.
I doubt that I shall ever eat as well."

—Such was the tale the Aardvark stopped to tell.

II

I say I heard the Aardvark tell
this mournful tale. He told it well,
it seemed to me. He had a touch
if not quite epic, nearly such.
And swung a picturesque detail
as freely as he swished his tail.

And yet he swung a crooked tongue
above, around, between, among
a file of ants that happened by,
and slurped them in with the same sigh
I heard him sigh for that great snack
he said he'd lunched on somewhere back
in Formicidia, in Peru.

Which made me wonder: was it true?

How can a man be wholly sure
of a self-stated epicure
who licks up dust while he's reciting
what menus regally exciting
he feasted on a lick ago?

He's like a lot of poets I know:
well spoken, even at times well sung,
but always poking a great tongue
through any dust, to slurp at sight
whatever crumb of passing mite
might move their gluttony.

                    I can't trust
a bon-vivant who licks up dust
and wags his tongue (coated with clay)
to claim he is a great gourmet.

And still I find some tales beguile
despite the teller. Art is style.
Some poets are a loathsome lot,
put face to face, or pot to pot,
or id to ego, or lust to greed.
Yet sometimes, when they die, we read—
soul to soul, and lie to lie—
truths a seraph could live by.

Idiosyncratic man,
like the doubtful Aardvark can
be a slob while singing graces.
Half at least of what the race is

half, but only half, refutes
our best go at the absolutes
we like to think we move among,
praising with a dirty tongue.

June 25, 1966

An Editorial April

Thomas Bailey Aldrich was a poet whose profession of the arts outran his own talents. Perhaps that is the imbalance from which all editors are born. Or perhaps it must be said of every poet that his devotion to the art outruns what his talent can make of it. Aldrich, in any case, made little enough of his, and rare is the man who can summon from memory a line from Aldrich's pen. Yet, in his time, Aldrich had an easy gift for literary success, moving in the esteem of most of his literary contemporaries, including even Mark Twain and—more pertinently to Aldrich's career—William Dean Howells, whom Aldrich succeeded as editor of the *Atlantic Monthly*.

Aldrich occupied that literary eminence from 1881 to 1890, but unfortunately forgot to take a vacation in April of 1887, for it was then, alas, that he wrote a letter, a copy of which I have before me through the kindness of Peter D. Witt of Chestnut Hill, Massachusetts, and the proof of which you may find for yourself in Ferris Greenslet's *Thomas Bailey Aldrich*, published by Houghton Mifflin back in 1906.

April 26, 1887

Dear Madam,—
Though I think this is a good sonnet, I do not retain it, for the reason that I have on hand more poems in that unpopular form

115

than I can conveniently use. The sonnet is essentially a poet's poem; I don't believe that the general reader cares for it.

Your sonnet is very carefully built, and the construction afforded me pleasure; but while reading the lines I wondered if we writers of verse did not give the public credit for more interest in our purely personal emotions than really exists. Why should we print in a magazine those intimate revelations which we wouldn't dream of confiding to the bosom of an utter stranger at an evening party? In what respect does the stranger differ from the public which we are so ready to take into our inmost confidence? The reflection was not new to me, however; it has saved me from writing many a verse that could by no chance have been of the slightest interest to the general public. I trust, dear madam, that you will not think that I write at this length whenever I decline to print a sonnet!

Yours very respectfully,
T. B. Aldrich

From this literary broomcloset above Madison Avenue to that genteel lounge on Arlington Street, my first thought on reading this letter was that April 26, 1887, was an easy day at the *Atlantic*, and that Aldrich was moved to indulge himself in a languidly pompous way. April has ways of betraying us all.

But only see what wheels begin to turn when an editor answers his mail as if it mattered, and especially as if he mattered. Not only does the office correspondence file begin to bulge beyond reason, but sooner or later a biographer comes to sift through it, a publisher edits it, a compositor sets it, a printer spoils paper with it, a sharp-eyed reader exhumes it and sends it to another editor, and that first foolish impulse is once more processed into print and onto more spoiled paper.

Whole provinces of Canada could be deforested for pulp in the circling of one such impulse. Had two editors been so moved once a day since 1887, the advancing dunes of the Canadian desert might already be sifting across the Pennsylvania Turnpike. Let April, I say, be a silence between us, preferably the year round. And yes, of course, I am being as selfish as a sparrow when I chuck your letters into the wastebasket, averted by such an enlightened selfishness!

116

And what on earth was that April editor saying in the first place? That ladies should be told not to write sonnets certainly makes sense, though I am sure Aldrich got small thanks for his pains. I have myself urged many a lady sonneteer of both sexes to learn how to cook and knit, and I cannot recall that any of them was grateful to me.

But I only objected to the fact that they wrote bad sonnets. Can Aldrich really have been objecting to the fact that his lady wrote a good one? He meant, of course—he *had* to mean—that what she wrote was good enough, but only good enough, and therefore worthless.

But how does an editor manage to object to a poem on the grounds that only poets will like it? Was Aldrich assuming that poets are a bad audience for poetry? They are, I submit, just about all the first audience a good poem is likely to find. Let a poem be written to satisfy today's poets and it will probably satisfy some of tomorrow's general public, but let it be written to satisfy today's general public and tomorrow it will not exist.

April, of course, is a sweet and lazy month in Boston. It tempts a man to open windows, and the windows then let in breezes that get in his hair in a distracting way. Come to think of it, I don't know whether or not Aldrich had enough hair for a breeze to play through. But bare scalps, too, can tingle in the right breeze. I am left to suspect Aldrich, bald or hairy, of suffering from as much spring fever as editorial pomposity can contract.

April or no, I am sure Aldrich was right in rejecting the lady's outpouring. Nor does it matter that the poem he was writing about is unknown. I have at least a dozen of the same sonnet in today's mail. Or should any day miss its quota, I could make it up on the spot: Take any surge of impassioned yearning, add an abyss or two of bereft time, fly in a pair of mating bluebirds, and night cannot fail to turn into a fire of anguish for what the fierce, implacable heart lets go, foreswearing kisses that still burn the soul.

But reticence is to be recommended only to the untalented. Should Shakespeare have been more reticent about Lady Macbeth or Othello? Should he have kept their expression within the bland proprieties of "an evening party"? It would be pleasant to send messages of fraternal solidarity from this office to the old

117

Atlantic's and from this April day to that one more than eighty years ago, but not all the imaginable bluebirds (of which there are none here) nor all the breezes of April (these being noticeably polluted) can persuade an agreement. The editor, I am afraid, was doodling at the feet of his own image.

I shall insist for April that poetry is the deepest plunge a man of talent can take into himself. Poetry fails (or—and much the same thing—it succeeds in a pointless way) only when it does not go deep enough. The true plunge outdives the privacy of any one man and becomes everyman's privacy. "What I am," art says, "you are."

No man can come to that saying easily. Yet how easily any man can scribble himself to one side of it. I have it from April, even in this polluted air that still wafts almost like a first again, that most letters are foolish letters. I think I may even burn the rejection slips and come to the office with a basket of new leaves, pressing one into each batch of poems on their way to the Out Basket. Who could complain at sending away a bad poem and getting it back with a green leaf pressed to the page? Or if I am wrong and send back a good poem, who will dare say he sent me as good a thing as I sent back? And right or wrong, where is the editor who can send a better letter from April to April?

April 15, 1967

Letter Writers

Readers of this magazine, as I have long since discovered, are Herculean letter writers. Whether to confirm or confound, the subscription list makes itself felt. Three qualified cheers for that. What is more disappointing for a writer than to drop his published words into a bottomless well of silence from which no echo is ever to be heard? But if only a man could wish for an echo without wishing-up a roar. I dare not count how many letters are at this moment spilling over my desk unanswered. They are unanswered for the good reason that to answer them would not be a chore but a career. And because I have other work to do.

One good reason, of course, for answering mail is that it is fun to receive it. But there are even better reasons for not answering, and certainly the first among them is the fact that many letters ought not to have been written in the first place. In terms of any reasonable social contract, the writer should have known better.

In the first rank of such social misdemeanors I certainly place the scores of letters I have received from misguided students fumbling at a term paper, who have blandly asked me in effect to write it for them. At first—because I have myself put in too many years as a teacher—I used to reply with a mild avuncular scolding, along with a brief summary of basic reference works available in any good library, and the assurance that the writer would neither lose social standing nor be shot down by the librarian were he to pass quietly through the front door and look for himself.

But no more. I am persuaded we have reared an unmannerly generation unto ourselves. Not one of the young whelps I wrote to took the trouble to say thanks. (One mother did write to thank me for the scolding I had given her young whippersnapper.) Not one enclosed a self-addressed stamped envelope. And not one knew enough to frame a considered (which is to say answerable) question, but only such hopelessly hopeful casts as "Please tell me what you think of William Butler Yeats. I am doing my term paper on him." I must insist on assuming that one is absolved when bad manners are added to ignorance, and that there need be no social debt to answer such letters.

The second rank of letters that must be discarded at once is made up of those that come along with a batch of bad poems (they are always bad) and a request for a personal critique.

Certainly I understand why a writer wants someone else to read his work and to comment on it. I have sought such reading and comment all my life. "Well, isn't that a debt?" one hears the letter writer thinking. Yes it is, and I do my best to repay it to my students. I try to repay it there because, there, repayment is more or less possible. I *can* criticize their writing—for better or worse—but only after at least a month of setting forth principles, rules of thumb, and a vocabulary of criticism.

What happens, on the other hand, when the editor confuses himself with the teacher? If a student passes in a poem whose diction is random I can say, "Show me how the overtones of your words bear any relation to one another." Or in another case I can say, "Break the poem down into its mechanical and meaningful stresses and show me what you think happens between the two." The student—at least the good one—will understand because he has been to the lectures that set up those criteria and because he has done supervised exercises in analyzing those elements of the poem.

But suppose I mention overtones to a reader? Or mechanical and meaningful stresses? I have not answered the mail, I have only multiplied it. Back comes another letter saying, "What is an overtone? And what is a mechanical and a meaningful stress?"

By that point the hour has struck. Nothing less than 10,000 words could begin to make sense. I compute that I am offered daily the opportunity to write roughly 500,000 such words, and I leave simple addition to attest that the answer must be no. Sorry, but no. And since that is the only possible answer, why answer at all?

The third rank in the army of the pestiferous carries a banner that reads "Chatty Pals." Between Bangor and San Diego there must be millions of literate and semiliterate people with nothing to do, and the itch to write long soul-searching single-spaced letters. To engage in two such correspondences would be a life work for an unfastidious Lord Chesterfield. Forgive me, dear leisured friends, but once again, the rest is silence.

I suspect we are all overcivilized these days, and it does in fact cause an uneasy feeling (at first) to leave letters unanswered. But in time the calluses grow. And in the name of reason, is everyman's mistake a duty upon me once any given writer has bought a postage stamp?

But to ask that question is a way of wheedling toward an easy self-justification. A writer has purer grounds within his own need. The Age of Public Relations is upon us all, and where is the executive, however majestic in his banker's eye, who has not established a routine for making some sort of acknowledgement of

120

every scrap of mail? He has heard the legend that the busiest and most important men always find time to answer, and since he is obviously busy and obviously important, he will not disappoint his own legend of himself. After all, it takes only a standard-forms book and a secretary who knows her business—both of them deductible items.

No thanks. I shall rest with the writer's purer refusal. What need he care about the legends of importance? He has the holy right of his own selfishness. His attention belongs to himself and to his writing. He owes no private pieces of his mind to junior college students in Minnesota, to hopefully hopeless young writers on Long Island, or to chatty housewives in Tuscaloosa. What he has to say is best said within the formalities of his writing. Whatever he has written well is there to be received by anyone able to read it, and nothing he might scribble out of a misplaced sense of public relations will take its place.

In the name of that indispensable selfishness, therefore, and to ask of such readers as are willing to grant it, their mercy upon selfish need, I hereby sweep the desk clean of all letters I have lacked the courage to chuck out before, and for such amends as it may offer, I begin this column in which I shall try to answer, among other things, some of the questions that crop up in the mailbag, at least such as involve matters of general interest. I have some thought of getting down to occasional specific discussion of poetic techniques. And obviously—along with every other columnist—I must take a shot at saving the world now and then. At saving it or damning it.

My plans are no more definite than that. Except to look at the mail when there is time, and to give most letter writers the fullest assurance that unless their letters are answered here they will not be answered at all.

April 15, 1961

A Letter

Dear N: I should have answered your letter long since. I have nothing to plead now but the purity of my selfishness. The more letters a man writes at the edge of his mind, the less he will write at his own center. Even now I am answering selfishly, because I sense in your letter a chance to speak not so much to you as out of myself. I am using you as an occasion for what I myself want to say.

Don't feel upset by editorial fools who tell you what to write. I'm an editor, too, and I'm ready to confess for the trade that any reason given for rejecting a poem is an irrelevancy after the fact. There may be saintly editors unknown to me, but, heaven's margin allowed for, a man rejects a poem because it does nothing to his dendrites. If then, for some reason, he feels obliged to return the piece with something more than a printed rejection slip, he makes up a few hems and haws toward the social graces. If he is also a fool, he pronounces.

I suppose it's fashionable these days for editorial pronouncers to tell a black poet he should write ANGRY and that he's lost if his poems sound caucasian—that, incidentally, is his lower case "c," not mine, and I'm moved to tell him that if he insists on his capital N, I want my capital C, though I'd a sight rather get together on a capital H for Human.

The problem's not new, though it changes labels and faces. Remember poor Countee Cullen forever trying to decide whether to write N or C, John Henry or John Keats? Remember his poem beginning "What is Africa to me?" I'll take that for a soul's cry in pain. Remember Baldwin in Switzerland playing one Bessie Smith record over and over because it gave him back the rhythm of his

122

own first idiom, back through those Harvard vowels he had tried to swallow as a way to a fake sufferance by what Auden called "a foreign code of conscience"? No one gets to his capital H the easy way, but the time is not yet when a black man can reach for his without some tussle between N and C. (I didn't make the world: I weep for it some in the act of trying to see it, and I try to live in it toward whatever H I can reach for. I do not endorse it. It hasn't asked for my endorsement.)

There will always be poetic pronouncers and programmers but they change nothing. A poet is a poet not in what he writes about but in his act of language. Be angry, be joyous, be urbane, or be primitive, but perform it full to the language itself.

I'm willing enough to sit around while the discussion goes to theory and etherea and the nature of the poetic mind. Let the bourbon be sour mash, and I'll even call the session something for nothing (like listening to Nixon while drinking good corn. Or should I write *good* corn?). But it isn't really my kind of session until the talk gets to specific poems, to specific acts of language, and to the management of that act. (Damn Chopin as idea: what does the pianist have to do *on the keyboard* to equal whatever experience Chopin is?)

Give a man mind and he has no way to avoid some sort of involvement in social causes. "Social cause" is only one of various ways of saying "good and evil." I don't know of any artist who hasn't been moved to his own wrestling match with good and evil, whatever his terms for that match. Poetry stirs the seedbeds and root-deeps of language, and what comes up from language at those depths is the closest I can get to what a man is in his bout with his first questions. That compulsion to language is not art for art's sake: it is language entered as a means of knowledge, and the knowledge is of man for the simple reason that he has spent all his generations to make language, and because the language he makes, makes him. It makes him and it enters him at reaches of himself he could not come to except through art.

I am setting the case high. That case is not lowered a fraction of a degree when the talk of poets turns, as it must, to nouns, to verbs, to adjectives, to stresses, to rhythms, to metaphor, to rhetoric, to forms, to the balances and counterbalances of the elements of specific poems. For, let's face it, the good poet is a

123

manipulator of illusion; nor does it change matters to say he's an illusionist of God, or of the feeling the idea of God used to be before we ran out of right words for the summarizing idea. (No matter that it doesn't exist.) Any cause come to in the fullness of the language is capital H Human, because the language at its full has nothing else it *can* be about.

And even cause is the poet's illusion. I'll grant you—I'll grant any man—wish, self, anguish, name, and all the crossings of his moods. But a poet puts words on paper. If he masters his means, a presence called John Donne is born forever and lives in the reader's mind as surely as any man lives. Or someone called Blake puts the order of words to his illusion and makes a tiger for the jungle of anyman's nervous system. Or a hophead named Coleridge sits to his page and makes a place called Xanadu, and it exists as if language were geography and Xanadu a visited place within it.

High theory or low craft, it is done with words that had no such power till a poet brought them together in a mastered illusion. I am winding up to the nastiness of saying I don't like the poems you sent me. I can't feel that you put words together in any way good enough for the miracle that leaves an artifact. Look at these excerpts: *falling leaves, huge waves, huge entering, shadows stalk, mighty trust, proud congruence, foolish rage, faded cares.*

Yes, they are ripped out of their contexts in eight different poems, and, yes, a genius might set one of these phrases in a context that makes the artifact materialize. And still you could have sat down on the dullest day of your life and made better word-jointures than these just for practice.

"Words alone are certain good." (That's Yeats, isn't it?) These words aren't good enough to be good. Whoever you are outside the poem, I don't see how you can get the illusion of that presence (that H) into the poem till your words coil closer to the root.

So I'm not only being nasty, but compounding offense by taking advantage of you, and turning what should have been a letter for your sake into a column for my sake. If you really mean to write poems, you don't need my mercy, and you had better learn to walk in terror of your own. Damn editors: Go break your head on language, not on publication. I'll be nastier yet: Having myself to track, I don't even care who you are.

124

But come to yourself in language enough, and I can then come to you in full selfishness, needing you, as I need every man who can awaken language for me.

Should some editorial pronouncer tell you there is any other reason for reading any poet, alive or dead, tell the man he is misted mad in no world. It's mortal time a man spends reading poetry, and no poet gets that time as a kindness: he has to earn it by the mortal rightness of his act of language.

Best to you, and the words for it.

January 11, 1969

Pigeon Mail

Dear Mr. Ciardi:

It is just possible that some sympathetic soul will write you about a unique way of banishing pigeons [*SR*, Oct. 16]. Should it be the same advice given me, I feel obligated to brief you on the results of the experiment.

Not long ago, in a moment of pesticidal desperation, I phoned an exterminator about the problem. After listing what I could not do legally, he conceded that since shooting was out, any first step would involve catching the pigeons. Having caught them, he implied that we might enjoy a midnight ride on some back road.

His suggested method was as follows: Get a large plastic bag and punch a few holes in it. Buy a box of bird seed and thoroughly soak in brandy. Scatter seed in driveway and wait, the theory being that this "on the house" fare would get them off the house and leave them staggering and unable to fly. Drop them in the bag and take off. Since there is nothing on the books about either intoxicating or transporting pigeons, this seemed an attractive idea.

I did hesitate when I discovered that our only brandy was Hennessey 4 Star, but this was no time to be pigeon-hearted and think of cost. The birds loved it, all the pigeons in the neighborhood attended the open house, but I couldn't get near a single boozy bird.

The only result of this ignoble experiment is that my husband, finding a new bottle of brandy practically empty, thinks I've gone in for secret binges. The chatter has increased, for the pigeons are still cooing about the party. Should you have better luck with gin or vodka, do let me know.

Sympathetically yours,
Mrs. Kenneth H. Bailey.

Flushing, N.Y.

Dear Mr. Bailey

I hope you will not think I am barging in where I have no right to be. I have something to say to you about your wife's drinking habits, and why should the fact that I am a stranger deter me from a good deed? When I was a Boy Scout I never insisted on a formal introduction before helping an old lady across the street.

Not that I imply Mrs. Bailey is an old lady—heaven forbid. I don't even mean to help her across the street, not in any literal sense. But I do find myself in a position to do a good turn, and you wouldn't want me to turn that down, would you?

What I mean is I don't want you to start brooding in any serious way about what is going on in your brandy bottles, or about what is going out of them. Mrs. Bailey, I happen to know, hasn't really turned into a secret tippler. It was the pigeons, Mr. Bailey. You can probably hear them in your eaves right now. Let me ask you just one question: do they sound innocent to you? Before you start thinking ill of Mrs. Bailey, just listen to them, and then ask yourself if you have ever heard anything guiltier than their cooing. See what I mean?

It all began, as nearly as I can make out, when the pigeons got a large plastic bag and began poking holes in it. After that Mrs. Bailey just had to soak the bird seed, and is it her fault if you keep only good stuff on hand? You certainly wouldn't want her to walk into the local liquor store and ask for any of that cheap pigeon brandy.

126

Then, to make matters worse, the pigeons refused to get inside the plastic bag even after holes had been poked in it. I know that leaves you with a damaged large plastic bag on your hands, but you can hardly blame Mrs. Bailey for that, can you? She really was trying her best and in a good cause, as I hope I have made clear to you.

I hope that setting your mind at rest in this way will be enough excuse for busting in on you. Believe me, Mrs. Bailey is not becoming an alcoholic but only has pigeons on her roof. That, as you will admit, could happen to anyone. Since you share the same roof, it is happening to you. Under my own roof, it is happening to me. So you see that puts us all in the same boat, doesn't it?

Shipmates forever,
John Ciardi.

Dear Mrs. Bailey:

I must thank you for your suggestions and I want you to know I am off to a glorious start even though I took time off to square you with Mr. Bailey about the shrinkage in the brandy bottle. I had set up the experiment as you outlined it, but I had hardly begun to lower the experimental level when I found myself thinking of Mr. Bailey pointing the dark suspicion of several missing fingers of brandy at you, and on impulse I sat down and explained the whole thing to him, even though the plastic bag over my head kept fogging up and kept needing to have more holes punched in it.

Let me confess I had to improvise in a few other ways. We didn't have any bird seed in the house, and the stores were closed, so I settled for a few bowls of puffy cereals. I think you will find they absorb liquids in a more satisfying way than bird seed does. I especially recommend any of those enormous blown-up oats.

The only brandy I could find in the house was a bottle of Remy Martin VSOP, but I did turn up a lot of vodka, and I decided to use that on the oats, reserving the Remy Martin for myself as a control group for determining relative absorption. Obviously, you can't have a real experiment without a control group, as I am sure you will agree.

I do not know how much the oats soaked up, but the control

127

group was doing fine until it fell asleep and woke to find that my little monsters had come down for breakfast, slurped up the bowls of specially treated oats, and subsided into beatitude. ·

If the end can be said to justify the means, the experiment—whatever it was—came to a lovely conclusion. I am a little embarrassed to say I can't quite remember what the experiment was supposed to get rid of, but I am sure it is gone. Thank you for the suggestion that made all this possible.

Not only were the results gorgeously conclusive, but though it hardly seems possible, my eaves are full of nightingales. Yes, I know that nightingales are not indigenous to North America and also that they are not supposed to sing in the morning, but believe me there they are—whole exaltations of them. Or is that larks? Anyhow, the air is full of their warbling. If I did not know better, in fact, I'd swear that I was hearing their trills and flutters from inside my own head. It's beautiful!

Let me only hope your own experiments will have the same, or at least comparable results. I am afraid I have a long way to go before I have compiled and correlated the final data, but the general conclusions are unmistakably promising.

With every good wish for your own experimental work, and with best regards to Mr. Bailey.

Yours gratefully,
John Ciardi.

December 18, 1965

Sense and Being

It is always a mistake to discuss poetry with a man who insists that it must make sense. It is just possible that sense is what we settle for only when we fall away from the fullest act of being.

128

Who, for example, expects a bridegroom to make sense? We all know him to be too busy with a more enviable condition of being than sense can make. "If I could only live at the pitch that is near madness," writes Richard Eberhart. And adds:

> When everything is as it was in my childhood
> Violent, vivid, and of infinite possibility.

Nonsense, of course. Or nonsense, that is, to the adamantly practical man. But take another look at that man. I see him coming toward me in the shape of a number of large male relatives who assumed the place of my dead father and who were moved by a kindly concern. I had gone to college with the idea of becoming a lawyer, but I got hooked on English courses and kept taking them until I was obviously unemployable. So the sensible avuncular concern of the tribe's senior males. "John," they would say to me, "It's nice to know about all those poetry things, but you gotta be practical." And I would mumble respectful evasions but I would also take a good look at each of them in turn and say to myself, "I wonder what practicality ever did for *him?*"

For the trouble with being sensible is not the sense it does or does not make but the life it never really manages to get to. Sense, as the insistently sensible man practices it, always manages to shut as many doors as it opens. I suspect, in fact, that it shuts far more than it opens. And one of the doors it always shuts, and always with a slam, is poetry.

The slam of that closing door is always the insistence that the poet expound himself in straightforward and logical order. But how can he? The act of writing a poem is never a simple assertion of meaning. It is an act of skill. And an act of skill is precisely one in which the performer must do more things at once than he has time to think about.

On a simple level, riding a bicycle is an act of skill. Let a man try to itemize and account for each of his thousands of balances as he rides his bicycle and he will fall off. The only way to ride it is faster than he can think it. Paradoxically, of course, he must also think it. A rider who forgets he has a bicycle under him is getting ready to fall off. A rider who is aware of the bicycle under him is forever keeping himself from falling: he senses each imbalance as

129

it develops, and his conditioning produces the counterbalance by reflex. But if he tries to make sense of his reflexive ride, the ride is over.

Let him try to over-rationalize those reflexes, moreover, and he will be in trouble. He might, for example, decide to write a sensible treatise on how to ride a bicycle in good rational order. It might even be a persuasive paper. But were he then to get back on his bicycle and try to ride it according to his own script, nothing could keep him from falling off. It has to be done multiply, by reflex; not monosequentially by theory.

Unlike the bicycle rider, of course, the poet can strike out any part of his ride and any of his falls. There is always that gift of mercy to the artist, and the artist would be a fool not to cherish it. Yet if the poem is to be an achieved act, it can only be brought off as a managed multiplicity, as an act of balancing upon itself, and as one that derives from the poet's whole experience both as a person and as a writer. Every poem he has ever written has a finger in this poem's pie; and everything he ever read, and every sentence he ever parsed, and every man, woman, and child he ever knew, and everywhere he has ever been, and everything he has ever seen, and everything he has ever thought, felt, and—to borrow a coinage from Robert Frost—*thoughtfelt* about any of these conditioning experiences. All these are stored behind the act of writing. Some may be there in neat and conscious storage. Some may be whirling there as some sort of originating chaos. Both the order and the chaos are there as necessary parts of himself, and he must summon both.

The magic of the act of writing is not in its power to make sense, but in its great power to quicken and summon this memorial mass of the self. As the poem begins to buzz, endless possibilities offer themselves; possibilities that were not there a word, a phrase, an image, a rhyme, or a cadence ago.

But these possibilities can only exist as a sort of side vision. Turn on them the full rational-cognitive stare of the logician as biomechanic, and they disappear. For one can no more demand them than he can demand the sequences of a dream. One of the blindnesses of the man of insistent sense follows directly from the fact that what he insists on is that full rational-cognitive stare. Instantly, then, his side vision is lost.

130

The poet knows better. He knows that language, rhyme, image, rhythm, and form are means of knowledge and that they are the means of a knowledge that cannot be acquired scientifically, or mechanically, or, in general, "sensibly" as the insistently sensible man means the word.

The human race has been shaping language from its earliest beginning, and language has been shaping the human race. Whatever else a man is, he is bound to be a product of his own use of language. By some process at least remotely related to natural evolution, moreover, language has adapted itself to man's needs. Let a man teach himself, not to make statements, but to hearken to his own fullest language, and the language will infallibly inform him as he works to bring it to form. How can he know what the language will say next?—he has to wait for the language to say it to him.

What he is waiting for is his act of language. Like the dream that most tells him who he is, it does not say things; it takes place. The important difference between the dream and the poem is that he has no control over the dream. He has to let it happen. And the poem he must *make* happen.

But what he makes happen is itself. There is, finally, no question of making sense, but only of making happen. The poem, like any work of art, must be made to happen not to anyone's notion of logic, sense, reality, practicality, or moral resolution. It must be made to happen in answer to itself. Only so can it be a means of knowledge.

Of what sort of knowledge? Imagine yourself as having stood by Shakespeare's deathbed watching his eyes. You might then find yourself in the context that might answer: it is the knowledge of everything that went out when those eyes closed.

It is the sort of knowledge no man can take by assault. It is the sum of what he learns by living his life in his mind's fullest waking. And that order of living, as I believe I have learned, can be won to only when the poet—or any other artist—has given himself in trust to his medium, because he knows his medium is a sentient and an active thing, and that wherever it takes him will be toward life.

September 19, 1964

131

Of Poetry and Sloganeering

Every literary generation has its would-be lawgivers who think to reduce the art to a set of slogans and who are themselves reduced by the attempt. Sometimes, as in the ferment of the Imagist movement, the slogans of the lawgivers are mostly literary. At other times, as in the mad Thirties of the Young Communist League and the Spanish Civil War, the slogans are directives to social action. The literary slogans, as it seems to me, are usually Thou-shalt-nots; the social slogans are usually Thou-shalts.

The literary slogans one hears on every hand today are anti-formal and anti-metric. So Robert Bly announces (as usual, without qualification) that the sonnet cannot be written in the twentieth century. (Thou shalt not formalize.) So Karl Shapiro, in his characteristic but always gifted zaniness, announces that it "makes him feel dirty" to write in iambic pentameter. (Thou shalt not tick.)

Nor can I entirely disagree with either Bly or Shapiro. The sonnet does not seem to be a likely form for our age (and therefore it has a chance to surprise a formalism into being). It may well be that the best of our poetry will be written off rather than on a strict metric base (except, of course, that such a master as W. H. Auden can make the ticktock of metric so compulsive that it becomes a power beyond its own saying). What defeats possibility in all sloganeering is never its total lack of point but the flatness of its assertion. Art is of the nimbleness of the mind and will not be packsaddled by such gross weights of certainty.

The social slogans of our times are primarily of the racial problem and of Vietnam. Thou shalt join in protest, they declare. Thou shalt picket. And well one may, for certainly there is cause

132

enough. But when the slogan becomes "Thou shalt write the poem that defeats police lines and that ends the war"—at that point poetry has been left behind and has been replaced by social passions that may well have their own nobility of purpose but that care nothing for literary possibility.

Within the last year I have had letters from several sloganeers who insist that, unless I write about the war in Vietnam, I have "sold out." They do not tell me what it is I will have sold out. What they want me to buy is the certainty of their convictions, and they always refuse to entertain the possibility that their convictions—even when I share them to some extent—are not literary.

Has everyone forgotten the Thirties? I want to ask. Has everyone forgotten the fulminations of the party line critics? Has everyone forgotten the Spanish War and the endless flow of bad poems that defended Spain, city by city, to be followed by another endless flow of elegies as each city fell? Where are they now, all those poems of social passion, of noble ideals, of burning and certified social conviction? It is hard even to remember the cities whose very names were once like the sounds of the eternal verities—whatever they are.

Of all those tens of thousands of published poems I am able to call back to mind only Stephen Spender's "Ultima Ratio Regum," a poem touched off, so to speak, by the Spanish War, but one that is in fact an elegy on the death of a young man who went forth to idealistic battle and who died under the olive trees—a poem that takes off from the social occasions of the age but that strikes agelessly to the theme of pity for blasted youth.

And Spender, let the young be reminded, is a man deeply involved in the social causes of his time. "Ultima Ratio Regum" was written almost concurrently with Spender's assertion that a poem could be a palpable, overt, anti-Fascist action, a sort of bullet fired in the war for freedom. What raised Spender's poem above his own lost slogans can only have been his own commitment to form and language. Once into the poem, because he was poet enough, he put by his own slogans, wrote to the language itself, and ended with a poem that has survived public causes and all literary slogans.

Spender, in this case, escaped, but the terrible power of slogans remains, and lies, as I must believe, in their way of taking over the minds of the sloganeers. The hopeful power of poetry is in a motion of a different sort. Poetry is a sequence from an opening in joy to a resolution in insight.

Esthetic joy, because it stirs forever toward new possibilities and new combinations of possibility, puts us into a mood to receive new impressions. It beguiles us to the horizons of ourselves and beyond. Our normal practical, dutiful steps through the "is" of daily schedules tend to limit and close us. Esthetic joy opens us to the full "as if" of our speculative powers. A man running for a train—or for any other certainty—is not likely to be moving toward the possible universes of feeling. A declaimer of simplified causes, however noble he feels his commitment to be, limits himself to his cause. Good art, on the other hand, reaches for an order itself calls into being. The poet cannot be certain of it in advance —cannot sloganize it—because that order simply was not there before the esthetic encounter had reached to the joy of form and language. As Wallace Stevens once wrote of the sound of a sonata (in a poem I cannot lay my hand on at the moment and that I may misquote), it:

Makes music seem to be a nature,
A place in which itself gives rise to everything else.

The esthetic motion does not declaim; it harkens. It waits for possibility to sound toward insight, and it reaches to insight in a glad serendipity. The man who is sure he knows in advance what insight his poem will reach to may be heroic in his own image, but he is not much given to poetry.

My thought is of the young. In the course of the year I find myself lecturing at many colleges, and I know, from the questions the undergraduates ask, that they have heard the sloganeers and are ready or half ready to be persuaded. Let me hope they may be better persuaded to put their esthetic faith in language and form itself. To be moved to poetry is to be moved to human concern. The poet, away from his desk, may be the activist of all causes. Once at his desk and into his poem, however, he must be a poet or nothing. Let him bring every living issue to the writing. But then let him write to the writing itself, toward the joy of sensing the language take form, from joy to possibility, from possibility to the sudden surfacing of those insights logic cannot come to and social issues cannot alter, and that only poetry can surprise into being in the act of hearkening to itself.

January 6, 1968

Poetry and Luck

In art, good luck happens only to those who have earned it. The minimum requirement for a good poem, I have argued in the past, is a miracle. It now occurs to me that I was simply restating Keats's thought that poetry should surprise with "a fine excess." The poem has to turn out better than anyone, the poet included, could have foreseen that it would, or could have expected it to. That is the miracle: the poem must in some way outrun what seemed possible. It must somehow be struck by lightning. As, say, Emily Dickinson was when she set out to describe her innate revulsion at the sight of a snake and found herself saying that she never came upon one

> Without a tighter breathing
> And Zero at the bone.

Think of the endless ways in which that line might have been nothing. An unlucky, unmiraculous, unlightning-struck poet might have written "And a shudder deep inside," or "And a shiver of the spine," or "And a tingle of revulsion." Had that same poet let those lines stand he would, of course, have been guilty of that esthetic immorality that tolerates shoddy as real stuff. But no matter how firm his refusal to stock bad goods, only a poet moved by lucky lightning could have struck from the page the ominous scraping *zizz* of that Zero.

135

Nothing but luck can do, but that luck is not free: the lightning must be worked for.

That work begins with the act of meaning the poem hard enough to reject such spineless bad lines as I have improvised as alternates, in refusing to settle for anything but true lightning. But it only begins there.

Having declared against all that is not lightning, how do the good poets get to the lightning itself, or it to them? For if to be struck by such blessed lightning is a piece of luck, it is a kind of luck that happens over and over to some people, and never to others. Some poets obviously know how to woo that lightning. It is in the wooing, in their devotion to the discipline of love, that they earn their luck.

Think of it in terms of a perhaps entirely frivolous figure. The good poet is a student of lightning. He keeps weather charts and he keeps them constantly to hand. He develops a feel for where the thunderheads are. He also keeps some sort of emotional helicopter ready. As soon as he spots a thunderstorm he is on his way to it. There he instinctively places himself under the tallest tree, makes sure he is soaking wet and standing in a puddle, wraps himself in chains for good measure, and holds up a lightning rod.

He won't catch the lightning every time. Luck cannot always be with him. But he is ready for whatever luck will come. He has earned it. And he must inevitably have more luck than the dry and stormless souls that live in Faraday cages.

A Faraday cage, in case you were asleep that day in first-year physics, is, roughly speaking, an enclosure shielded from outside electrical forces. An automobile is more or less a Faraday cage, unless it is grounded by a chain, as fuel trucks are. A mental Faraday cage is an emotional inclosure shielded from the storm of ideas. It will get you from womb to tomb dry and unshocked— unless the road gives out or you wreck it. But it runs to one side of poetry.

The good poet earns his luck by living closer to the weather.

But if there is no esthetic luck without devotion, it is still in fact luck, and devotion alone will not bring the lightning down. If all men are created equal as a political premise, what follows their creation spreads them out with considerable differences between them. How many men are created as equal as, say, Robert Frost?

136

There has to be not only devotion and risk but a talent for the weather. In poetry, that weather talent is locked into the poet's feel for words and images and rhythms and forms as living systems of things. He generates meaning—enduring and dramatic enactments of what it means to be a self-registering personality in a self-consuming body. But it is not meaning as such he pursues. He is after the *thingness* of the word, the image, the rhythm, and the form. The *thingness* is his weather. He has no need to mean it: he lives it. He does not tell a poem: he experiences it. He experiences himself into it. It comes to him as a cloud and he enters it, not knowing where he will come out, but certain that whatever essential lightning there may be in his life has to be in that cloud or another like it. And certain, too, that when the lightning does strike—if it does strike—he will know that it is in fact lightning, and not "a shudder deep inside," nor "a shiver of the spine," nor "a tingle of revulsion."

That is the other thing about lightning: one has to learn to accept no substitutes. But how? How can one be sure that he hasn't been settling for static electricity, which his nerves have been registering as lightning? I suspect one never ultimately knows. Perhaps it is more nearly a matter of praying for rather than knowing. I have known men I surely believe to be bad poets who were yet entirely and prayerfully convinced that they were toward the lightning. So perhaps do all men delude themselves. It is always possible to fail. But one tries at least to fail into the weather.

If there is any luck to be had, that's where it is.

October 21, 1961

Rhyme

Driving the family cross-country to Missouri to see Grandfather and Grandmother can get dull and long and games can help. One of the games our minnows have had good times with is Rhymes. They have, by now, pretty much outgrown the simpler versions, but we can still get some mileage out of trying to match such rhymes as *Mephistopheles/with the most awful ease.*

If nothing else our games taught me that rhyme is not necessarily an entirely simple concept, as witness Benn at age three and a half asking, "Does *love* rhyme with *hate?*"

A number of recent (and earlier) letter writers to this column turn out to be not much more subtle than Benn in their notions of rhyme. In Benn's defense, moreover, let me say he is three years older now, and no longer needs to ask that question. He knows whether or not it is a rhyme. But all he does recognize as rhyme is what must properly be called "syllabic" rhyme. It is worth noting that syllabic rhyme is only one of several possibilities.

Basically, rhyme is important in English simply because it is hard. Many languages—Italian for example—offer hundreds and even thousands of possible rhymes in cases where English offers none or few. *Self, life, love, star, womb,* to take a few examples, are the words for key concepts in poetry, yet the rhymes for them are generally so few that the pairings quickly become standardized and the rhymes tired. Thus Alexander Pope's dig at poets who jog along

> While they ring round the same unvaried chimes,
> With sure returns of still expected rhymes;
> Where'er you find "the cooling western breeze,"
> In the next line, it "whispers through the trees."
> (An Essay on Criticism, II, 348–351.)

A poet is not required to rhyme, but so long as rhyme is difficult poets will work at it for the pure fun of the difficulty, and so long as they do rhyme, the English pairings will grow more and more familiar.

So long, that is, as one is speaking of only syllabic rhyme. In more recent English and American poetry a number of new ways of rhyming have been tried, and their claims are worth a look.

One well-established way of rhyming, borrowed into English primarily from the French, is *assonance,* the sort of rhyme in which one rhymes simply the stressed vowel sound of the rhyme word, letting the consonants pretty much fall where they may. MacLeish's "Conquistador" is certainly our most ambitious effort at assonantal rhyme.

In general, however, I confess that I am not able to respond richly to assonance in English. Such rhyme is native to French, but I cannot sense that it is native to English. I have no over-whelming brief against assonance: I simply am not drawn to it.

Consonantal rhyme, on the other hand, is an immediate and rich resource and one that can certainly lend new pleasures to English poetry. Consonance is rhyme in which the vowel sound of the rhymed syllable is varied while the consonants, fore and aft, are kept the same. Some examples of consonantal rhyme are: *run, rain, Rhine, ran, ruin* (as an interesting vowel-to-diphthong variant within the consonance), *strewn, brawn, wren, Irene.* Wilfred Owen has probably made the most systematic use of consonantal rhyme in English.

Consonantal rhyme is no loose matter. The unattuned ear may resist it, but it is certainly as precise and demanding as syllabic rhyme, if not more so, and it has the advantage of making fresh and pleasurable combinations possible to the ear long familiar with the available syllabic rhymes of English.

Inevitably, then, there follows a more relaxed rhyme suggested by some combination of assonance and consonance but not strictly of either. Such rhyme has been called *approximate* or *half-rhyme.* Emily Dickinson abounds in such rhymes and even looser ones, and their use has spread widely among modern poets. Some examples of approximate rhyme are: *fox, backs, exacts;* or *summer, somewhere;* or *witch, scotch, patch.*

The orthodox reader may want to argue that this is not rhyme

139

at all, but why can the poet not argue back that it is at least more rhyme than not-rhyme? Such rhymes do have at least part of a sound in common.

I am not sure, for that matter, but what one could defend a purely phonetic theory of rhyme based on the idea that any words ending in sounds that are pronounced in the same phonetic groupings are in fact rhymes. All gutteral sounds, for example, are made by basically the same speech muscles and are physically related, as are all sounds made off the teeth, off the lips, off the roof of the mouth, etc. One could rhyme by the mouth areas in which terminal sounds are made.

It is not, of course, theory that matters but the ear of the poet. Poets are word-sensitive men. Nor do the good poets try to dodge out by short cuts. When they experiment with rhyme they do so in answer to a demand from within themselves. When enough of them have been satisfied by the results of such experiments, the audience will eventually learn to respond to that new satisfaction and to find the poet's pleasure in it. What one was taught (and only half understood at that) by a teacher who did not know more than so much about such matters, is not necessarily a limit to poetic possibility.

One fascinating possibility that has not, to my knowledge, been explored thoroughly is a structure of rhyme-chords based on alternating syllabic and consonantal rhymes, thus: *rant-runt-punt-pint-point-joint-jaunt-haunt-hint*, etc. A series of such structures seems, in theory at least, a natural and engaging rhyme chord for a complex stanza form, one such chord to a stanza. But, though I have played with the theory for some time, I have never been able to apply it in any satisfactory way. Perhaps it is too elaborate a stunt, though I do not see why. All I can really report is that I like the theory but that it has not worked for me.

Certainly it seems to be a basic fact of English poetry that elaborate rhyme-stunts hurt serious poetry and are best confined to light verse. A serious poem can stand only very limited amounts of cleverness; its food is something heavier than that.

It can in fact do very well without any rhyme at all. But if one does rhyme, he must never look away from one basic rule: it is not the last words that must rhyme but the whole lines. The rhyme words must fall in place in the inevitable flow of idiom

and be firmly locked into the structure of their total lines. Lunge
for that rhyme word and then lead the line limpingly to it, and
all is lost. *Lost* rhymes with *cost*—which is to say no poet can
afford it.

September 16, 1961

The Middle Drawer

The middle drawer of an average desk may be described as a sliding box, about two and a half inches deep and about two and a
half feet square, beginning with a pencil rack and ending in
oblivion. Such, at least, are the estimated dimensions and the obvious organization of the antique but average desk at which I sit at
SR, when I am sitting there, which I do only irregularly, and only
as the spirit moves me.

The average pencil rack with which this average middle drawer
begins was designed to hold the pencils that lie scattered across the
desk top. The remaining cavern, for whatever purpose it was designed, is the oblivion file.

Moved by what might be called an obscure impulse (to obscure
my average reluctance to get to work), I recently fell to taking
inventory of my average pencil rack and came up with the following itemization: two red pencils (unsharpened), one black
grease pencil, one ball point and one fountain pen (both broken),
one mailing sticker that had curled up into a small tube and which
I unrolled to find that I had once printed on it with some care
my social security number (032-10-1228), one purchaser's receipt
for a money order in the amount of $7.15, one theater ticket stub
(R 108) for the opening night of *The Rise of Arturo Ui*, one sec-
ond-best (and therefore unused) letter opener, one spool of J. &
P. Coats black thread (15¢, 125 yards, number 60, origin and pur-

pose unknown), one dentist's tool (broken, but obviously useful for picking things out of things if I had anything of that sort to pick related things out of), two nail files, one pair of cuff links, one metal pill box (empty, origin and purpose unknown), one glass marble (probably a souvenir of a visit from Benn), one four-for-a-quarter-while-you-wait-press-the-button photo taken, as I recall, at, then, Idlewild Airport and showing Jonnel and me looking at one another in some sort of fond but unsubstantiated pride, one twenty-cent stamp (1938 Presidential issue, James A. Garfield), two rubber bands, one pocket comb, a litter of paper clips, one 1889 quarter (to give to the kids for their collection as soon as I am sure they will not spend it on candy), one Canadian dime and one British halfpenny (to be given to them any time), one air-mail sticker, two six-penny nails, three thumb tacks, two match folders, one broken tie clip (probably repairable), one small screw driver (in case any small screws show up to be driven?), one pocket pack of Kleenex, one pair of paper scissors, one staple remover, assorted grit.

It was, I concluded in an average glow of identity with all mankind, an irreproachably average holding, and carried away by good will toward average man, I pulled the drawer wide to explore what lay beyond.

Let me forego itemization for a more shapen thought. Can the years of man's life be brought to mere inventory? Let any man look into his own average heart and desk for his own average litters and so learn to describe himself to himself.

My one perhaps off-average accumulation consisted of about two pounds of individually wrapped sugar cubes, a hoard I come by because the coffee I send out for, and which I drink black and without sugar, always arrives with its quota of sugar cubes, which I always think of saving for the kids until I always remember that they eat too much sugar without my adding more, but which (to round out this month's exercise in all-out sentence structure) I can never bring myself to throw away, their average cavities and my more than average disorder notwithstanding, and because on days when I am not cleaning out my middle desk drawer I can always play blocks with them. There is always some way of not working.

This sugary hoard aside (I finally took it home and put it in the

142

cupboard against such time as I could use it to ruin the coffee of such friends as insisted on its ruin), I finally dumped out on my desk top several pounds of rulers, erasers, and irrelevant hardware, and a ream of papers. And there they were: memos, file-and-forget letters, photos, clippings, receipts, brochures, news releases, notes to me, notes to myself—my whole cemetery of dead intentions.

To it all I have now given proper burial, but from it—as one ghost sighing among many—let me cherish a transcript of a freshman girl's answer to an examination question about one of my poems. The letter that once accompanied it was long since lost. It came, I gather, from her instructor in his limbo. So, in the litter of things, I cannot thank him by name, but as one average ghost saluting another across that limbo we call "the norm," let me send a ghostly thanks. Toward the contexts of this world, let me here reproduce the poem (copyright 1958, Rutgers University Press), and then, as its own example of that average litter known as the student mind, your and my daughter's commentary.

SNOWY HERON

What lifts the heron leaning on the air
I praise without a name. A crouch, a flare,
a long stroke through the cumulus of trees,
a shaped thought at the sky—then gone. *O rare!*
Saint Francis, being happiest on his knees,
would have cried *Father!* Cry anything you please.

But praise. By any name or none. But praise
the white original burst that lights
the heron on his two soft kissing kites.
When saints praise heaven lit by doves and rays,
I sit by pond scums till the air recites
its heron back. And doubt all else. But praise.

And herewith, one child's garden of mental mists:

My version of the poem is that it is a snowy night and a cold winter snow is flaring across the trees. I do not know what the author means by the heron leaning on the air. I believe that this old man is out in the weather and is without a name. He is crouched or cuttled up to make himself warm. The snow is blowing through the cumulus of trees which must be a strong, blowing wind. He is looking toward the sky for help and then the thought leaves him. St. Francis comes to his mind which tells him he is the happiest person on his knees and is looking for guidance from the Father which is God. Cry anything you please is telling the man to speak to God and tell him your troubles because no one else can help him the way God can.

I am not for sure what he means by praise only that God is praising the old man for the work he has done.

The connotations in this poem is crouch and cumulus. Allusions are lit by doves and rays which is taken from the Bible. I cannot recognize any paradox or metonomy in the poem. Personification is used when the author says a praise without a name. He means a man without a name. No simile's are given in the poem.

Gone now, all gone. For all of two weeks my middle drawer opened on order and efficiency. Then back to litter. As worlds go. Yet in my desk's tidiest hours I heard this ghost weep through it, warning of that litter to which every hope must fall at last in the dead averages of time.

October 3, 1964

Did I Mean That?

From time to time my wife comes up to my attic study and looks purposefully at my desk. On such occasions she always wants to

144

know how I keep track of anything. To which I reply that I never really lose anything. To which she replies that I can never really find anything, either.

As it happens, she is wrong in this case. I do constantly find things on my desk in the process of looking for something else. To be sure, I seldom find what I happened to be looking for just at that moment, but no matter—that will show up some other time. All one need really do is acquire a sense of sidereal time and everything will happen.

Somewhere in that infinite continuum, I was stirring things on the top of my desk looking for I-forget-what, when I came on a clip of correspondence dating back to May of 1961. In *SR* for April 1, 1961, I had published a poem and one of the students of Professor John R. Bryden of Wayne University had written a paper on it. Professor Bryden had thought I might like to see that student paper.

This column may seem to be a tardy acknowledgement as the Winchell flies, but think again how the orbits swing. Not even such a cosmic gadabout as Halley's Comet has reappeared. The interim, in fact, hardly gives me time to be surprised over again by the student's ingenuity.

But to begin at the beginning, here is the poem:

ON FLUNKING A NICE BOY OUT OF SCHOOL

I wish I could teach you how ugly
decency and humility can be when they are not
the election of a contained mind but only
the defenses of an incompetent. Were you taught
meekness as a weapon? Or did you discover,
by chance maybe, that it worked on mother
and was generally a good thing—
at least when all else failed—to get you over
the worst of what was coming. Is that why you bring
these sheepfaces to Tuesday?
                                   They won't do.
It's three months work I want, and I'd sooner have it
from the brassiest lumpkin in pimpledom, but have it,
than all these martyred repentances from you.

The student who wrote about the poem got the surface situation and its mood beyond any question. He was, in fact, surprisingly sensitive in that part of his discussion. Then, having described that much, a disastrous phrase occurred to him. "On a deeper level," he began—and suddenly I find myself buried in Norse mythology. Here is the part of his paper that leaves me gasping:

On a deeper level, the poem says much more. Not only does it juxtapose the conflicting matriarchal and patriarchal principles of our society, but it also analyzes the positive and negative aspects of Christianity in juxtaposition with northern mythology symbolized by *Tuesday*.

Indeed, the word *Tuesday* is the key to the entire poem. Technically, we note that it is the only word that does not rime or near rime with any other end-word of a line. Furthermore, it climaxes the first ten lines of the sonnet, forcing the reader to a halt, and leads to the spondaic "They won't do" and resolution of the final three lines.

Tuesday, we remember, is the day of the week named for Tyr, the Norse god of battle, and here represents the patriarchal principle, which demands that children earn their parents' love (here it is the teacher's "pass") as opposed to the matriarchal principle that counsels giving love *regardless*, and is symbolized by *mother*.

Of course, *Tuesday* might simply be the day of the student's class or conference, but symbolically it is also the Norse god of battle, the patriarchal principle, and the teacher himself.

Several words in the poem call up Christianity: *election, meekness, mother, sheep-faces, martyred*. One is at first shocked to see *decency* and *humility* labeled *ugly*, but one soon realizes that the poet is saying these traits can be beautiful when they are *elected* (Christian theological overtone) by a "contained mind" (connoting, perhaps, a disciplined and disciplining God) and not by an "incompetent mind" (connoting self-indulgence and an overpermissive God).

Mother, of course, is Mary, and *sheep-faces* and *martyred* call up Christ. The poem might be saying that patriarchal Christianity (God's love must be earned) is good, while matriarchal Christianity (God's love is for all) is bad, or that a dogmatic, insti-

146

tutionalized church (mother) is bad, while a militant Christ (*Tuesday*) is good.

Tyr willingly had his hand bitten off by the wolf, Fenris. Isn't it ironic that *sheep-faces* come to him, and isn't it more than coincidental that Christ is supposed to have said, "If your hand offends you, cut it off"?

The poem then is a plea for individual responsibility: Tyr would rather face a wolf than a sheep. The patriarchal principle calls for a deserving child. A teacher vastly prefers a pimply upstart who works and thinks to a "nice boy."

What astonishes me about all this is its combination of acumen and obtusity. The conclusions are right enough, yet all sorts of things are incidentally wrong, as for example, the poem is not a sonnet, and "Tuesday" is not a line end, but the middle of a line, the rest of the line being dropped because the tone of the poem changes in mid-line.

Somewhere between precision and fumble, moreover, this student decided to turn a corner that wasn't there. Obviously the boy had been reading up on Norse mythology and he happened to be loaded up on Tyr and Fenris.

For all that about Tuesday is an obvious derailment. Had I said Monday he would probably have come on with moon symbolism, and so on through the week. For the name of any day can be taken for this sort of symbolic ride—and when I say "ride" I am thinking of Rhakaday from "rakateah," one of the goon Norns of Shickagoan mythology, who on orders from Ahlkhapohn rode people out of this world to the symbolic terminus known as Thurivver, where they were embraced by the goddess Seement.

But I really shouldn't josh this boy. On something like the same level he is exactly right about the Christian overtones of *election*, *meekness*, etc. Those words were all chosen for a purpose.

But how is a student to know he is right in one set of identifications and wrong in another? It is the residual teacher in me that asks that question, not the writer of the poem. And I think the teacher has a reasonable answer.

How do you *know*, asks the student, that *Tuesday* wasn't meant as a symbol? Because, says the teacher, that possibility is never returned to in the poem.

Any poet who intends a common word to acquire the extraordinary symbolic weight this student gives to *Tuesday* will reinforce that possibility by returning to it somewhere else in the poem. The Christian overtones of the poem are a theme because they are developed into a theme. *Tuesday* is simply a day of the week because had the poet wanted to evoke Tyr, or Tiw, or Thing, he would have brought the phrasing back to that possibility somewhere else in the poem.

January 16, 1965

On Leaving the Bench

I have always shied away from invitations to judge literary competitions. I confess to a distrust of those who have an appetite for such appointments. A hunger for literary authority, I suspect, is a symptom of literary insensitivity. I am not sure I can defend the rightness of my mistrust. I do know that all of my feelings are conditioned by such a doubt and that they have been for most of my life. In World War II, for example, I managed four GI years in which, it is almost possible to say, I never took an order nor gave one. I don't imagine any such score can be perfect. I do like to believe that I scored high. Whatever percentage points I must surrender to ugly fact, I know my intention was pure and that I have always meant it to describe the way I should like to live—as in Dante's heaven all souls are brothers and sisters and there are no titles of authority though many of esteem.

From time to time, however, a sense of duty is likely to infect even the purest intention. I have in my time been helped to prizes, and so into print, by esteemed and duty-ridden seniors. When, eventually, my own name began to appear on the spines of books,

148

I was easily persuaded that I, in my turn, owed to the competing young such doubtful endorsement as I could give them.

At that time, moreover, I was a teacher, which is to say, a hired sympathy inured to the dreariness of most student manuscripts. I knew they were poisonous, but I had persuaded myself that, like Mithridates, I could immunize myself by progressive dosages. It took me most of twenty years to find out that my psychic hair and fingernails were falling out, that I was dead every June, and that if I managed some sort of rebirth by August and enough vital energy to keep me writing for the first month or so of the school year, I would soon begin to dry up to next June's point of death with the ever recurring panic that this time there could be no rebirth from such a tomb. It was in despair that I finally gathered the courage to resign my professorship. Now when former colleagues ask if I regret my action, I can point out that in the four years after I left I published eleven books—projects, for the most part, that had been mired and caked over while I graded papers and went to committee meetings.

My final decision to quit teaching was taken after two years in which I could find no students worthy of even a teacher's desperate sympathies. So it is with my decision to judge no more undergraduate poetry contests. In the last two years I have shuffled the papers for a dozen such assortments of prize-seeking manuscripts, under instructions to list the first five, or the first eight, and in one case the first twenty in order of merit.

Desperate work! How does one rank mush, and particularly mush that has been watered and (possibly) stirred but never cooked? I could not have dreamed that poets would be discovered in every competition, or even in any twenty, but if what I have read these past two years is evidence, this generation of undergraduate would-bes doesn't even mean to write, but thinks of a poetry competition as a subagency of the welfare state: A distribution is to be made and why not fill out the forms on the chance of getting some of the goodies?

I confess to seeing no point in addressing the students whose manuscripts I have read. Let me, rather, not only imagine that there is one unknown among them who is mad enough to want to be known as a writer but who actually wants to write. If that man will take me on trust, at least to the point of doubting me seri-

149

ously, I should like to sermonize my impressions of the student manuscripts I have been reading.

To begin with, these students obviously think that writing poetry is easy and that it takes no preparation. Some of them, I will even guess, honestly believe they have put a real effort into their poems. If that is so, then I can only conclude that they have no sense of what real effort involves. "A poem," said one of the French poets—I forget which one—"is never finished; it is abandoned in despair." To which I must add that it makes a lot of difference whose despair it is abandoned in. If the undergraduates I have been reading touched on anything like despair, they obviously reached desperation before they had worked up a sweat. I want Mr. X, my unknown hope among them, to know that a writer has to *mean it*, and that he must mean it with an intensity I find no traces of in those of his peers I have read.

Part of the act of meaning it consists of preparing oneself. One expects students to lack a background in depth; to say that a beginner is a beginner is no charge against him. But please, Mr. X, consider how many "poetic authorities" are encouraging students to scorn all background. Your generation has been told by some of the names on the spines of books that it must shout social causes, that meter is reactionary, that rhyme is decadent, that language distinction has Fascist overtones, and that formal structure is an Establishment sellout.

What measures then? There *are* what we call "free" forms, but "free," when we speak of a form, can only mean "free of traditional measures because it has invented its own." Take "free" to mean "without measure," and you are dead in the egg, chick.

I will go a reactionary step further. Measure, I will insist, must be learned, and it can be learned only within meter, rhyme, and the old forms—and, yes, I mean the couplet, the sonnet, the sestina, the rondeau, the rondelle, and any other "archaic" form you care to list, "archaic" here signifying "generally pertinent to a past age and way of life only, though always (see Auden) capable of becoming forceful when transformed by talent."

In the face of many of your generation's Pooh-Bahs, Mr. X, I beg you to think of such formalities as being archaic in about the sense the roots of a tree are. I do not urge you to dig up and air tree roots. I am saying that until they sink in, nothing can come

150

up. The best radical is usually the one who knows in the greatest detail what he is rebelling from. The past is your base. Until you make it your own, you have no standing—not even a place from which to attack it. Think of yourself as beautiful and facile, or as having hit upon such truths that it is enough to shout them without laboring to shape them into form, and no good can follow. And remember, Mr. X, what your peers seem never to have known: It is enough for the poem to be beautiful; there is no need for the poet to be.

OF FISH AND FISHERMEN

Fish are subtle. Fishermen
are gross and stinking and they lurch
hauling their nets. Which clod of them
could shimmer like a cod or perch
through blue and green and purple spells?
It isn't shimmering grace that tells
in the long run. It's being taught
to track and set and haul and stink.
If stinking's part of it. It's not?
It needn't be? That's what you think.

March 13, 1971

And the Frame Around It

Sometimes I think the music critics have all the best of it. They are free to feel as passionate as they please about the music, and at the same time they are free to talk as technically as they please about its management. Anyone who reads them is prepared to accept the technical concern as part of the passion. But let a writer

try to suggest that a poem is a passionately technical performance of an orchestra called language, and he will infallibly be accused of committing an indecency at the shrine of Absolute
Beauty.

I have no choice but to insist that a technical awareness is no
more offensive to poetry than to music, and that it is as necessary
to a true accomplishment of the one form as to the other. Those
readers who resent any effort at technical attention have made
the fundamental mistake of confusing the art form with the subject matter. Force them into a stubborn consistency with their
own premise and they would have to conclude that there is no
difference between a portrait and the model who sat for it, the
ideal function of the ideal portrait being to give the viewer not a
painting but a person.

There is not only a sentimental moral fallacy in that argument,
but it is always touched with a defensive love of The Vague. It is
comforting to brush aside the disciplines of technical management,
for then one need not go to the trouble of studying them. Instant
Beauty is much more satisfying. Just add hot water and serve.

It is a lazy argument, then. But it has been a persuasive one, and
perhaps it will help to establish a better persuasion if the rebuttal
can go out to meet it halfway. Both sides can agree that there has
to be some sort of relation between the model and the portrait:
why else do painters go to the trouble of hiring models? Never
mind, for the moment, in what way the two are alike. Let it simply be granted that there is some sort of likeness. But "some sort
of likeness" must also imply "some sort of difference." Let me suggest, as the most immediately obvious difference, that there is a
frame around the portrait but none around the model,

Now, if the Absolutely Beautiful will still insist that the ideal
function of the ideal portrait is to offer a likeness, they must at
least concede that what is really offered is not only a likeness but
a likeness with a frame around it.

To be sure, we all knew that all the time, but it is still useful to
get it said straight out, for once the frame has been let into the
discussion, any man may discover that he has always known something about how a frame works.

Suppose our hypothetical man is an enthusiastic mountaineer.
And suppose, moreover, that he is the sort of person who goes

152

around passionately mixing metaphors about "getting into tune with the rhythm of it all." He likes mountains, and he likes nature "as it is," which is to say "in the total communion of things as they are." He is currently on a month's vacation in the Rockies. And he has just bought an expensive camera. He has, as a matter of fact, told a number of his friends that he is out to photograph "the real essence of mountain nature."

If that is what he really wants, does it make any difference where he points his camera? Does nature care where any particular mountain rises or what shape its outline takes? As far as nature is concerned, everything out there is Rocky Mountains in whatever sequence it happens. An aerial surveyor running his cameras up and down the whole shebang has the same liberal sense of it. He is out to get the whole thing and he cannot care what lies next to what in what order. Just let it happen and his cameras will record it in their kind of unselective absolute.

And so might our hypothetical man, if he were a real absolutist. If all he wants is Rocky Mountains somewhere in their absolute natural sequence (whatever that is) he is free to shut his eyes and photograph at random—anything his camera catches will be equally of the total nature of things, and who is prepared to argue that in the total of the universe a brook is more than a rock or a rock more than a tree? Just click the shutter at random and the absolutes will concur.

But who ever heard of such an indiscriminate reliance on the absolute nature of things? Our man, in fact, has spent a lot of time looking at the Rockies through his view finder. And everyone knows that as soon as you put your eye to a view finder, you put a frame around your imagination and begin to rearrange nature to suit your sense of the frame. You refuse, now, to take things as they happen. You select. So with our man sizing up Mount Massive. A minute ago it existed as itself in infinity. Now he is juggling it around to get it into the left half of his frame, because he wants to balance it against a triangle of sky (with that one cloud in just the right place) in the right half.

Surely everyone knows that much about a frame. And knowing that, he must know something else. He knows, or is ready to recognize at once, that a daub of color put on an infinite plane is nowhere, but that the same daub, once it has been framed off from

153

infinity, is in the middle, or in the lower right-hand corner, or the upper left, or anywhere else, but somewhere. And he knows that if he puts in a second daub, it immediately comes into relation not only to the first, but also to the frame. And so on for a third, and a fourth, and for as many as can be, until something called a composition (*i.e.*, an intrarelation) has taken place.

By now, in fact, it should come to our man as no surprise at all to discover something else he had always known about the frame and how it works: *sooner or later (and, as a matter of fact, very soon) whatever is happening inside the frame becomes more involved in itself than with the nature of any unframed point of departure.*

And so ends the parable. For it is, of course, a parable, and the real name of that frame is formality, and all those daubs and all those bits and massifs of the Rockies are the elements of anything that happens inside a formality.

For let any man be as absolutely beautiful as he can manage to be inside his own soul—he must still know what he knows. And once he knows as much as everybody knows about frames and about what happens inside them, how can he fail to know that it takes a passion for the handling of technical details to get anything beautiful into the frame around it?

December 5, 1964

On Form as a Language

The more I hear teachers talk about the meaning of poetry (by which they always seem to mean paraphrasable content), the more I suspect them of talking that way because they never learned how to talk about form. I do not mean to imply that poetry has no meaning. Meaning in poetry is inevitable but secondary—still as-

154

suming, that is, that by "meaning" one means "paraphrasable content."

If, however, "meaning" is taken to mean the "intention" of a poem, then let it be added that the meaning is never in the subject content but always and only in the way that content is fused into form. Form is always first.

For the poem is not a statement but a verbal artifact. It exists as a painting or a piece of sculpture or a piece of music exists. It is a wrought entity. It is not simply a sequence of words and phrases. It has *thingness*. It exists as a form.

The act of the writing is the act of reaching for the completion of whatever form offers itself. Nor is the poet opposed to meaning in that act of reaching. Rather, form is the language in which he means. The poem is finished, so to speak, when the form has signaled itself to a close.

There is nothing mysterious about the way a poetic form signals itself to a close; every reader knows something about it. He has at least noticed that when Shakespeare writes a soliloquy in blank verse, he is likely to end it with one or two rhymed couplets. The rhyme serves as the closing bell. The listener hears it and knows the passage has been brought to rest.

It is, to be sure, a bit more complicated than that. The rhythm of the saying, the sound of it, the emotional enlargement of the dramatic situation, and the paraphrasable content of the passage must all be manipulated in such a way that they come to rest together in those final chimes. But even a gross simplification of the case is enough to suggest one general rule: *form tends to conclude itself by some increase in formality*.

And the rule so derived from Shakespeare's use of blank verse will apply as readily to poetry written in other conventions. If the poet is writing in rhymed couplets, for example, the addition of one more couplet will not in itself signal the passage to an end, but some other increase in formality can do so. Alexander Pope is likely to conclude his paragraphs of rhymed couplets with a particularly pointed parallelism, with a balanced antithesis, with some other grammatical or rhetorical formality, with a particular management of the sound and stress of the voice, or with some combination of these.

Just as certainly, a series of double rhymes can be rounded

155

home on a final chord of triple rhymes. And many poets have given the closing signal to a sequence of iambic pentameter couplets by ringing in a final alexandrine. An alexandrine is technically no more than an iambic hexameter, but when it is used in this way it tends to be further characterized by a rather formal pause in the middle with the rhythm and grammar (or both) of the last three feet repeating or complementing that of the first three.

Pope, I must note, thought badly of alexandrines. The famous passage of "An Essay on Criticism" in which he ticks off, while imitating, the bad habits of poetasters concludes:

> Then, at the last and only couplet fraught
> With some unmeaning thing they call a thought,
> A nameless Alexandrine ends the song,
> That, like a wounded snake, drags its slow length along.

English teachers, however, ought not to assume that the whole law has been spoken in a single deft lampoon. The alexandrines Pope had in mind may have been pedestrian, but the need for them was formal, and there is nothing to keep a good poet from writing such alexandrines to good effect. They remain a still usable, though minor, technical resource.

Another sort of formal completion is the one I think of as *thematic*. It consists of getting two different tonalities going in a poem and of bringing the poem to rest by blending the two into one. Marianne Moore's "Nevertheless" is a particularly firm example of this sort of form. The poem begins (and the title must be read as part of the saying):

> you've seen a strawberry
>   that's had a struggle; yet
>   was, where the fragments met,
>
> a hedgehog or a star-
>   fish for the multitude
>   of seeds.

The poem continues in this tone for six stanzas, reveling in minutely observed details of such particularities as prickly pears

156

and the "leaves of *kok-saghyz*-stalks" (*kok-saghyz* is a species of dandelion from the roots of which the Russians make rubber; the *WNW* spells it without the *h*). Then, between the seventh and the eighth stanzas, a new tone enters:

> as carrots form mandrakes
>   or a ram's-horn root some-
>   times. Victory won't come
> to me unless I go
>   to it;

Thereafter the poem returns to the first tone until the last two stanzas, which read:

> The weak overcomes its
>   menace, the strong over-
>   comes itself. What is there
> like fortitude! What sap
>   went through that little thread
>   to make the cherry red!

What has happened? Let me suggest that the reader can readily enough find out for himself either from these fragments or from the total poem (it may be found in the *Collected Poems*, published by Macmillan).

Let him begin by calling that first tone "botanical observations" and the second "moral statements." Then let him go through the poem underlining every "botanical observation" in blue and every "moral statement" in red.

My hope is that by the time he finds himself underlining the last two and a half lines in purple, he will have discovered for himself something about the way in which form is its own language.

October 31, 1964

157

The Artist and Society

"As everyone knows," one of my students once wrote in the course of a term paper, "the eighteenth century was the Age of Reason, and then came the Romantics who found all sorts of things they chose to be mysterious and irrational about."

He was botching an oversimplified notion, to be sure, but I was ready to guess he had remained at least half awake for at least half of the opening lecture. Somewhere between, let us say, Alexander Pope and Lord Byron the terms of a central assumption had shifted in the minds of literary men. The highest order of creative mind, once identified by the possession of "wit, taste, dignity, and fit measure," had come to be reconceived around such terms as "genius, *je-ne-sais-quoi*, divine madness, nature, and inspiration."

Every age has its set of natural assumptions. The natural assumptions of the Age of Reason held art to be a social function, its forms transmitted by society and regulated by the practice of the classic masters. "Taste" in art consisted on the one hand of knowing the masters and on the other of avoiding "enthusiasm." An "enthusiast" was what the seventeenth century called a "fantastic," and approximately what the twentieth century calls a "beatnik." To possess "taste" meant to feel a rapport with the standards of intellectual society. The individual entered the equation primarily as the possessor of "wit," a compound of talent, restraint, and learning. The good artist danced as all intellectual society danced; the measure of his excellence lay in the fact that he danced the same dance more gracefully than did others.

The romantic idea of "inspiration" was unmistakably an opposed notion. By divine gift, and scorning the social restraints implicit in "taste," the inspired artist made his own rules. But to

158

make one's own rules is obviously to reject those of society. Thus the romantic was, by definition, a rebel and antisocial. "Look in thy heart and write," may be taken to state the case for the individual genius. "The proper measure of mankind is man," may be taken to state it for the social, which is to say, the cultivated poet.

Nothing in the history of art is, of course, quite that simple. Byron had read his classic masters and could himself have turned out a discourse on "taste." And Pope certainly honored that spark that marks the superior artist. Art, that is to say, is something like a balance—or an imbalance between the individual artist and society.

The nature of that balance—or imbalance—is especially pertinent in our times, of which it can be said categorically that no good artist embraces wholeheartedly the values of the society in which he lives. (Not, at least, outside the USSR.) Yet at the same time, he must recognize that it is society and only society that stores from the past and transmits to him his traditions, his forms, and even the world view and the sort of passion that make his work possible.

No genius has ever flowered apart from society—without a passionate immersion in the traditions society has stored up for him, and without a zealous joy in remaking what society has made possible. Let him be as anarchic as Dylan Thomas or as orthodox as Tennyson—the teeth of the true gift must be in his own mouth, but only from society can he take the food that will build the body of his special genius.

Art has had few such geniuses as Mozart. It is almost possible to think of him as coming from the cradle—if not from the womb—with his genius already formed. And that enormous native genius, though battered by social and physical adversity, swelled from one creative triumph to another, not only seemingly unexhaustible but ever mounting, up to the hour of its tragically early death.

To be sure, that enormous inherited gift happened to be born in the son of the greatest music teacher of his age, a master attached to a court in which great music and great musicians were a daily routine. If natural genius is the all-absorbing sponge, the sponge that was Mozart was plunged by fruitful accident into the clearest waters of its age. So goes happy chance at its best. But now try imagining.

159

Imagine that the enormous inherited gift that was Mozart was snatched up at birth by a time machine and transported to the Greek Golden Age. Can one doubt that, barring fantastic mischance, the transported Mozart would become a master musician of that other age? Who knows what he might not have accomplished with lute, flute, reeds, drums, or as a rhapsode? Marvelous things, one must suppose.

But (leaving out the quartets, ensembles, operas) how many symphonies could he have composed? He could not have had even the dimmest concept of symphonic music. The very idea of the orchestra had yet to be formed by society. The individual instruments that would bit by bit blend together to form that idea had hardly begun their evolution. It is for these reasons that the natural genius of twenty Mozarts could not have composed a single symphony. Society had not yet made such a thing possible.

And now, with all fantasy in gear, imagine that this transported Mozart, having been fully formed in the Golden Age, is suddenly transported in his maturity to a concert hall in which a symphony orchestra is flowering forth in the full passion of a Mozart symphony as we know it. What would he hear?

An excitement perhaps. A marvelous stirring of confused possibility. But no language. Only by being born of the evolved language can one learn it. Only in society could he have acquired the ears that could listen to that music. The inherited musical genius would still be there—the chromosomal possibility—but as a seed without soil to flower in.

Society is that only soil. It is by the power of genius that men make essential new connections, but the elements among which it has its connections to make are forever from society.

Some see it as the tragic schizophrenia of our times that the artist, forever dependent on his motherhood by society, is somehow forced by his honesty to reject most of the values of his society. Tragic? Well, perhaps. But given what seems to be happening in Russia, where the artist makes it his career and passion to embrace even the most glaring slogans of the party leaders, we may think of ourselves as lucky in having artists who dare rebel. The fact is that their rebellion is never really from society. Rather, they insist on holding up to all levels of society

160

that society's own best levels. The health of that rebellion is the health of us all.

November 23, 1963

Metaphor and Parlor Games

My fabulous friend, the late Fletcher Pratt, once came up with an idea that has stayed with me and done a bit of fermenting on its own (for which he need share no responsibility). In one of his volumes on Napoleon, Fletcher described how the Austrian heavy infantry marched into battle in parade formation and was chewed to pieces when Napoleon, from his inferior forces, sent seemingly random clouds of skirmishers against the parade ranks. The parade, designed to be impregnable against a counter-parade, was confused into a rout by the whirling and skipping tactics of the French.

Those skirmishers, as Fletcher saw it (they had approximate antecedents in the American Revolutionists), struck the blow that was to be the death both of parade-rank warfare and of the kind of society that produced it. In a brilliant insight, Fletcher pointed out the same sort of breaking of patterns on other levels of Western life and society. The flashing and improvised Napoleonic tactics were to the Austrian parade ranks, he argued, as the reeling metric of "Kubla Khan" was to the courtly measures of the "Essay on Criticism," and as the impassionate movement of the mature Beethoven was to the stateliness of Mozart. The flaring of a new, wild impromptu sense could be felt everywhere in Europe.

It was an irresistible sort of master metaphor and we chewed away a happy night guessing out various ways of taking it. Metaphor, to be sure, proves nothing. But neither, to work in

161

another metaphor, does a seed. Both, however, can grow and flower. And this one kept growing and flowering toward the possibility of a true insight into one of our history's most enormous times of change.

The change was there, but what was the change? A change of rhythm, I suggested. "No more than that?" Fletcher asked. "As much as that," I said. Fletcher thought a minute and then nodded. "For that," he said pouring, "you get a drink."

As always when Fletcher poured, it was a good drink. But neither of us was entirely satisfied with letting it go as a change of rhythm, though rhythm was much of it. My clue came sometime later. I was browsing one night through something titled, as I recall, "An Encyclopedia of the Dance," when I came on a definition of the waltz as "a dance in which two figures rotate about their own axis." An odd definition, I thought, but then instantly it brought that other evening's talk to mind. The change we had been trying to identify was essentially the change from the minuet to the waltz. The minuet, of course, is a dance in which every dancer keeps himself in strict relation to a larger inclosing pattern.

I had my metaphor. Let no lawyer apply for admission to it. The joy of good metaphor is not juridical. It is the joy of guessing out analogies. Call it a parlor game if you like, but I mean to live in that parlor. That change from the metaphoric minuet to the metaphoric waltz, already well underway in 1800, was to produce more changes in Western man in the course of the next 100 years than had been brought about in the total history of civilization.

The master metaphor of any social order is, of course, government, and it was government that underwent the most drastic changes in the new waltz-time. The minuet of the old monarchies was breaking up in a revolutionary collision with the waltzers of the new democracies until the few surviving kings and queens were to remain as little more than national heirlooms. What is the force of monarchical theory if not that every man takes his place in relation to an overriding and divinely sanctioned order? And what is the force of democratic theory if not that every man is more or less free to rotate around his own axis?

As for government, so for all social organization. At the same time the thrones were being shaken by the democrats, the old agrarian estates were being shaken by the Industrial Revolution.

Money rather than land was to become the basis of social standing.

As for the economics of life, so in time for the tenor of that life and its ideas. In philosophy, the pre-established orders of Leibnitz that had provided so much of the rationale of eighteenth-century thinking and that had drawn so much from that rationale, were falling before the radical individualism of Rousseau and of the Transcendentalists with their leaning toward Oriental teachings. In literature, the bastions of "taste" (the product, of course, of a selective and academic education based on the observance of approved precedents) had crumbled almost at a touch, and on the ruined parapets a dark Byronic figure labeled "genius" was reaching for guidance into his own inspired madness, dancing to the waltz of his own impulses.

What was genius? I believe it was the Frenchman Boileau who first called it a *"je ne sais quoi."* What can a *"je ne sais quoi"* have to do with social pattern and selected precedents? It has no choice but to waltz around itself.

Impractical perhaps, but in an area as practical as physics, Michael Faraday, born in 1791, was to find himself fooling around with a *je ne sais quoi* that ran along wires and was called electricity. How does a practical man make firmly patterned sense of an invisible-undefinable that is nevertheless there and that can be shown to make a bit of metal rotate when placed between magnets?

If the physicist was to have his eighteenth-century foundations waltzed out from under him, what was the theologian who believed the world dated precisely from biblical times to do with the new heresy called geology? What were his firm notions of divine origin to do with an impostor named Charles Robert Darwin? What was his son, who became a banker, to do with a madman named Karl Marx who argued that money was not money but only hours of work? What was any proper man of the mid-century to do with the madness of those Frenchmen and the blotches they painted?

If there was any part of Western culture that did not stop

minueting and begin waltzing in the wake of that basic change, I'm blessed if I can think what it might be. Try it for yourself in your own parlor. There is no need to prove anything. Everyman, by the grace of metaphor, his own social historian.

And then try another game. If the minuet is the basic rhythm of the eighteenth century, and if the waltz is the basic rhythm of the nineteenth century—what is the basic rhythm of ours? There will be no parlor answer to that one. If we produce a monumentally great poet in this century, he will be the one to find that rhythm and its pattern for us. And once he has found it, less perceptive men will be able to recognize it.

For that matter, we all know what some of the parts 'will be. Jazz has some parts of it. So have the newer composers. You can hear it for yourself in the sound of the highways, at airports, in subways, and in the way we speak because of our lives on highways, in the air, and underground. The seeds of that rhythm and pattern are in everything we do. In how we move. In how our machinery moves around us. In our dread that it may stop moving around and start moving over and through us. But what we lack until some great poet gives it to us is the synthesis. When we hear the whole—if we ever do—we shall know more about ourselves.

November 18, 1961

Games

My recent lecture tour left me a good goat's leap ahead of the tax collector but several bad months behind my accumulated mail, and I now begin to realize that in my hurry to get through it I misled Mr. R. Hugh Ulmann, who wrote me from Kansas City to quote a friend of his as saying, "The status quo is just about the same," and to ask if I could identify that statement as a figure of speech. Without thinking much about it I dictated something to the effect that it might be an Irish Bull and flipped over to the next letter.

For some reason, however, it stuck in my mind after the letter had been mailed and second thought told me that I was, of course, wrong. It might have qualified as an Irish Bull had my correspondent's friend said, "The trouble with the status quo is that it is always changing." As quoted, however, it is a simple tautology, and I hereby file my correction and apology.

By error and retraction, in any case, I found I had the Irish Bull on my mind without being entirely sure I had the beast identified. The only one I could recall with any assurance ran, "The weather in Dublin is so inclement that most of the inhabitants live elsewhere."

And there it is, but what is it? "An Irish Bull," I tried saying to myself, "is a statement whose meaning makes no sense whatever." I think that turns out to be another Irish Bull, but it hardly does as a definition. "An Irish Bull," I tried again, "is a smoothly paved highway of meaning that no one can drive on because of the subsurface bumps." I guess that turns out to be another one, but it obviously tries too hard, and it still misses the essence.

The essence of it is contradiction. Off the cuff, an Irish Bull seems to be a plausible and perhaps even weighty statement that turns out, on second thought, to be absurd.

With that, I thought I had it, and was gratified on turning to Webster's unabridged to find that the sons of Noah and I were substantially in accord:

A grotesque blunder in language;—now usually applied to expressions containing apparent congruity, but real incongruity, of ideas.

In which I was cheered to find that Webster's definition seemed at least as labored as my figure about the highway of meaning. And to which, I was gratified to find, Webster's had added a fine example of the species:

He remarked in all seriousness that it was hereditary in his family to have no children.

So to the commuter train and a Pennsylvania week of trying to make up Irish Bulls. (A Pennsylvania week, let me explain, consists of ten hours of riding back and forth on the Pennsylvania Railroad, one hour each morning and one each night for five days running.) My first, I am afraid, was my best, and it was an outright gift of the Pennsy's management. "The conductor," I noted, "is so ugly that he would look better if he were invisible."

Thereafter, in slow but inevitably descending progression, I came up with the following jottings:

If automobiles get to going any faster you won't be able to move in the traffic jam that will result.

It is only natural for some girls to be artificial.

When you take a real look at this plethora of modern art you will begin to understand why no one wants to paint that way.

Some people are so rich they impoverish one another by comparison.

Time ages all but the very young.

From a single girl's point of view the best thing about bachelors is that most of them are not married.

Secaucus used to smell so bad that even the odors wouldn't stay there.

It gets so dark in those woods that you can't see a light before your eyes.

His club is so snobbish that it turns down applicants just for not being members.

Switzerland has carried internationalism to the point at which practically all of its citizens are foreigners.

Price resistance is when all your customers do their buying in another store.

The defendant shouldered the entire guilt, testifying that his accomplices had not been involved.

The train schedule to Metuchen considered, it is small wonder that our New York guests never come to see us.

One look at the rush-hour jam in the subway and you know why no one rides it any more.

During a depression everybody is unemployed because all the jobs are already taken.

166

The only thing that makes his poetry so popular is that no one can read it.

Despite the fact that no one understands his ideas, they have had a tremendous influence on contemporary thinking.

And let that be enough of that. I do these things only to amuse myself when there is no diversion available. On the Pennsylvania Railroad you have nothing to do anyhow—in whatever form it happens to take. A man could look out at the view, but in New Jersey there is never much of it in sight. Or he could strike up a conversation with the man sitting beside him, except that he has always just left the train at the last stop. Or he could read the newspaper, except that it is hard to unfold because someone has always just gotten on and taken his seatmate's place. It leaves a man hard put for nothing to do.

August 8, 1964

In Boston

It must be thirty years since I used to drink Moxie without thinking anything about it. My uncle used to like it and kept a supply on ice. He was given to aperitifs made of sweet and dry vermouth with a shot of Ferro-China bitters, and Moxie, he said, gave him a related taste. I can myself testify that the two tastes are close enough to be pleasant when one concentrates on the moment of the taste, and irrelevant as soon as the moment has passed. I do at times recall mixing a little Moxie with other soft drinks to kill their oversweetness and give them a little zing. I suppose a person given to a taste for medicinal bitters might even do something with Moxie and vodka, and I mean to try it the next time I am in Boston, though I make myself no promises in advance.

167

In any case, I was in Boston not long since and, being offered a bottle of chilled Moxie, I accepted and poured it into a glass. "Can you get it in New York?" my host said. I told him I had never seen the stuff out of Boston. Then, for nostalgia's sake, I took a sip. Not bad, really not bad at all.

"It tastes like a tonic," I said.

"What else should it taste like?" my host said.

I had forgotten but I was reminded: in Boston all carbonated soft drinks are classified as "tonic," and may be bought regularly at soda fountains called "spas." I had, in fact, been brought up in Boston on "orange tonic," and with that memory as a point of departure, I could recall reading of baseball games in New York where the fans drank "orange pop."

It had sounded exciting then—"pop"—and I could remember thinking it had to be a delicacy. I was, of course, building up to a disappointment and the disappointment came. Orange "pop" turned out to be neither up nor down the scale from orange "tonic," but the discovery that they were identical did remove one more expectation from the world. Is it better to dream there are wonders yet to be tasted, or to taste the wonder and to find it is no more than you have already known, and that a word you could once dream on has popped its bubble?

How much of what we set our taste buds for is the flavor of the name and how much is the flavor on the tongue? What are our years but our habits?

Then, of course, years pass and we find ourselves reminded with a sense of strangeness of those very things we once took to be norms. Whatever its merits, Moxie is a Boston norm and is aptly called a tonic, suggesting compounds of bitterroot, quinine, and Indian snake oil, though I don't know that it actually contains any of those substances. It is my private guess that Moxie is descended from the days of medicine men, folk medicine, and the spring drench to which husbands and children were subjected while the ladies took something equivalent out of the pharmacopoeia of Lydia Pinkham. I suspect, moreover, that Moxie must have something to do with the survival of "tonic" as the standard name for a Bostonian's soft drink.

In any case, the language of Boston remains its own feast. In Medford, we used to have Fourth of July athletic competitions

168

for which posters were nailed up announcing a long list of "field sports" and "aquatic competitions," the list always concluding: "and divers other events." The competitions were held in various parts of town, most of the "field sports" at Winthrop Field and most of the "aquatic competitions" in the River Basin (before it became polluted), but for years I wandered around looking for those other events the divers put on. Where but in Boston is confusion so easily come by?

Even Tufts College (now Tufts University), which is my school, and I its patriot, slid over the edge of caution and into dangerously inflated Bostonese at one point after my time, though I am not sure I can blame Boston and I remain reluctant to blame Tufts, the new nomenclature having been introduced by Leonard Carmichael when he came from Rochester to become president, before going on to the Smithsonian as its director. Leonard Carmichael is a distinguished man and an admirable one, but perhaps on coming upon Boston from the outside he was awed by its idiom and decided to live up to it and beyond it. I do know it was in his administration that the Bursar's Office became The Bursary and acquired a suite called The Counting Rooms, that the old Cafeteria became The Refectory, and that the Snack Bar became The Kursaal.

Even for Boston, that nomenclature struck me as being a bit gamey. The least one can do for a cafeteria become a refectory is to get rid of the baked macaroni steamtable special. On the other hand, it does make Tufts the only university in town with a genuine hamburger and malted-milk Kursaal.

Language, of course, is a habituated taste. Future Tuftsmen (and Jacksonwomen) may come to think of a Kursaal as the one natural place for a cherry frappe or for a dish of frozen pudding, unless they go off campus to get theirs at the local Spa. And some future Boston adolescent, reading of "soda fountains," may yet dream a Tivoli of cascading flavors, only to visit the Outside and learn it is no fountain at all, but only a Spa or a Kursaal.

Such reveries come easily in Boston, which is not in the State of Massachusetts but in the Commonwealth thereof, which does not have a State Legislature but a General Court, which does not adjourn but "prorogates." A man from the Outside might reasonably expect from such a combination a flavor of rhetoric unknown to mere legislatures, though he is more likely, alas, to hear—as I once did—those guardians of marble principle call for a factual discussion of the issue by shouting, "Let's get down to the meat and pudaders!"

You must, that is to say, take Boston as it is. It will toss a Refectory at you now and then, but once inside, it's pudaders you're going to get. If you can't find a Refectory, there is always a Waldorf. In Boston the Waldorf is not a hotel, but any one of a chain of cafeterias spread through the town and into the suburbs.

"Let's scoff," my Irish brother-in-law once said to me as we passed the local Waldorf.

"Let's what?" I said.

"Scoff," he said. "Time for the feedbag."

His translation given, I filed the word away as a piece of South Boston slang, but when I got home and looked it up, Webster's had it down as slang for "to eat" or "to eat greedily," but derived it from South-African Dutch, a source I could hardly connect to my brother-in-law's idiom.

Boston vowels being what they are, he may have been saying "scoff" or "scaff," or something in between. I turned to "scaff," therefore, and that was it—not slang but proper Erse, meaning "to provide food," and plausibly from the Old Sod itself by way of South Boston.

As far as I know, that leaves Boston as the only place on earth where a man may go to the Waldorf to scoff meat and pudaders. I almost wish we had gone in for that at the Tufts Refectory, but one can't have everything. As it was, he made a heaping good meal of it. I know because I sawr it.

P.S. Think of a word, you'll hear it spoken: In the cab to *SR*'s offices to deliver the typescript of this column, my Jewish driver said, "I scoff raisins by the handful."

April 20, 1968

170

What's a Mokko?

I was browsing the unabridged and extensively titled *Random House Dictionary of the English Language,* when I happened on the word "mokko" and found it identified as a word of Japanese origin signifying (total definition quoted) "a tsuba having four lobes."

Was I justified in thinking the *RHD* had led me up to "mokko" but had mumbled the introduction? I certainly wasn't about to stand there at the word party, first on one lexicographical foot and then the other, trying to exchange knowledgeable sweet nothings about tsubas and their lobes. Nor was I about to give up "mokko" —who knows but what that very same mokko might offer me my moment of supreme triumph at the climactic point of some yet unbegun game of Scrabble?

No help for it: I was out to track it down. I turned, accordingly, to "tsuba" and found it defined as:

the metal plate, usually elliptical, serving as the guard of a Japanese sword or knife, having an opening for the tang of the blade, a blank area, or seppa dai, sometimes bearing the maker's signature, and sometimes one or two lateral openings, or riobitsus, for a kogai, a kozuka, or both.

I saw at once that it was going to be difficult to work up a spirited conversation with the words at *RHD*'s party, but my mood had turned stubborn. "Tang" stopped me for a moment. In context it suggested itself as another word of Japanese origin. Then I refocused and remembered that it was a sound and seasoned English word for that metal extension by which a blade, or

171

a tool, is fixed to its handle. The "seppa dai," I further learned by cross-checking that entry in the *RHD*, is a blank space around the tang. "Riobitsus," I gathered from the definition of "tsuba," is a plural form, but when I turned to it as a separate entry, *RHD* gave me "riobitsu" as the singular and the plural as "-su."

I still don't know which plural to go for in case I should meet more than one riobitsu at the same time, but I let myself guess that when an opening (a slot?) in an ellipse is lateral, it is aligned with the long axis of the ellipse. Immediately, then, I began to wonder if it would not, rather, be aligned with the short axis? At the same time, I found myself wondering how one would go about putting four lobes on an ellipse, and where in relation to either axis, and what on earth for. Such thoughts, however, were getting me nowhere. I dismissed them and turned to "kozuka" which I found defined as:

a detachable dagger blade made of a plate of steel and a plate of iron welded together and sharpened with a bevel on the iron face, used with an elaborately decorated handle, and worn mainly with the wakizashi.

I let myself assume that what the blade is detachable from is that elaborately decorated handle, and I thought I understood the trick of that bimetallic laminate, at least enough to guess that the iron provides the cutting edge while the steel prevents the brittle iron from snapping. But why on earth would anyone want a knife that detaches from the handle? And how does even a samurai pull out his trusty snicker-snack when its handle has other handles sticking up beside it? Was *RHD* deliberately trying to confuse me, or were all its editors dropouts from the Bureau of Federal Prose?

I suppressed the thought and turned to "kogai":

an ornamental pin carried in a sheath in the scabbard of a waki-zashi or katana.

A sheath in a scabbard?—well, yes: a scabbard is specifically a sheath for a sword or knife, but a sheath is not necessarily a scabbard. I managed a picture of a small pocket in a scabbard with an ornamental pin slipped into the pocket, but only in time to find

172

myself in trouble with that riobitsu in the tsuba into which, when last heard from, the kogai was supposed to fit. Was I now to think of a riobitsu as a sheath in a scabbard? If so, what was it doing playing around among those lobes on the tsuba—always remembering that a tsuba lobe is a sometime thing?

It was getting murkier and murkier at Random House, but I was getting stubborner and stubborner as I turned to "wakizashi":

a short Japanese sword carried by a samurai, usually equipped with a matching doggai and kozuka: used for fighting and for suicide. Cf. katana.

What a measly evasion that "equipped" turns out to be! Equipped in what way? In reason, I wanted to imagine some sort of belt fitted out with various loops and danglements. But what was I to do with whatever the plural is of riobitsu "a" and "b," those two slots that are still sitting there in those tsubas for the kozukas and maybe the kogai to fit into? I was back to that image of a samurai trying to draw his good old wakizashi but having to fumble with a fistful of handles sticking out of one tsuba, with a kogai lurking somewhere, either in a riobitsu or in that scabbard sheath.

I trudged on to "katana":

the long fighting sword of a Japanese samurai, having a gently curved blade with a single edge and a long handle continuing the curve: occasionally equipped with a kogai and kozuka.

I confess I blinked at "Japanese samurai." Is there another kind of samurai? RHD itself defines "samurai" as "a member of the hereditary warrior class in feudal Japan." It would follow, therefore, that there are no non-Japanese samurai, but by that time I was in no way surprised to find evidence that the RHD's editors, if any, did not read one another. For my part, it had been a long hunt, and I was still not sure whether I was in the presence of a samurai or in the cutlery department of Abercrombie and Fitch. As a matter of fact, I was still not sure I had identified either "mokko" or "tsuba" beyond all reasonable doubt.

But I was still not ready to give up. There was "doggai" yet to

173

go, and what can be more dramatic than the last minute clue that seals the case?

I found the right page and ran my finger down it: "dogfish" . . . "dog fox" . . . "dogged". . . . Had I missed it? I checked again. No "doggai." Random House was keeping that one to itself.

It is, you can see, a mildly frustrating game. Yet, there are all sorts of psychic types in the world, and those who like to be defeated in intricate ways may find this sort of *RHD* word hunt exactly to their taste. Should anyone care to try for himself, let me suggest starting with "raguly" (pronounced, approximately, RAG-yuh-lee):

Heraldry, noting a partition line or a charge, as an ordinary, similar to the embattled but with the indentations sloping in one direction. [? cf. GULES]

You get *partition line*, *charge*, *ordinary*, and *gules* (if you want it) as starting clues. First one back with a clearly defined raguly (this one can actually be run down to an almost decipherable diagram) gets a Lexicographical Cross and first chance to buy my slightly used *RHD* cheap. (Or will trade.)

April 12, 1969

What Is a Dictionary? (*a Meander*)

For weeks now I have been playing mildly frustrating games with the unabridged *Random House Dictionary of the English Language*. Those frustrations keep driving me back to the *RHD* to ask more questions of it, and, I am sorry to say, I am not at all pleased by such answers as I have come on.

Let me assume that the primary work of a lexicographer involves phonetics, etymology, usage, and definition.

I have no questions to ask of *RHD*'s phonetics, in part because phonetic scholarship is so readily available to the lexicographer that he can relegate that portion of his work to a computer, in part because I am not phonetically qualified and can, therefore, ask no questions of the *RHD*'s handling of phonetics, and in part because of my probably arrogant but, by now, ingrained assumption that the rules of English pronunciation do not concern me since any given word is properly pronounced exactly as I happen to pronounce it.

Aside from many questions about the quality of the *RHD*'s definitions, there remain matters of etymology and of usage, which in my view, readily become one.

Usage, as I understand it, is a double thing. It involves, first, the lexicographer's attention to the status or tone of a given word or phrase, as for example, a lexicographer might reasonably be moved to suggest that the expression "Oh, yeah?" is not likely to be used during sittings of the Supreme Court, and that a lawyer who does use that expression in addressing the Court might find himself cited for contempt.

The fear of any such comment on usage derives from the credo of the newly enshrined structural linguisticians. They call themselves linguists, but I must insist on reserving "linguist" to signify "one who has mastered various languages." Linguisticians, on the other hand may not be linguists at all. They set themselves, primarily, to parse the structures and mechanisms of one language.

Under the charge of those linguisticians, recent dictionaries have shied away from comments on usage. They seem to have assumed that any such comment implies a judgment of right and wrong. Language, they charge, does not go by moral judgment; it is simply a matter of what people who are native to a given language happen to say when they speak it. I suspect the linguisticians of an oversimplification here. I hold it to be a part of any dictionary's function to report, without moral judgments, on the sort of social or situational context in which a given word or phrase is likely to be used at the time the dictionary is compiled.

There is also the question of historical usage, which is to say, of

175

the way given words and phrases have been used at different periods in the development of the language. Comments on historical usage would note such matters, for example, as the fact that the word "luxury," as used in Shakespeare, always and only meant "lust," and that it has since developed a quite different meaning, even to the point of having lost its original sense.

Usage in this sense immediately involves etymological derivation, a point that becomes obvious when we stop to consider that most of the words we speak are mispronounced Latin and Greek on the south side and mispronounced Norse on the north. Historical usage and etymology, therefore, blend into one consideration, the etymologist tracking a word's usage before it entered the English language, the commentator on usage tracking it thereafter.

Some attention to these qualities of words is absolutely necessary for the man who would use his native tongue well. Not only does one become aware of both the root meanings and the evolved meanings of words, but of the possible interplay of the two meanings. Certainly no lexicographer has done his work thoroughly until he has responded to these meanings and to their possible interplay within a given word.

"Starve" offers an excellent example of the historical changes a word can undergo without ever entirely losing its root sense. The *RHD* derives it, rather skimpily, from:

[ME *sterve* (*n*), OE *steorfan* to die; c. G *sterben;* akin to STARE]

The unabridged *Webster's New International Dictionary*, Second Edition, does substantially better:

[ME. *sterven* to die, fr AS. *steorfan;* akin to D. *sterven*, G. *sterben*, OHG. *sterban* to die, ON. *starf* labor, toil, *stjarfi* epilepsy. See TORPID]

Neither dictionary, however, does well enough for the word-lover. The various Nordic roots and the Anglo-Saxon *steorfan* meant not simply "to die" but specifically "to die any slow, lingering, painful death, as from torture, exposure, deprivation, or disease." When walled towns were besieged, they were said to be

176

"starved" (later "starved out") in this sense of a slow death. As it happened in those days before refrigeration and canning, the first thing to give out was likely to be food, and the slow death most common among stubborn defenders was likely to be by deprivation of food. So it was that death by being deprived of food, originally one of the many meanings of *starf, steorfan, sterven*, usurped all of our "starve," except in such surviving usages as "he was starved for affection," which may, as a matter of fact, be either a survival of the root meaning or a later metaphorical usage of "starve."

Are such word probings excessive? The click-click let's-get-on-with-it mind (and the *RHD* does, alas, suggest such a tone of tidy but shallow efficiency) is likely to think so. Yet I must insist that a lexicographer's duty is not simply statistical. He must love words and have a feeling for them as living forces with characters, histories, and shifting powers. Every word is a work of human genius. Any list of even ten English verbs is a cultural achievement and a cultural possibility of more enduring value than any monument in England.

May 24, 1969

Mumpsimus

I am grateful to Mrs. John A. Ward of Carlisle, Pennsylvania, for calling my attention to the word "mumpsimus" of which Webster's Unabridged, Second Edition, has the following to say:

mumpsimus: n. [A blunder for the L. *sumpsimus*, "we have received," the story running that an aged priest, when corrected for saying *mumpsimus* in the service, declared that he had said *mumpsimus* for thirty years, and would not change his old *mumpsimus*

177

for the new *sumpsimus*.] A bigoted adherent to exposed but customary error; also, a custom or tenet so adhered to. *Archaic.*

Doctors *mumpsimusses* of divinity.

Tyndale.

I had not previously come upon the word, but I want Mrs. Ward to know I welcome it. I am sorry to note that Webster's classifies it as archaic, and I hereby declare my allegiance to it, pledging to do all I can to restore it to good usage. So mumpsimus a world as ours is cannot do without so useful a label.

For whatever pleasure it may offer Mrs. Ward, and for whatever help it may be to philomumpsimuses, my most memorable bird of this plumage was a sweetly determined aged schoolteacher I met in Kansas City in the summer of 1940. I went to Kansas City University as an instructor in English in February of 1940 and, lacking carfare to get out of town, I stayed on to teach summer school. Let me say I was in no unfriendly haste to leave Kansas City, and I meant, in any case, to return in the fall. Kansas City does, however, remain a good place to be away from during the summer. I could easily have been bribed away by an airline ticket to, say, St. Moritz. I can even confess that it was only because no one made any effort to bribe me in this way that I remained in town, teaching school for eating money.

Among the subjects I found myself teaching was American literature, and I was more than a bit uneasy to find that I was younger than any of the schoolteachers who were taking the class. I had just turned twenty-four, an age that gave me a bit of an edge on the seniors of the regular session, but that gave everyone in the summer school class an edge on me. Among my white heads was Miss Mumpsimus, who must have been within a year or two of retirement, and who took several occasions to imply that the maturity of her certainties was a better thing than the greenness of my confusions.

All went reasonably well, however, till we got to Longfellow and to *The Psalm of Life*. Longfellow has always been a poet toward whom I feel a massive lack of interest, but cribbing from my graduate school notes, from *The Cambridge History of American Literature*, and from a busy weekend in the library, I hope I managed to describe the work accurately, confining my

178

unfavorable criticism of it to an analysis of its metrical monotony.

I had no sooner paused, however, than Miss Mumpsimus was upon me. "About the beginning," she announced, and she read:

> Tell me not in mournful numbers,
> Life is but an empty dream! . . . .

"Yes?" I encouraged in my best-practiced professorial tone.

"Why do you say the poem is addressed to other poets?"

"Who else writes poems?" I asked.

"What's that got to do with it?"

"Everything, I should say. The very first line says, 'Don't tell me in sad poems.'"

"Sad poems?" said Miss Mumpsimus indignantly. "And where do you get *that* idea?"

"From 'mournful numbers,' of course."

There was a great deal more of that sort of thing, as I recall, but I finally understood that Miss Mumpsimus was taking "mournful numbers" to mean "sad multitudes," and I set out to explain where she had gone wrong. I cited Pope's "I lisped in numbers since the numbers came." I cited "Grief brought to numbers cannot be so fierce," though I still cannot remember who wrote it. I cited the fact that John Donne's religious poems are titled *Holy Numbers*. With these as examples, I pointed out that numbers means "metric quantities" and by extension, poetry in general. Miss Mumpsimus was having none of that.

Finally, however, she did agree to accept the authority of the dictionary, and to make the proof the weightier I went down the hall to my office and returned with Webster's Unabridged, from which I read the fifteenth meaning given:

15. Poetry & Music. a. Regular count of syllables or beats, esp. with alternation of accents. b. *pl.* Metrical, esp. syllabic, verses or measures; hence, verses or verse.

Miss Mumpsimus read it for herself, bending over the desk, then straightened up to look at me with the disdain that must have shriveled generations of students. "For forty years," she declared, "I have been teaching this poem according to one of the very first meanings of the word 'number.' Do you really expect me to give that up for the *second* part of the fifteenth meaning?!"

If only I had known enough then to turn a few more pages of the dictionary to "mumpsimus" and to have her read that definition!

In any case, thank you, Mrs. Ward. And thank you again for helping me to establish something like a record for "remarks that come to us as we walk home from that party." It has taken me twenty-five and a half years to think of the right answer. I submit, however, that it was a dull party, and that I have not thought about it exclusively in the years between.

Mrs. Ward made me a present of "mumpsimus" by means of a photocopy of page 1611 of Webster's Unabridged (2nd), and having drawn a red line around "mumpsimus" she proceeded, for its own sake, to draw another red line around the next word, which I am happy to pass on here, for its own (and sufficient) sake:

mumruffin: *n*. The long-tailed titmouse. *Local Brit.*

May 7, 1966

Whose Usage Counts?

Is there no final question of right and wrong in English usage?

My first real tussle with a qualified linguist occurred when I appeared on Bergen Evans's TV show some years back and found myself at odds with him over his willingness to accept the usage "a crusading Egyptian newspaper." I hope I am stating his position fairly when I say he was ready to accept the word "crusade" in its extended sense as meaning, roughly, "any campaign or concerted

180

action toward a good cause." I, simply enough, was not willing to give away the word "cross" locked into the roots of the word. A crusade is, literally, "an act of [going to] the cross." The Egyptians, I had to insist, were clearly on the other side of that one.

Professor Evans does, to be sure, know about word roots: I was prepared to grant this point that the word "crusade" does function in its extended sense. By "extended sense" I think I mean "away from root meaning." Obviously no man can expect all those who speak a language to respond sensitively to all the roots of all its words. I cannot myself pretend to know enough roots in enough languages to speak English with that ultimate distinction. In the particular case of "crusade" I am ready enough to accept the word in its extended sense in almost any Christian context. But I must draw the line there. I cannot accept Egyptians as crusaders any more than I can accept the Union Army as the Confederate, or *vice versa*.

Words, of course, are constantly evolving things. That process of extension away from root meanings is as sure as the force of living language. A language is dead at exactly the point at which its words can no longer acquire new shades of meaning. A century-old Latin dictionary can be as useful as a new one. A century-old English dictionary is out of touch with today's usage. It is in the nature of living words to change as the life of those who speak the language changes. How else could language be able to meet our demands upon it?

The word "broadcast" is a fair example of one way in which words change in response to the lives of those who use them. For centuries the word signified the act of a country-man in scattering certain kinds of seed in his fields. He marched back and forth carrying a sack of seed and cast it about him with a broad sweep of his arm—a broad cast.

Such a firmly pictorial word inevitably lends itself to metaphor. I have no doubt that metaphoric extensions of the word can be culled from every century of English Literature. I suspect, however, that anyone in the past who used it in a metaphoric sense was aware of his metaphor, for every man of the past would have had in his head a picture of that unchanging sower at his work.

Then, in the 1920s radio came along and it seized upon the

181

word—as a metaphor. By repeated usage, however, the word went far toward losing its original metaphoric force. At the same time the United States became increasingly urbanized. And also at the same time, farmers were generally turning to new sorts of machinery to get their sowing done. The ancient broadcaster of the fields was no longer a common figure. His image disappeared from both the world and the word as far as most Americans were concerned. The image they then began to see in the word was more likely that of a man with a microphone in his face, or of a great steel tower with diagrammatic lightning shooting forth in all directions.

And now, mutation upon mutation, even that changed word is going out, all but replaced by the coinage "telecast" or the British "transmission."

So will it ever be with language; its power is that it lives, and to live is to change. But is every usage permissible simply because some sort of linguistic Gallup poll demonstrates that more people than any other illiterates spoke "like" for "as"? Yes, I know the Elizabethans did, too, and that I am in danger of arguing for the fossils, along with Jonathan Swift, who held the usage "mob" to be an ignorant corruption of "*mobile vulgus.*" It was as offensive to his ear as "rep" for "reputation" is likely to be to yours (and certainly is to mine).

At this point I am in the center of my confusions with nothing to trust but my own firmly prejudiced ear. Usage, to be sure, must rule in the long run, but to let it assume rule without resistance is to enshrine ignorance as the chosen force of language. Can the School System, for example, permit the blurring together of "imply" and "infer" without destroying a resource of the language? "Infer" does seem to be taking over for both words these days. That is usage. But whose usage? How could such a usage come about except through ignorance, which is to say, through the failure of the School System to teach the firmness of the language at those points at which the language is discerningly firm, as it is in the difference between "imply" (to fold into) and "infer" (to carry into).

The case is not easily put. I once had a brilliant student who wrote a piece about his experiences in the Navy. In it he wrote, "We arrived at our midocean rendezvous point." Because he was a good student I raised a finicky point. English "arrive," I sug-

182

gested, is simply a slightly changed way of spelling and pronouncing Latin *"ad ripam,"* meaning "to the bank." Could one *"ad ripam"* at midocean? He chose to brush the point aside. So be it.

But can one fail to hope that a few students will yet be left to remember that words come to us with richly usable histories attached? Among the diehards, I am forced to believe that our School System is in fact turning out some sort of intellectual rabble in the name of democratic education. There was a time when an ignorant man at least knew that he was ignorant. Today we run our ignorant young through the entire School System, and through college to boot, and certify their illiteracy with a diploma and a degree. There stands the young graduate, incapable of his own language in any informed sense, but shining nonetheless in the cap and gown bestowed upon him by Universal Illiteracy and Humane Enlightenment (Division of the Low Pass). He is not only ignorant, but he has been told he is educated. Where can he hope to acquire the humility to acknowledge the usages of his intellectual betters?

I have no answer. Only this suggestion. Our English Classes seem enthusiastically dedicated to an exercise called "vocabulary building." Fine. Build high. But, teacher, when you send the kids to the dictionary, take a look for yourself at those parentheses between the word and its definition. There, tightly condensed, is each word's history, its roots. Teach them "usage" if you must, but teach them history, too. If you can teach both forces of the word, and teach them as great and equal forces in the making of language, the chances are you will have justified whatever custodianship you had in mind when you walked into that classroom.

October 27, 1962

Aphorisms

Writing about J. Frank Dobie and some of his sayings reminded me that I had once made a happy game of making up aphorisms, and sent me searching for a small box of three-by-five file cards on which I had jotted them, transferring them from the pocket pads I carry on planes and trains, and sometimes salvaging one from a discarded poem or prose manuscript. The box would not show up at once and as I rummaged I found myself mulling over the word "aphorism" and a whole family of related words. By the time I did find the box, I put it aside to reach for that grand book, "Webster's Dictionary of Synonyms," in which I found the family given as: saying, saw, maxim, adage, proverb, motto, epigram, aphorism, and apothegm. I don't know why "slogan" was omitted and I charge the editors to fill out the family tree by including it in any future edition.

"Saying," the word that categorizes the whole family, signifies any habituated remark including those in current fashion. "Adage," on the other hand (from Latin *ad-* plus *aio*, "to say," and meaning literally "I say to"), implies both a well-aged saying and one containing a moral precept. When the saying has become so worn by usage that it may be thought of as faceless coinage it may qualify as a "saw" (from Anglo-Saxon *sagu*, related to our word "saga") meaning at root "say" but implying that the saying is about old things, hence once more connoting antiquity. Though Webster does not make the point, I further sense, without being able to demonstrate, that a saw is the most likely of all this family to be phrased in street-and-country colloquialism. "Proverb" also connotes a well-aged saying, the word from Latin *pro-* (for or before) plus *verbum* (word) thereby implying perhaps, though

184

doubtfully, that the wisdom of the saying existed before there were words for it. Continuing this genealogy, we may take both "maxim" and "epigram" to signify a time-honored saying with the difference that a maxim (from the Latin term *maxima propositio*, "the greatest premise") is specifically a rule of conduct ("Do unto others," etc.) and an epigram (from Greek *epi* plus *graphein*, "to write upon") derives from the name of a kind of poem and has come to mean any pithy saying, with the clear implication that the phrasing is more literary than the colloquialism of the saw. The unabridged "Webster's" (the good one, not the new edition) also notes that the epigram is usually antithetical in structure and offers as an example "Crying is the refuge of plain women, but the ruin of pretty ones," a perception that must certainly be underlined for the special notice of the curriculum committees of all women's colleges.

The motto, which may or may not be an ancient saying, is a special case of the maxim, a briefly stated guiding principle generally attached to a specific person, group, or project. The word derives of course from French *mot*, "word." The motto is narrower in its application than the maxim and rather closer to the slogan, from Gaelic roots meaning "the cry of an armed band," i.e., "a battle cry," though the word now connotes not a battle cry but a catch phrase for a political or advertising campaign.

The remaining members of the family of sayings are the aphorism and the apothegm, both implying a certain freshness of coinage, an elegant pithiness above the colloquialism of the saw, and a generally traceable individual authorship. The distinction between them is harder to find than their similarities. "Webster's" derives "apothegm" from Greek *apo-* (from) and *phthengesthai* (to cry out) and defines it as a terse saying that is specified to be "sharply pointed" and "startling." "The Dictionary of Synonyms" offers as an example Johnson's "Patriotism is the last refuge of a scoundrel."

"Webster's" derives "aphorism" from Greek *apo-* (from) and *horizein* (to bound), hence meaning "to mark off, to set limits to, to distinguish from," and hence, one may conclude, "to define." "Webster's" then defines the word, rather weakly, as "a short, concise statement of a principle." The "Dictionary of Synonyms" offers as an example Mark Twain's "Heaven for climate, hell for society," surely as sharply pointed and as startling a saying as

185

Johnson's. Let me conclude that the shade of difference "Webster's" has not made clear either by definition or example lies most clearly in the roots, and that "apothegm" implies a crying-out in some heat, whereas "aphorism" implies a more dispassionate, more precise, and, by root implication, even mathematical exactness of wit.

Having completed these researches, I was free to start thumbing through my file, and immediately bogged down in my effort to decide whether a given saying should be listed as a saw, bachelor-proverb, crypto-adage, maxim, motto, apothegm, epigram, or whatever. I could not fail to note at once that I have already worked some of them into pieces I have written for *SR* wherein they passed as simple (though—who knows?—perhaps even coruscating) sentences. Any of them, it seemed to me, might serve as the text for some future column, whereupon I decided at once that some of them would. Reserving that right for the future, therefore, and deciding to take the risk of lumping them all together as aphorisms, I offer the following examples from the dusty file, with more to come in a later installment.

Nothing in nature offends nature.
Religion has ten commandments; reality has five senses.
The most human expression is the smile of seriousness.
Why die of a sniffle? Contract a real disease.
Be selfish. Nothing else makes the human race predictable.
Athletes do their thinking while their bones heal.
Nothing is curable, but the sickroom can be swept out.
There is no difference between the official and the inhuman.
A fox is a dog that found out about mankind.
Don't talk to me about complexity: I have a daughter.
I don't care who is calling: tell him to put it in a letter and that I never answer my mail.
Everything will happen.
A savage is a man who has not had enough news from the human race.
Everyone is in trouble when he looks at the stars.
The weight of the world is in the thumbs of the clumsy.
A man wise enough to learn from a fool may be trusted in any company.

186

It would be easier to grow sentimental about motherhood were the prerequisites higher.

To respect a sick age is to be in contempt of eternity.

Don't dislike good people: avoid them.

April 14, 1962

Teach Them Tongues (If You Can)

An *SR* reader, who asks to remain anonymous for fear of identifying and perhaps embarrassing young innocence, writes that she teaches religious education to teen-age girls of her parish and recently found that her girls seemed badly confused by "chastity" and "celibacy." Accordingly, she lectured them at some length on the mint-markings of the two words and on the differences between them, and made the point of checking back later as part of a written quiz. She has sent me some of the answers uttered by those mints of young virtue and I pass them on herewith as some sort of coinage, undoubtedly genuine but of intellectual lands unknown:

Celibacy is mostly for the single state person. If you are married or in the religious you cannot use this at all. Chastity can be used by both kinds of people, but makes priests and nuns the best.

Chastity is the belief that you should refrain from sex outside your own family, but among the family it is all right.

The difference is that in the single state you have the responsibility of staying chaste, while married celibacy means that you cannot go around with other men. This is for women of course. Men must have this responsibility in married celibacy.

Chastity is pride and negligence; I am not sure what celibacy is, but I don't think it's very good, either.

KIDS: A second correspondent, a lady I shall myself leave anonymous among the literal-minded of this world, writes to rebuke me for having referred to children as "kids." The lady even went so far as to copy out what she took to be the entire dictionary definition, though—and significantly—she left out the dictionary's parenthetical matter on the roots of the word (which, in the case of "kid," to be sure, is inconclusive, but which I mean to die insisting is essential to any dictionary's discussion of any word). She then asked, with firmly footnoted disapproval:

Where does "children" come into this definition? I am not the only one who shares this opinion. See *Elementary English—A Magazine of the Language Arts*, October 1962, page 608.

And she concluded in what I take to be at least low dudgeon:

Please use the correct word "children" not "kids." I am a teacher of children, not of goats.

Dear teacher of (if you insist) children, I have chosen not to see *Elementary English*, page 608. I do not know where children come into it, or into your dictionary definition. But "kids" comes into my usage as a heart's metaphor. In another mood I might have called them chicks, cubs, fledglings, fry, piglets, puppies— you summon it from the young of the animal kingdom and my mood will find the occasion on which to use it as that moment's metaphor. "Kids," I shall insist, is never used for "children" except as a metaphor. Because the metaphor is so right, it has passed into such frequent usage that the literal-minded see only the frequency of its usage and forget its rightness. Yet it remains the best all-purpose metaphor in this particular family of metaphors. There are moments when those things you teach resemble every variant of the young of the animal kingdom, but for a metaphoric summary that fairly represents the energy content, the noise level, the quality of motion, the attention span, the usually uncurried attractiveness, and the recurring smelliness of most of the human young most of the time, my heart will still cry "kids" against all your half-read dictionaries, into the teeth of *Elementary English —A Magazine of the Language Arts,* and—though their cohorts range far as the eye can see into the horizons of the school system —against every persuasion of all its subscribers.

APHORISMS (AND SUGGESTED PROPOSITIONS): Children are leaky receptacles into which the world pours. Adults are locked doors against which the world beats. Given your choice, be a child.

Habit is blindness.

A child is an act of faith about which one grows increasingly uncertain.

Posterity is a 6 A.M. noise from the children's room. What am I doing interrupting my sleep to dabble in futures?

Endure a change of imagination.

On Mother's Day think what gave birth to Caligula.

No dogs, no cats. In this house we beget our livestock.

The unimaginative are those who find it easier to get into Heaven than into Hell.

AND BACK TO PROVERBS: Ours is not, relatively speaking, a proverbial age, but every society, to some extent, gives off from itself metaphors and self observations that will serve as general rules of conduct or as the word patterns of a revelation. One of the best of the twentieth-century proverbs—impossible to have come by before our own time yet meaningful, now, to all time— has been around for some years now and says simply: "A camel is a greyhound designed by a committee."

I am indebted to Richard Ellmann for another he told me years ago and that I have never again run into, perhaps because its meaning is not clear without a particular voice emphasis I shall try to indicate by italics: "The stomach *seeks* its ulcer."

A dark and darkly pertinent thought, and one that reminds me I am also indebted to Richard Ellmann for the darkest proverb I know, a sort of elixir of the bitterness of poverty. As I recall, it is taken from the Arabian, and though the righteous may think it blasphemous, I submit that it speaks more from suffering endured than to blasphemy intended. It reads: "If you see a blind man, kick him—why should you be kinder than God?"

189

Curiously, I think I find a distant cousin (on the other side) of this thought in Dante. In the Twentieth Canto of "The Inferno" Dante looks upon the grossly distorted souls of the Fortune Tellers and Diviners and bursts into tears at the sight of such suffering, only to be scolded by Virgil, who declares:

There is no place for pity here. Who is more arrogant
within his soul, who is more impious
than one who dares to sorrow at God's judgment?

June 8, 1963

Mail Bag: File X

The first letter was in answer to one of the notes I had written on poetic style, and no matter which; almost any remarks on style might have provided equal occasion for this correspondent. His letter read:

Dear Sir:

Although you said it nicely, I'm sure you realize that it is not possible. To paraphrase slightly—habituated speech cannot be shattered. There is no essential language that can be called into being by an esthetic experience.

The requirements of precise communication have subjected language—including the essences of style—to electronic analysis. New knowledge has destroyed the traditional beauties of mere words giving in return the greater beauty of understanding. The doom of the glittering but meaningless phrase has arrived. No longer will mere cleverness with words be mistaken for knowledge. Only the clean bone of clear indices will remain. Whether

190

reality will be considered to be beautiful or ugly is merely relative to the trained response of the esthete.

Sincerely
X
(Not for Publication)

The note under the signature had, of course, to be honored, and so my reply.

Dear Mr. X:

I am about as close to your point of view as I am to Martian psychology but I must say you lay it on the line.

You note that your letter is not for publication. Would you allow me to use it while protecting your anonymity? I have so many disagreements that I hate to miss such a target.

Sincerely yours,
John Ciardi

In reply to which, Mr. X, in the course of giving me a dizzying historical eminence in a straight line from Chaucer to Ciardi, also gave me the permission I had asked, along with some fateful warnings (the only real answer to which is: I should live so long):

Dear Sir:

You have the permission you requested. The views expressed in my first letter cannot rightly be mine since I did not originate them. The words are mere epitomes of the rather grossly expressed original reports of linguist and habit studies of which I have only sufficient knowledge to support the more picturesque synthesis you believe will be useful. My personal preferences may or may not be in accord. You cannot know them unless I thus state them.

You have a reputation to defend in history; I have not. The need for sensualized mathematics and the exigencies of programing will have more effect upon the future of language than anything any writer will say today and this is not a modern phenomenon. No English writer from Chaucer to Ciardi has had the power to prevent the erosion of the very meanings he has put down on paper. Rare indeed is the author who even partially reads

191

the way he wrote. Beware lest Ciardi also become a footnote curiosity of antiquarians.

Sincerely,

X

There the file concludes. But now that Mr. X has granted his permission (for which thank you, sir) I hardly know where to begin disagreeing. For one reason or another there are a number of Mr. X's phrases I mean to be wary of. His first letter is especially potted with semantic quicksand and I am not about to be sucked into a defense of "mere words," of the "glittering but meaningless phrase" or of "mere cleverness." If electronic analysis can get rid of all such when the combined satiric powers of a Dryden, a Pope, and a Byron have failed, why plug in the analyzer and let 'er rip. I must even pass up a temptation to argue that an esthetic experience certainly can call an essential language into being, largely because I am not at all sure what Mr. X has up his semantic sleeve when he slips in that "essential." And though I certainly resist the idea of a style that has to pass an electronic analysis in order to emerge as "the clean bone of clear indices," I am going to dodge that one, too, at least for the time being, on the ground that Mr. X gets a bit stylistic himself when he starts rhapsodizing those indices of his. I begin rather with his second letter. As Mr. X points out there meanings do shift on the page when custom and the language have shifted. There, at least, we have an agreement to start disagreeing from.

Yet it is certainly to the point that no great work of Western literature has suffered enough from such changes as to lose its recognizable force. Even with the help of scholars and translators we cannot hope to read Homer as the Greeks did, or Horace as the Latins did, or Dante as fourteenth-century Italians did. Yet, to take Dante's writings as an example, it is likely, and may be certain, that we read him more sensitively than his contemporaries could, our reading informed by a massive and sustained scholarship.

"Experience" is the key word here. It is the essential nature of literature as experience that will forever make boobs and yokels of electronic linguisticians, sad souls who have no interest but in the elusive hardware of information-prose and who dream, therefore, of reducing language, and even poetry, to a mathematical

192

symbolism in which X means forever exactly and only what has been assigned to it as its meaning.

If such a language will do for the "clean bones of the clear indices" Mr. Electronic X is looking for, one simple solution is already available: he need only learn to program his electronic gizmos in Latin, or in any other dead language. The lovely humming-and-buzzing electronic utility of a dead language is just in the fact that all of its words have lost all of their possibility of undergoing a change in meaning. The roots of those words have, to be sure, passed into other tongues. But within the idiom and syntax of the original and now dead language, *rigor mortis* has set in. The Latin dictionary you buy for your own use, if it is a good one, will be equally useful to your great-grandchildren's great-grandchildren.

In the living language, however, I will not be told I am having syndrome X when I hear the liquefaction of Julia's clothes, nor will I compute "this morning's minion" as part of some avian index, nor will I stop looking through any "magic casements" I can find, not on electronic command. You stick to your hard facts, boys, and take it as one more hard fact that writers will go on calling into being an "essential" language that does not transmit indices but that creates esthetic experiences.

Life comes to our experience of it uncomputable (or at least uncomputerable) but full of elusive and active presences. And if any of you electronic X's doubt the pertinence of those presences, or that a good artist can render them with exacting control and precision and achieve thereby a kind of knowledge that is otherwise unknowable—then may that man be so far gone in madness that he asks the computer to pick him a programed wife, and may he marry her click by click in the witness of all transistors. The fact that he might actually achieve with her as much as his low-order nervous system can grasp of the idea of a satisfying relationship is all the evidence there need be of his cross-indexed non-existence.

January 15, 1966

Bringing Down the Odds

The story as I have it is hearsay and I have no way of verifying it. True or not, its point remains to confirm or to terrify all of us who scuttle through the turnstiles of the calendar into who-knows-what electric-eyed future.

Some of the boys in Norbert Wiener's cybernetics lab at the Massachusetts Institute of Technology—so the story goes—got playful and assembled an electronic gizmo that played tick-tack-toe (spelling courtesy of "Webster's New World Dictionary," which also offers the variant "tit-tat-toe"). In what I take to be the nature of things to come, the gizmo ("a gizmo" is of course a "whatsis," neither of which is listed in the NWD) turned out to be unbeatable. "Computer-wise," as my man said in engineer-English, "the job was duck soup."

I live on a checking account that balances only by the introduction of such variables as "We pay bank" and "Bank pays us." Let no man trust my mathematical rendering. I gathered, however, that the gizmo made no mistakes. It could, therefore, be played to a draw. But let its human opponent make any mistake and the machine would win.

The problem there, of course, is that even the least fallible of human beings will tire. And also that human beings tire most readily, as we all know, by not having a chance to win.

For all of us and our machine-lashed psyches, therefore, let me salute the unknown and perhaps legendary hero of this story—an engineer who, either whimsically or moved by an impulse as deep as the will to survive, attached to the gizmo a lever for bringing down the odds. When the human player has been sufficiently affronted by the gizmo's calm 100 per cent efficiency,

194

he can pull the lever toward him and reduce the gizmotic grasp of the situation to 98 per cent or to 95 per cent or to whatever mechanical I.Q. level, right down to idiocy, will give the human player a chance.

As far as I know, that lever has not been christened. My man called it, if my memory serves, an impedance. If I understood him, it was some sort of rheostat-but-not-exactly-that, and its function was to introduce random "blips." And "blips," as I do or do not understand, are electrical impulses containing bits of information or directions to which the machine is supposed to respond.

Random blips, as I gather through my dark glasses, throw irrelevancies in with relevancies and confuse the gizmo by leaving it to decide which is which—a condition so close to the constant state of mankind that, in the absence of prior claim by the engineers, I hasten to dub our hero's device The Humanizing Lever. For bringing fire to mankind, Prometheus was doomed to eternal surgery of the liver by a hungry eagle. May our hero, for bringing humanity to the machine, be visited by nothing but vegetarian and singing birds. And may no engineer in all of time lose sight of that lever, of its powers and its possibility of eternal hope, as he designs the boxes and the blinking eyes that seem ready to entrap all our fallible future in their calculating but incalculable perfection.

PAST, PRESENT, AND FUTURE: Speaking of man's eternal squinting into the crystal ball brings me to a quotation from Macaulay's "Democracy and Progress" that has long sat in my files, and that has long since become detached from the letter bearing the name of the *SR* reader who sent it to me. My apologies to him with my thanks. Macaulay wrote in 1830:

The present moment is one of great distress. But how small will that distress appear when we think over the history of the last forty years; a war, compared with which all other wars sink into insignificance; taxation, such as the most heavily taxed people of former times could not have conceived; a debt larger than all the public debts that ever existed in the world added together; the food of the people studiously rendered dear; the currency

195

imprudently debased, and imprudently restored. Yet is the country poorer than in 1790? We fully believe that in spite of all the misgovernment of her rulers, she has been almost constantly becoming richer and richer. . . .

If we were to prophesy that in the year 1930 a population of fifty millions, better fed, clad, and lodged than the English of our time, will cover these islands. . . . that machines constructed on principles yet undiscovered will be in every house, that there will be no highways but railroads, no traveling but by steam, that our debt, vast as it seems to us, will appear to our great-grandchildren a trifling encumberance, which might easily be paid off in a year or two, many people would think us insane. We prophesy nothing: but this we say: if any person had told the Parliament which met in perplexity and terror after the crash in 1790 that in 1830 the wealth of Europe would surpass all their wildest dreams, . . . that men would be in the habit of sailing without wind, and would be beginning to ride without horses, our ancestors would have given as much credit to the prediction as they gave to Gulliver's Travels. Yet the prediction would have been true. . . . We cannot absolutely prove that those are in error who tell us that society has reached a turning point, that we have seen our best days. But so said all who came before us, and with just as much apparent reason. . . . On what principle is it that, when we see nothing but improvement behind us, we are to expect nothing but deterioration before us?

With Macaulay I "cannot absolutely prove that those are in error who tell us society has reached a turning point." I am, in fact, afraid they are right. And I am left with the rueful thought that what would have seemed such foresight as only genius could soar to, had one read Macaulay's words as late as 1930, or even 1940, seems darkly to one side of the question today. There seem to be too many reasons for foreseeing nothing but deterioration ahead. Nor, nowadays, is reason itself a window into hope. I am left with my shy hope for that Humanizing Lever, and with the dream that somehow some machine "constructed on principles yet undiscovered" will build that lever into the Eternal Gizmo.

November 17, 1962

Raising the Stakes

Not long ago I found myself at a banquet seated between two distinguished men of science, one a British astronomer and the other an American biochemist. These two impressive men fell into a discussion of the future of scientific research and, having little to contribute except the admirations of my ignorance, I played a rapt game of ear-in-the-middle as they forecast the next hazy turnings of the technological revolution.

As dinner discussion will, theirs ranged far—as far even as to the possibility of extracting brain substances that might transplant acquired learning and acquired abilities from one organism to another. Such transplantation of learned processes had, or so I gathered, already been accomplished in a primitive way among primitive organisms. In the easy ramble of dinner talk my two scientists were iffing wistfully. If only there were some way of injecting scientific knowledge into research men, they were dreaming. Sadly, however, neither the biochemist nor the astronomer foresaw any likelihood that some sort of Einstein extract, for example, could ever inject the mystery of genius into a young Johnny Doe.

It would, they both agreed on their way back to reality, continue to take most or all of thirty years and intense training to turn an especially gifted Johnny Doe into a good research man. And as scientific knowledge became increasingly complex it would take longer. The astronomer estimated that after each twenty years of scientific development it would take an additional five years of training to bring a good man up to the jumping-off point at which he could leave the known and push into the

197

unknown. And the biochemist agreed but thought the astronomer's estimate might turn out to be a bit conservative.

As befits the scientific mind, however, their iffing was not entirely random. Both of my dinner companions were convinced that scientific research could not continue to expand and proliferate in the future as it has done in the past. And both thought that the problem of training enough competent research men would probably be the one to fix the critical limits of future research, though there was the almost equal problem of financing the endless projects in which science is interested.

The astronomer was convinced that the next step in our space program would be planetary rather than lunar, and that by 1975 such a program would be costing about $60 billion a year—about the amount of our present annual defense budget—and with nowhere to go but up. Even granting a fantastic development of the economy, the appetite of science, as the astronomer believed, would outrun all public and private resources of men and money. Eventually, he foresaw, each nation would find itself abandoning certain kinds of basic research in order to continue with others.

One consequent possibility might be that each of the major powers, as well as some of the secondary ones, would be pushing its own sort of research into areas other powers had abandoned. Any sort of basic research, moreover, may conceivably turn up a new weapon capable of producing a dramatic shift in the world's balance of power.

Were the scientists of all nations about equally involved in about the same sorts of research, such an imbalance would probably not last long. But if, for example, nation A abandons space research in order to concentrate on neural phenomena, while nation B continues to pour its resources into space study, while nation C concentrates on wave phenomena; and if such a divergence continues for, say, ten or twenty years, it will have become a near certainty that no one of the nations could retrain and retool to catch up with another in the field the other had chosen.

If, then, the researches of any one of the nations produces a super-weapon (a neural impulse capable of immobilizing populations, a space-source capable of mass annihilation, or a wave phenomenon capable of destroying life on a truly enlightened scale), then the nation that first happens on that particular technological breakthrough will have life-and-death powers over the others, who will not have the means for developing a similar weapon, or one to counter it.

So, by brandy-and-cigar time, two reasonable and learned men had drawn a picture of a technological gamble that seemed to be approaching with something like mathematical certainty. And though I could hardly meet my companions on their own grounds, I found myself at last on grounds of my own.

I had once spent four years in a research unit then known as the United States Army Air Force, and I had personally compiled extensive test results on certain mathematical near certainties involved in the permutations of the top surfaces of two cubes, the sides of which were numbered from one to six in such a way that the numbers on opposing faces of each cube always totaled seven. By repeated experimentation, I discovered (to cite only one mathematical near certainty) that if one of my co-researchers (called "the shooter") were to set himself the problem of turning up two faces totaling four, six, eight, or ten before turning up a combination totaling seven; and that if he were offered odds of seven-to-one that he could not make his particular total by turning up paired numbers (*i.e.*, "the hard way"); and that if the shooter were stupid enough to take the bet (as many of my co-researchers were, I am happy to say, abandoning mathematics for the mystique of long odds), then it would be (and is) a mathematical near certainty that the researcher offering the bet might sometimes drop $700 in the course of chasing a mere hundred, but that over any substantial period of time he would achieve what may be called positive results.

I had, then, only to remind myself that what we call history is basically the record of the longest sustained crap game of which we have any knowledge, and I could once more be reasonably certain about where I stood in the misty sequences of time. Science, I am now able to conclude, has not changed the nature of the game. It has only raised the stakes.

January 8, 1966

Elephantiasis

I see from a long-buried newspaper clipping that Kenya is suffering a giant case of elephantiasis. Tsavo National Park, its main wildlife preserve, is a tract of 8,000 square miles, and now contains about 15,000 elephants; a disastrous result of over-protection that leaves the hypothetical average elephant an area of about half a square mile from which to forage about two hundred pounds of leaves, grass, and bark daily.

Eight thousand square miles, as it happens, is about the total area of Massachusetts, and fifteen thousand may be just about the number of Republicans the Kennedys have left standing in that preserve, though not as a result of over-protection. The situation in Massachusetts, however, does not threaten over-crowding, for the Republicans there are no longer allowed to eat more than once every twelve years or so, and not much then.

These differences aside, and Kenya's greater urgency noted, the problem in Kenya and in Massachusetts becomes much the same. Since there seems to be no way of improving the grazing grounds, some of the excess elephants and Republicans will have to be shot in order to preserve a token herd for the admiration of future generations.

The real elephants of Kenya, as it turns out, seem to be a lot harder to kill than are the political elephants of Massachusetts. As Jeffrey Poley estimates the situation in Kenya—in a special report to the *Herald Tribune*—an experienced hunter requires an average of at least three days to track and kill an elephant. A hundred a year would be a high score for even the most experienced hunter. Thus, with at least 5,000 elephants to be killed off before a reasonable ecological balance can be restored,

200

the job would require at least a year's work by fifty hunters, each of whom would need the support of about twenty men to handle the carcasses and to get the ivory out. And Authorities further estimate that it would take at least two years to clear and register the tusks of 5,000 elephants.

At about this point in the report it began to occur to me that someone who passed for an Authority in Kenya was more than somewhat confused about the nature of his problem. Was he (the hypothetical person in Authority) out to kill off 5,000 elephants before some larger number starved to death, or was he out to preserve the white-hunter motif, and to make sure the carcasses were properly handled, and the tusks properly "cleared and registered," whatever that means?

I found myself ready to make a suggestion. The Colonel Blimp of this report might do well to arm himself with some modern weaponry. If the problem is too many elephants in the act of despoiling the forage in too few square miles, then the thing to do is kill off the elephants and to let the carcasses and the tusks fall where they may. Given a couple of fast scouting cars and a couple of helicopters equipped with radio and armor-piercing fifty calibers, or bazookas, or whatever popgun the armament boys decide is the right elephant-banger, there must certainly be a half-dozen venturesome lads now lounging around the United States or the Commonwealth nations, who would be glad to take on the job as a contract, and to get rid of those 5,000 elephants within a year at a flat fee per head, with or without the ivory thrown in. Meanwhile, the authorities might let subcontractors have the carcasses in return for haulage. Or they might simply let the carcasses go back to nature for organic soil enrichment, as they will in any case when the elephants starve.

Anyone in actual Authority is certainly bound to tell me my notion is wild, impractical, and probably illegal, but I am left, in rebuttal, to point out that the authorities haven't even been able to define their problem, which does seem to indicate that their notion of it is not predictably helpful.

I had these thoughts in mind when I found myself lounging next to no-one-in-particular one afternoon at the verge of no-where, and to dull away that day's tooth of eternity, I brought up all this business of the elephants. I was only making idle talk, but my co-idler immediately fell to berating me for a callous failure to sympathize with nature's noblest animals.

What can sooner spoil an empty afternoon at the edge of nowhere than to have idle talk turned into a flagrantly moral cause? Must all chitchat be brought to the barricades by the high-minded? My erstwhile co-idler made it painfully clear that he was high-minded to the point at which his moral altitude made anoxia inevitable. Nor was I tempted to chase him to such heights, even with full oxygen equipment. I prefer to believe that he is a fool of a species I keep encountering, a sort of moral mush-grubber that most resembles a vegetarian praying mantis. Give such a mush-grubber the thought of a symbolic animal and he is all for defending it to the point of letting it starve.

I found myself accused of not taking Kenya's elephants seriously. The fact is I hadn't taken them at all, except as one more statistic of the sort I keep expecting from the world. I know I had no intention of pulling the legs off elephants. If there were any legs to be pulled, they must belong to those zealous animal lovers who overprotected the herds until they outbred their feeding grounds and ran up against the sentimental gift of starvation.

Elephants in large numbers in a wildlife preserve, I should have thought, were a natural product to be harvested from time to time with a shrewd eye to the balance of nature. I do not know why they should be more sacred than, say, a Texas steer. And though I can pity their plight, I cannot make it a first order of pity when I think of Filipinos bent double in their rice paddies, or urchins foraging for nothing in the streets of India, or slum children snarling themselves into knots nearer home. Kenya's elephants may have my passive pity, but if pity is the act of identifying with what suffers, I am not sufficiently large souled to encompass an active pity for all mankind, and neither are you, and neither was my co-idler, though all of us must try. And what I really want in all this, is that my former co-idler find these words, so that I may tell him, and all of his species, that to substitute an indignant and generalized pity of far-off beasts for that effort to identify with what matters first, is mush-headedness while the elephants starve.

May 14, 1966

A National Culture Center

Every now and then, when my worst fears are in danger of evaporating into hope, I stumble on a passage from the *Congressional Record* or on the transcript of some Congressional hearing, and I am instantly restored to the serene assurance that things really are as bad as I always knew them to be.

Make no mistake: serenity is no posy-picker in Pollyanna's meadow. The only real serenity arises from recognizing things as they happen. "Right," says the serene man as the next thing comes into view, "just as I expected." And no matter what he sees coming—be it a tidal wave, the tax collector, or the next Four Horsemen out of Washington—he is serene who finds himself confirmed. Bless the Government Printing Office, for in its output any pessimist may find his confirmation.

It must be nearly two years since I received (and left lying around my study unread till just a few days ago) a pamphlet cumulatively titled "Federal Advisory Commission on the Arts: Hearings before a Subcommittee of the Committee of Education and Labor, House of Representatives, Eighty-Fifth Congress, First Session, on H.R. 3541 and Related Bills to Provide for the Establishment of a Federal Advisory Commission on the Arts and Other Purposes." The pamphlet was sent to me by the office of Representative Frank Thompson, Jr., a mover in the cause of government sponsorship of the arts, and was part of a lengthier documentation I had been receiving in the course of a correspondence with interested persons in government who asked my support of a project—now considerably more advanced than it was then—to create a National Culture Center. Congress had already approved the project on condition that $25,000,000 be raised by private donations.

I could not then, and I do not now, doubt the motives of anyone involved, but the idea itself, I must conclude, is a dud on its way to a disaster. In principle, I must insist, the best thing government can do for the arts is to stay away from them. In art, what is official is inhuman. What can there be left in it for the silent psyche by the time the Honorables from The Dark Below the Grass Roots have done investigating it? Even as mild a program as the Fulbright exchanges has been assaulted by the hog-callers. And when the Bollingen Foundation, loosely affiliated with the Library of Congress, gave an award to Ezra Pound on defensible if debatable esthetic grounds, the resulting political furor forced the Bollingen Committee out of Washington to find refuge at Yale, which despite opinions still current in Cambridge, remains a better government of minds than any now known to Washington.

By nature the arts must always be venturesome, or even out-rageous. The worst thing that can be said about an artist is that he lacks talent. But it is almost as bad to say that he takes no chances. Don't give that poet a home: give him a limb to crawl out on and to saw off behind him. His business is not to win honor and status. His duty is to fail. It is his duty because he must want so much and must reach so far for it that he cannot hope to succeed. As such, his failure is a better success than all the killings on Wall Street and all the posies of the public wreaths. The artist has no right to trust government. All he can trust is in himself and in the demands of his form. He has no way of knowing where those demands will lead him, but he is on his way with no other road to travel. In glad selfishness, he has a right to grab any handout that will keep him functioning. But the instant he begins to tailor his way of doing things in the hope of making himself more available to the handout, official or unofficial, then he has begun to destroy himself.

Speaking for poets generally, as I hope, but for myself certainly, there must be no truck with Congressional art. I will believe we have better disasters than that to engage us.

For the official process cannot help but destroy officialdom's best intentions toward the arts. The official process has no way

204

of distinguishing between art and pseudo-art. And the fringes of the arts are forever infested with pseudo-artists who know exactly how to set themselves up in quintuplicate for official purposes, but who will remain dismal artists from now to the time the next ice age scrapes Washington clean.

What I value in the tardily scanned pages of hearings on H.R. 3541 is the monumental darkness with which it confirms my serenest pessimism. For these hearings the committee summoned to speak in support of the bill "persons who are widely recognized for their knowledge, experience, and interest in one or another of the arts."

Now there, I submit, is an interesting venture. Who should be called? Who are the persons a wise Congress might summon to its councils as "widely recognized for their knowledge," etc.? The foolishly hopeful will immediately start to compile lists of artists. Let's say Douglas Moore, Copland, Barber, and Piston to speak for the composers. Say Graham and Limon for the dancers. Make your own list. And add lists of poets, novelists, painters, architects, sculptors. Let it be your heart's own directory of the living names that speak each form.

Then choke on your ignorance for having been human rather than official. The committee's alphabetical list of the "widely recognized" spokesmen of the arts runs: Mrs. Hortense Amram, practicing weaver; Hon. Ralph E. Becker, legislative representative, National Association of Legitimate Theatres and the League of New York Theatres, and the American National Theatre and Academy (how the official ears must prick up at the sound of such titles!); R. G. Beelke, Office of Education, Department of Health, Education and Welfare. And so on.

Of Mrs. Amram, Mr. Becker, and Mr. Beelke (to whom I intend no slightest disrespect), I know nothing except that their names fall at the top of a five-page alphabetical list of representatives, associates, union spokesmen, guild officials, and every other sort of agent of the arts. But I note, to my serenity, that no composer, dancer, painter, poet, novelist, sculptor of national reputation—and in sum no artist of hopefully final consequence—was called into consultation with Congress on the matter of a National Culture Center. Not at least in these hearings. I doubt that it would occur to a Congressman to ask artists about art. Not while the functionaries of the artistic fringes have what votes there are.

And yes, of course, we are all going to hell in a hand basket, but for my part, I shall lie among the other wrinkled fruit and glow as smuggly as I can in the serenity of having been sure of it from the start.

November 3, 1962

Open Letter to a Congressman

Dear Sir:

You take me to task for finding no hope for poetry in the proposed National Culture Center and, in what I take to be a now characteristic gesture of the federal mind, you express your disagreement by charging me with "a lack of faith in our form of government."

Given worse luck on my part or more accuracy on the part of the Japanese fighters and flak, I might once have gone down in the golden role of supreme sacrificers in defense of. I confess to having had strong personal feelings on that score, and even to a sustained distaste for the thought of burning to death in a B-29. But given my partial distrust of all government, I would still have granted then, and do now, that ours outshines its faults at least to the extent of being worth that highly personal death if it had to be called for. That offer may not sound sufficiently enthusiastic for your taste, but it stood as a firm offer and it will have to do.

I am, to be sure, glad I did make it back. But the best reason for having been there in the first place was in defense of free disagreement. Congress, I believe, is likely to be an emotional disaster where the arts are concerned. We disagree on that point, and welcome to your view. But within our disagreement you must allow me the right to censure any elected representative

206

whose mind so readily equates disagreement with lack of faith. You be faithful, sir, if that is your notion of faith. I have disagreement itself to defend.

Within that disagreement, I am not at all sure we can find common terms. Certainly, however, you are talking in general about the performing arts, I was talking about the creative arts, and specifically about poetry.

Yes, I think Washington can use a center for the performing arts. If all this talk about government-endorsed culture comes down to nothing more than getting a good symphony orchestra for Washington, Washington clearly enough stands in need, and let need be met.

But I still see no way in which such a center can do anything for poetry, and I shall continue to advise poets to stay away from it before they, too, are charged with lack of faith by the publicly righteous.

For poetry must be lived as a venture beyond the proprieties of state forensics, and at a depth far below what T. S. Eliot called "the face that you prepare to meet the faces that you meet." A few months ago I found myself in a group of American writers exchanging views with a group of visiting Russian writers. The talk turned to children's literature and the Russians declared that they tried to write stories and poems that would teach children to love one another, to be kind and good, and to find their places in society. At that point I asked what the writers did about helping children to *rescue* themselves from society. The question, need I say, drew a blank. As far as the Russians could understand it at all, they seemed to think I was joking.

I was not joking. In the nature of the social contract, the psyche has to give something away in exchange for public order. But in the nature of the esthetic contract, the psyche can give none of itself away. For that reason the best creations of many poets are likely to seem to be acts of anarchy. They never are, for supreme language always tends to unite men by shaping for them a deeper image of themselves, but I must believe that such a truth of the poetic experience lies at a depth not readily visible to the public-minded. In any case it is not the declarations of government the poet must trust first, but the language, the images, the rhythms, and the forms of his medium. And in loving and trusting them he

207

may as often as not find himself compelled to affront the habits of the official mind.

Nor is this thought a passing one with me. In 1950 I concluded an "Elegy for G. B. Shaw" with these lines:

> Consider his crimes: He would not commit our diet.
> He opened our tombs. He sold his medals for cash.
> His laughter blew out our anthems. He wiped his nose
> On the flags we die for—a crazy Irishman
> Who looked like a goat and would not be serious.
> But when we are finished, he may be our times.
> And all times may be nothing in his eye.
> All marshals, kings, and presidents we obey.
> His presence in men's minds is contempt of court,
> Of congress, and of flags. So must we pray
> That he be born again, anarch and rare.
> The race we are not in the race we are.

I do not ask you to defend these lines, or even to say you understand them, though they are clear enough. But I do suggest that were we to be friendly, your opponent in your next campaign could put an excerpt-lifter to work on them in a way that might serve to label you as a friend of persons with unsound sentiments. You, of course, may rise above such considerations. But you will grant me, I am sure, that the Congress as a whole would take them seriously. And I am foreseeing that any public debate that occurred on the subject of such lines would first distort them, and then attack them on grounds entirely removed from the question of esthetic competence.

Robert Frost, as you point out, has been honored by our government, and praise the fact. But is government ready to honor Ezra Pound in his fallible mixture as a deplorable public figure but as a source of real esthetic power? My bookshelves must so accept him and so honor him, and for that reason I shall believe them to be a better government of the arts than Congress can offer. Nor is Pound alone in this. Has government made a just peace with William Carlos Williams? Government fired Whitman from his clerk's desk. What would it have done with such originating forces as Baudelaire and Rimbaud? What agency of Congress

208

thought to honor e. e. cummings in his lifetime? Yet I shall believe his irreverences were a better sound from mankind than all the deliberations of all the committees ever assembled in Washington. Among the current poets, I could say as much of Kenneth Rexroth, Karl Shapiro, Delmore Schwartz, Langston Hughes, and Theodore Roethke, to name a few in no order of rank. They speak, I believe, a psychic language all but unknown to the Congress, and I must believe they will do better within the privacies of their own silences than they could do on any platform Congress could offer them.

There is no way to help a poet, in any case, except to leave him alone. If Congress wants to assist the creation of poetry, let it form a panel of established poets to make grants to younger poets of promise, and let it pledge itself to bar all public debate on the propriety of the grants awarded by such a panel. Not until Congress will set such a limit upon itself can I, in conscience, advise the poets to seek federal endorsement.

You conclude by doing me the honor of asking my advice. Granted that the interest of such a culture center is primarily in the performing arts—who should be asked to testify before your committee? The answer seems simple enough to me. You offer a long list of musical experts, from fiddlers to executive secretaries of associations. You even list one composer. Start with him if you want expert testimony. Start with Roy Harris. And then try adding (in alphabetical order): Samuel Barber, Aaron Copland, Ross Lee Finney, Lukas Foss, Paul Hindemith, Gian Carlo Menotti, Douglas Moore, Walter Piston, Roger Sessions, and Igor Stravinsky.

With the best reflections of these creators of music available to you, go ahead and call in as many honorables as you like, and certainly your list includes some fine intermediaries in music. But until Congress learns by heart that the creators must come first, there will be little enough for a Center of the Performing Arts to perform, and nothing for it to give to the creativity of the American arts. Begin with such men and there will be music. And let there be music. But let your councils summon one creator to twenty presidents of associations, representatives of guilds, and agents of unions and you are on your way to nothing but the quasi-arts. Which, as you will recall, was my original charge against the way the various committees of Congress have been going into the question of the arts in America.

John Ciardi

January 12, 1963

Expert Witness

I like my world by easy clocks—what is time but a journalist's dogma, a commuter's penance, and a lover's prayer? I hope, therefore, Mr. John Pekkanen of The Middletown (Connecticut) *Press* will not stand on his professionalism so strongly as to reject my leisurely thanks for his letter of April 10 in which he inclosed one of his byline stories of January 27. Let him take delay, rather, as evidence that what he reported by the day still reads by the year. And though a good reporter must find himself forever racing deadlines, surely there lurks in him the hope that what he writes will survive the turning of the next day's presses.

Mr. Pekkanen's report covered one more in this world's series of "obscenity" trials, this one involving a tabloid called *The National Insider* in a proceeding brought before the Ninth Circuit Court of Connecticut and originally instituted on complaint of a Mrs. Lucy Bradshaw of Deep River, Connecticut, who also appeared for the prosecution as an "expert witness" on obscenity. She and Defense Counsel Elmer Gertz seem to have had a long if insubstantial discussion on her expertise, and it is Mr. Pekkanen's report of that discussion that has just turned up from some substratum of my desk, to my dateless delight. As the account opens, Attorney Gertz had just shown Mrs. Bradshaw a copy of *The National Insider* with the headline: "Exposed: The Wife Swappers" and Mrs. Bradshaw had declared that it appealed to prurient

210

interest. He then showed her, on an inside page of the same issue, a photo of Carol Baker in a partially transparent dress and Mrs. Bradshaw declared that it was obscene. Before turning the narrative over to Mr. Pekkanen, let me explain that Mrs. Bradshaw also works for The Middletown *Press* (the Deep River office):

Gertz then told her it (the photo of Carol Baker) was a United Press International picture and he claimed it had appeared in The Middletown *Press*.

"You don't regard The Middletown *Press* as obscene, do you?"

"Not taken as a whole, no. I do know that we receive a great deal of material that we do not use." She said she did not know why.

Gertz then digressed briefly to ask Mrs. Bradshaw about the American novel.

"Do you regard yourself as a student of the American novel?"

"I wouldn't say a student," she replied, noting that she had only about two hours a day to spend on reading literature.

"You really aren't familiar with the American novel of today, are you?"

"Not in the technical sense, no."

Returning to *The National Insider*, Mrs. Bradshaw began to examine it. She pointed to a picture of a girl she said had an "abnormally large bust." She said it appealed to prurient interest.

At this point both Attorney Gertz and Mrs. Bradshaw seem to have become singularly disoriented to the pluralities in question but the majesty of the law forged on without taking notice:

"If they were normal size busts it would be acceptable?"

"Yes, I believe it would."

Another headline mentioned the word "homosexual." She said it was obscene.

"Mrs. Bradshaw, are you maintaining that the mere use of the word 'homosexual' is obscene?"

"Yes sir."

She pointed to another article, one by Carol Leslie, a Hollywood starlet, that stated she had once contemplated suicide. Mrs. Bradshaw said it appealed to prurient interest.

211

"Does this article mention anything about sex?" Gertz asked.

"No."

"Not a word?"

"No."

"Anything about nudity or excretion?"

"No."

Gertz then gave her an exposition of the obscenity law which defined "prurient interest" as "morbid or shameful interest in sex, nudity, or excretion."

"That's correct," she said, "but I think you will find when defining the word sex, that prurient appeal works in different ways."

Mrs. Bradshaw's may not have been a logician's dream in the matter of formulating definitions, but unhampered by such restrictive influences, she was the better able to be positive about what "appealed to prurient interest" identifying as such any mention of Playboy bunnies, a reference to a girl's measurements as 36-23-32, *Irma La Douce*, and any article on Marilyn Monroe (because "Miss Monroe had become known as a sex-symbol").

Mr. Gertz [and it was obviously not his day] then asked: "When did you become an expert on obscenity?"

"The first time I became aware was when I started getting into this and realized I had a broad background in experience and training."

Thank you, Mr. Pekkanen, for these glimpses into the name and nature of expertise, and thank you Founding Fathers, for the due process of law. I am beginning to realize that I, too, have a broad background in experience and training. And with a little more reading time than Mrs. Bradshaw seems to have available, I have managed to pore through a number of trial transcripts of just this sort of stuff. There seems to be something in the nature of "literary obscenity" trials that unhinges the sense of definition not only of witnesses but of the judges. Mr. Pekkanen's report is especially useful not because it documents a rare case but because it distills the usual.

The makers of college textbooks are forever hunting out exer-

212

cises in orderly and disorderly composition. Let me recommend Mr. Pekkanen's report to them as a useful exercise. Any class that can parse out and label the logical sequences of the exchange between Mrs. Bradshaw and Attorney Gertz is forewarned of the world and armed for it.

I am not sure what judges read these days, but let me recommend Mr. Pekkanen's report to them, too, and let me make it their assignment to read and re-read it until they manage to locate a reasonable connection between this sort of thing and the due process of law.

As for the rest of us, I am assuming that we are here for the fun of it, and I want to thank Mr. Pekkanen for that.

January 1, 1966

Tropic of Cancer

The American publication of Henry Miller's *Tropic of Cancer*, long the under-the-counter and smuggler's classic of our times, touched off another series of court cases, all following what has become a standard pattern. Books singled out by the local censors have to be defended in a seemingly endless number of jurisdictions. The publisher must take on the burden of fighting the same case over and over, with the likelihood that he will lose by exhaustion despite the merit of his legal position. I do not have all the details of the series of legal battles in which Grove Press has found itself since publication day, but I have seen it reported in the New York *Times* that Grove has been involved in over sixty cases (more than one a week) at an estimated cost of over $100,000. The multiplication of cases has become one part of the standard pattern.

As the standard pattern of the defense, Grove Press has called

213

upon critics and other expert witnesses to testify in court or to submit sworn affidavits in support of the book. All such depositions begin with the expert identifying himself under oath and declaring that he is thoroughly familiar with the book. He then states his position in the case, lists his qualifications (degrees, publications, honors, and positions held), and proceeds to a defense of the book, beginning usually with some generalizations on the nature of artistic merit.

The standard pattern of the prosecutor is to do his best to assemble a plain-as-mud jury and to dismiss all such learned experts as strange eggheads who in no sense understand the "average man" whose sensibilities are supposed to have been assaulted by the book.

In countering this anti-intellectual pattern of the prosecution, the experts have developed a more or less firm pattern of defending *Tropic of Cancer* on the grounds that it is "a great work of art." It is the wisdom of such a defense that I must question.

To describe a contemporary book as "a great work of art" is a temptation to which all enthusiasm is liable. It is a temptation to which I have myself succumbed at times. But it is finally to attribute to that book qualities that only time and the judgment of succeeding periods of varying literary taste can certify. One may safely say that *The Divine Comedy* is a great work of art; one can only assert as much about *Tropic of Cancer*, or about any other contemporary book. I do not mean to deny that *Tropic of Cancer* will survive the test by time. I believe it will. But I must also doubt that it will emerge as the central monument of twentieth-century writing.

Right or wrong, what service do critics perform for literature in rushing the verdict because a book is under local attack? Or in making the central defense of a book nothing less than its "greatness"? Shall there be no mercy for the less-than-great? Are serious writers to have no legal protection from the book banners simply because they happen to be minor writers?

The one defense of freedom must defend all. *Tropic of Cancer* must be defended, but not as "a great book." It must be defended as the work of a serious artist enlarged by talent and passionately engaged in giving form (and thereby meaning) to his view of life.

A prurient person could, of course, single out passages describing specific sex acts and feast his immature eroticism (whether or

214

not disguised as puritanical repugnance) on those. A sick-minded person could as readily go through a book of art reproductions and cut out every female breast, foot, or thigh, perhaps finding some sort of queer thrill in such fetishism. But the paintings in the book he so mutilates were never intended for such abuse. Neither was *Tropic of Cancer* intended for the sick snatcher of erotic details. Read from the beginning, as published and offered for reading, the book is, if anything, boring in its detailing of filth, of ugliness, and of the various acts of generally unattractive sex. It is only as one understands and responds to the author's full intent that such itemizations of unattractive matter become charged with meaning and, therefore, interesting.

There can be no question of that intent. The book sets out to portray the rescue of the individual life-impulse of the artist (and, therefore, of any man) in his necessary revolt against a society he takes to be shabby, grasping, hypocritical, and sterile. *Tropic of Cancer* is a novel of protest. Its protest is against all that stifles the essential life-impulse. It is also a novel of praise. What it praises is the dignity of the individual who will plunge into any experience, and welcome poverty, hunger, and ostracism, so long as he may escape hypocrisy.

Miller's protest includes mockery, a great roaring laughter, and a certain violent joy in flouting all the values socially accepted as sacred. He flatly refuses to do society the honor of taking it seriously.

But the violence of that mockery is inseparable from the moral stature of the book. Only as the author scorns what he feels to be false can he praise what he feels to be true. Were he to draw back from his assault on the social sickness he sees, were he to pass himself off, even for an instant, as a man of probity and respectability, he would have offered himself to the sickness he combats. The esthetic integrity of his affirmation would be lost at once.

The point of all his mockery, of his posturing, and even of his animal high jinks, is always in praise of the free soul. His cry of anguish at what society does to the individual is inseparable from the yell of animal joy with which he celebrates his escape from stultification.

Tropic of Cancer must be defended not as an ultimate peak of

215

greatness, but because, whether it succeeds or fails, it is written with power and compassion, and because it is charged in every passage with the author's esthetic devotion to his form and with his humane devotion to the joy of life. To remove such a book from the experience of mature readers on the grounds that the prurient may use it abusively is an assault upon the esthetic experience. It is a denial of freedom on the queasy grounds that men are not fit for freedom. It is to say that the least of men shall dictate the diet of the rest.

To base a defense on the claim of greatness is to abuse good cause. What must be defended is the right of the serious artist not to succeed, but to try.

June 30, 1962

The Book Banners

The following ten writers are arranged in alphabetical order: Balzac, Baudelaire, Faulkner, Joyce, Lawrence, Henry Miller, John O'Hara, Swinburne, Edmund Wilson, and Zola. What they have in common is that all of them have won a place of esteem in Western letters, and that all of them have found themselves, either literally or through their writings, summoned to court on charges of indecency, obscenity, or some related offense against public morality.

These ten are only a partial list of authors who have so suffered at the hands of the law, but they are enough to indicate that the law has no cause for pride in the history of its excursions into literature.

To be sure, every seriously written book eventually wins free of the restraint of censors. I have heard it argued, therefore, that censorship can be brushed aside as, at worst, a temporary nuisance.

216

So is an unfair jail sentence, but it manages to be nuisance enough in its time. The fact is that book banning, unless it is systematically and vigorously opposed, could intimidate publishers into shying away from every piece of writing in which the author breaks away from convention.

For though the battle does pass on from one title to another, the publisher engaged in defending his editorial judgment, his freedom of the press, and his commercial investment, is made to fight against unfair odds.

As John O'Hara and his publishers learned in the unsavory persecution-at-law of "Ten North Frederick," legal actions against a book, against a bookseller, or against author and publisher can be initiated in so many jurisdictions that it becomes impossible to defend every front. In one of many instances, O'Hara's book was successfully defended in Detroit only to have the same action brought against it in the next county. No publisher can afford to carry his legal fight across the nation, or even across a single state, county by county. The book banners can make themselves a nuisance not necessarily by right, but by exhaustion of the means to defend the right. The publisher, moreover, having committed his funds to the publication of a book he values, must often spend in its defense far more than the book can earn.

The position of the book banners is further strengthened by the fact that actions to suppress are now almost always initiated by public officials. There was a time when private organizations, such as Boston's fusty but adamant old Watch and Ward Society, brought actions in their own name, pursued the actions with their own funds, and left themselves responsibly open to countersuit for damages. Whatever else one may think of such fuss-budget organizations, they had the character to stand legally responsible for the moral positions they assumed.

Today, however, though book banning is often instigated by private organizations (such as, for example, the National Organization for Decent Literature, a Catholic censorship group whose lists of unloved books have provided the basis for many book-banning incidents), the action itself is legally initiated by a local prosecutor or chief of police. Such men cannot be counter-sued to any purpose. They have nothing to lose, they may well have something to gain in publicity, and they are, in fact, drawing public pay for the performance of duties that include their suppressions of books. But while the book banner's action is publicly underwritten, the publisher's defense must be paid for out of private funds.

Recent court decisions have made it all but inevitable that a publisher defending any seriously written book will eventually win his case if he fights it hard enough, long enough, and high enough—which is to say, expensively enough. The publisher's legal position is as firm as his pocketbook: he has the right to publish, but only if he can afford the legal fees.

Nor are the publisher's financial liabilities in such cases limited to his court costs. It is easy for him to be penalized commercially in the course of winning legally.

An action to suppress may begin as a civil action *in rem*, which is to say against the book itself. In Massachusetts, such civil actions are the usual procedure in book-banning cases. In other states, however, it is more likely that a criminal action will be brought and that it will begin with the arrest of a bookseller. The bookseller must then get in touch with a lawyer and undertake to pay a substantial fee. The fee, in all likelihood, will equal the profit the bookseller might have made from the sale of hundreds of copies of the book. Assume now that the publisher enters the case and, at considerable expense, wins it. Soon thereafter, the publisher's salesman calls in triumph upon the bookseller to take orders for the book. But the bookseller has had enough time in court and enough of paying lawyer's fees. How can he be sure a new action will not begin? He plays it safe and refuses to have anything to do with the book. The publisher has won in court but has lost his customer. In the "Ten North Frederick" case, O'Hara's publishers won only to lose in just this way.

It is, on all counts, an uneven contest. To defend his book, the publisher must pit his private resources against nothing less than the public till. He must face a needless multiplication of cases. (On this point it is worth noting that in its defense of "Tropic of Cancer," Grove Press repeatedly offered to withdraw the book in a given jurisdiction until a pending case in higher court had decided the issue, but that the local prosecutors refused the offer. They seem to want these multiplied cases, since obviously nothing

218

but good publicity can follow for them in the local press, and without the disadvantage of offending any local interests worth political consideration.) And, finally, the publisher stands likely to lose commercially even after he has established his expensive legal right—a right that was amply clear from the beginning. These are, I submit, patent abuses of the law.

The law is, of course, a cumbersome thing. But if the law lacks the ability to rid itself of abusive procedures, then it is no longer law but a legal *rigor mortis*. Freedom of thought and freedom of the press are inseparable from the idea of the American democracy. The law that affirms these freedoms in spirit cannot safely permit their destruction by the cumbersomeness of its own procedures.

Freedom would be that much closer for all of us, had we a fairer procedure for censorship cases. One way to even things would be to speed all such cases to federal courts, the higher the better. Such cases properly belong there, since they involve both freedom of the press and interstate commerce. In such courts, as happens all but inevitably, the book would be cleared. If such clearance is then followed by a federal injunction against interference with the book, the local censors will be deprived of most of their unfair advantage.

Such a procedure is difficult if not impossible under present law, and to be sure, right and legality cannot always coincide. But when the law cannot solve the technical problems of bringing itself into consonance with the right, it has lost its final claim to existence. Law that breeds abuse is bad law. We need new legal procedures for censorship cases, or new legislation, or both.

June 23, 1962

Last Exit to Nowhere

Someday, and soon I hope, the Supreme Court will hear a book-banning case and issue a ruling that not only clears the book but enunciates legal principle so firmly that the everlastingly reiterated harassment of books by the lower courts will be brought to a halt.

For though the higher courts all but invariably clear any book that is brought before them, police agencies and public prosecutors continue to bring new cases to the lower courts, leaving it to the defendant to find his expensive way to higher justice. These lower court actions, moreover, are invariably brought on the same grounds. The book is charged with contributing to juvenile delinquency. Or it is charged with offending community standards. Or with both.

Could I have all my wishes in the matter, the Supreme Court would be unequivocal in destroying the legal basis of these two charges.

It would rule first (so let me dream) that no book may be banned on the grounds that it contributes to juvenile delinquency, holding that there is no demonstrable connection between juvenile delinquency and any reading habit, and that the very existence of any least trace of a reading habit is more likely than not to be a deterrent to juvenile delinquency. The court may, with my blessing, exempt comic books from the ruling, finding them to be primarily an exercise in ogling rather than in reading. But, with whatever reservations it finds necessary, it will rule that few men and no children have ever been corrupted by holding in front of their eyes a series of pages.

It would rule second (my dream continues) that a book is incapable of offending community standards, holding that a book

220

has no way of intruding upon the community, that it is available only to one reader at a time, and that it cannot thrust itself upon even that reader as an offense to his standards since the reader is free to close the book whenever he feels that he is offended.

The second principle may be stated as the proposition that if an offense cannot occur by itself but must be deliberately sought out and brought into being by the person who then feels offended, that person can claim no redress at law.

On the chance that the Supreme Court does not have handy a precedent for such a ruling, let me cite the case of Bitsy O'Grady *vs.* Muscles Mike. The magistrate in this case was Officer Sam, Bitsy O'Grady bringing a complaint of indecent exposure against Muscles Mike. Officer Sam, investigating the complaint in person, was led by complainant to the window of her apartment and asked to look for himself at the window of Muscles Mike's apartment, where he was assured he would see Muscles Mike in near total undress and in obscene postures of rigorous exercise.

Officer Sam did look as directed but found he could not see into Muscles Mike's window, it being at a slightly higher level than complainant's and at an angle to it. "Ah, to be sure," testified complainant, "but just try standing on this chair and holding up this bit of a mirror I've tied to the end of my broomstick, and see if it isn't enough to give an honest soul palpitations!"

In this case Officer Sam found for the accused, ruling that if two shades have to be up at the same time before offense can be given, then complainant had sufficient protection in her own shade and needed none at law; and, further, that a mirror on a broomstick is the visual equivalent of wiretapping and not admissible in evidence without a prior court order.

Somewhere between tears and whimsy there is the further point that reviewers are reluctant to attack a bad book for fear that an excerpt-lifting prosecutor will use some passage of the review in evidence against the book. Sometime ago, I wrote about Cleland's *Memoirs of a Woman of Pleasure*, arguing that the book was not censorable but that it certainly was pornography. And within two weeks I had been entered in evidence by a public prosecutor as if I had pleaded for the book's suppression.

My damnation on any man who quotes me in support of any book-banner, for that man is a cheat and a liar. But now there comes upon the land the case of *Last Exit to Brooklyn* by Hubert Selby, Jr., and if I may pause to wish a case of Job's boils on any prosecutor who distorts my sentiments into a legal case against the book, then let me cite Selby's effusion as the season's and the century's post-ultimate event in the literary swill-slopping contest.

Last Exit is the gutter-to-sewer chronicle of a depraved gang of young hoods who hang out at the Greek's, "a beat-up all-night diner near the Brooklyn Army base." These specimens of the bestialized young live on what they can pick up by muggings, but their taste for violence is in no way limited to professional engagements. In the opening episode, the gang cripples a young soldier, standing around him in a circle and methodically kicking in his face, ribs, kidneys, crotch, and whatever else offers itself to marksmanship. Selby clearly has not only a knack for the details of vomit and crunching cartilage, but a literary taste for it.

After such a beginning, one can hardly expect surprises. Yet by the time the eager author has rung the changes on every detail of mayhem, homosexual violence, bloody dives, back-alley girls, and a mass fornication of the viciously feeble-minded slut called Tralala—by that time, I say, any fair-minded reader is bound to confess Selby has outdone his own advance billing.

For *Last Exit* is a well-chosen title. Whatever road our creative young apes have been traveling in their addicted denial of every human affection, this is certainly the last exit before someone comes up with the final epic of sodomy, cannibalism, and Caligulan ingenuities. The denial of love in any form is certainly an essence of it. There is only the reality of the man-beast to cling to. There is no memory in it of what a reasonable man may still, and honorably, call the humanities. And there is everywhere in it the assumption that ignorance plus a boiling energy is all the literary preparation a man needs.

Yet Selby's book is not depraved because of its subject matter. The depravity of a piece of writing is always located in the author. Nelson Algren, for example, can write about Skid Row and infuse the story of his lost souls with a sublimely tragic sense of compassion. There is no need to ask of Algren why he writes what he does as he does: he loves his people and we are made to love them, too.

222

But when I ask myself why Selby should be moved to write as he does about bestialized humanity, I can come up with no answer except that he is a literary fraud; skillful enough as a writer, but moved to the writing by no other purpose than to out-vomit, out-rape, out-bash, out-smear, and out-stink every other literary roughneck on the scene. "These guys think they can write rough, huh? Well," the author seems to be saying, "I'll show them!"

And he does, he certainly does. For no book as bad as this one gets written by accident. Only a man with a firm sense of direction could have turned it out so entirely to no human purpose.

No, it is not to be banned gentlemen—I did not say that—but damned it must be.

April 3, 1965

The Marquis de Sade, I

The Marquis de Sade is an aberration that has remained firmly a part of European literature for almost two centuries now despite a haphazard scattering and destruction of his papers and manuscripts, despite the serious intent of most readers of literature to bury him in silence, and despite extraordinary efforts at legal suppression. Nor did outraged society attack only his writings. Sade lived to be seventy-four and died in confinement after having spent most of his adult life either in prison or as a fugitive from various warrants. Whether as a nobleman under the King of France or as a citizen under the rule of the Republic (a transition he made with a whole skin by grace of the fact that he was a prisoner of the wicked monarchy when the Revolution broke out)—as aristocrat or commoner, it was Sade's compulsion to offend society and his vocation to be a prisoner. It seems oddly harmonious with his life that it should be his fate to become a

223

generally misunderstood word in most, if not all, the languages of Europe.

"Sadism" is current today in all psychological jargon to signify a range of sexual perversions that find their gratification in inflicting pain on the sex partner, and by extension it has come to signify in common usage any sort of behavior that finds pleasure in inflicting pain on others. Perhaps common usage is intuitive in sensing that there may be a sexual base to all active cruelty. But what Sade preached—and he was in essence a demented preacher—was no subcategory of perverted behavior. It was nothing less than a total philosophy of life.

One of the premises of that philosophy is an assertion of the sickness of the state. As Sade saw it, law exists only as a means of imposing the will of the aristocracy on the suffering masses of this world's slaves. Only two sorts of men can escape from slavery. They are, first, the aristocrats who make the law and who are thereby above it and, second, the great criminals who break the law and who are thereby beyond it.

All law is understood to be an artificial and largely whimsical imposition. Against it stands Nature (always with a capital N), in whose eyes all men are equal. Sade sees Nature as absolute and godless; no man, in fact, has attacked all religion more fervently and more abusively.

In Nature, each individual exists to seek his own pleasure, which consists simply of imposing his pleasure upon other individuals, as, for example, the lion imposes his pleasure upon the zebra, killing and eating it with no slightest concern for its victim's feelings.

But even the lion moves within its pride. For Sade, each creature is its own solitude. In Nature, it would follow, a man has no real function but to seek his own pleasure. Man's function in Nature is to resist Law, for within it he can only be a victim, whereas outside the Law he can fulfill himself as a victimizer.

Only such an absolute and leonine egoism offers man a life worth living. But Sade goes further: life itself is meaningless except as a man fills it with pleasurable sensations, and for Sade a deliberate and thoughtful criminality is one of the most satisfying of sensations. To impose physical tortures on others (including their painful murder in the act of achieving sexual gratification)

224

is erotically pleasurable, and the more criminally or sacrilegiously outrageous the act, the greater the erotic pleasure.

Finally, of course, there will come the time when the most ravening beast will weaken and itself become prey to a stronger. But Sade embraces even the victimizer's final fate as a victim. The one aim of the individual is pleasurable (*i.e.*, erotic) sensation. To the individual who is utterly true to his perfect denial of all but sensation, therefore, his own final death by torture is nothing to whimper at, but rather a goal to embrace as the exquisite consummation of the ultimate eroticism.

These are Sade's basic declarations. In expounding them, he became the first Western writer to construct an entire philosophy on personal sickness. Such writers as Poe, Baudelaire, Nietzsche, Kafka, Rimbaud, Celine, and on to our present-day Beats, have all, in one way or another, followed Sade's lead. And from Baudelaire and Swinburne down to Simone de Beauvoir, leading writers of every age have found reason to press extraordinary praises upon him. One might think the madmen have identified the world.

And may not that thought identify Sade's relevance? What man of mind has not found reason to wonder if reason itself may not be the cruelest madness? When the perverts and madmen of the world are assembled for judgment and are brought face to face with the chancellors of reason and the doctors of scientific destruction, what evil could the madmen claim as their own without finding it a triviality as compared to the savagery the world has endured in the name of reason and progress and legitimate national aspiration? All terrible thoughts, but where can one hide in what world to escape them?

There is even a sort of sick heroism in the ruthlessness of Sade's preachment. Yet it must be noted that the heroism stops with the preachment. The *soi-disant* beast of his own imagination turns out to have been a sordid sexual bungler in his escapades, and a self-justifying sniveler in his letters. Where is the ruthless splendor of the beast in Sade's letter to his wife written from the Bastille and dated February 20, 1781?

I am a libertine but I am neither a criminal nor a murderer. . . . I am a libertine, but three families residing in your area have for five years lived off my charity. . . . I am a libertine, but I have

225

saved a deserter from death. . . . I am a libertine, but at Evry, with your whole family looking on, I saved a child—at the risk of my life—who was on the verge of being crushed beneath the wheels of a runaway horse-drawn cart. . . . I am a libertine but I have never compromised my wife's health. Nor have I been guilty of the other kinds of libertinage so often fatal to children's fortunes: have I ruined them by gambling or by other expenses that might have deprived them of, or even by one day foreshortened, their inheritance? . . . . How, therefore, do you presume that, from so innocent a childhood and youth, I have suddenly arrived at the ultimate of premeditated horror? No, you do not believe it. And you who today tyrannize me so cruelly, you do not believe it either: your vengeance has beguiled your mind, you have proceeded blindly to tyrannize, but your heart knows mine, it judges it more fairly, and knows full well it is innocent. (As translated by Richard Seaver and Austryn Wainhouse in *The Marquis de Sade*. Grove Press. p. xiv.)

Yet Sade does refuse to disappear. Something about his madness remains relevant to the thoughtful despite the brashness of his style, and I am more than half inclined to guess the mark of the prison cell may be part of it, that men of our time, if they think at all, have reason to think of themselves as prisoners battering at fantasy for some escape that does not come. And for that, or for whatever other reasons, Sade persists—a bore, a pervert, perhaps even a lunatic, but still a force that whispers what we may not be pleased to hear but must listen to all the same.

June 18, 1965

The Marquis de Sade, II

Last week, as a necessary preliminary to a perhaps broader but in any case more immediate discussion, I offered an amateur sketch of the Marquis de Sade as a sick man and sick philosopher whose writings, though repetitious, tendentious, and all but styleless, have somehow refused to fade away despite all of "polite society's" efforts to ignore them. The occasion of the sketch, and of the present remarks on Sade, is the publication by Grove Press of the most substantial sampling of Sade's works ever to be openly published in America. *The Marquis de Sade* is compiled and translated by Richard Seaver and Austryn Wainhouse and presents, unexpurgated and in colloquial translation (which is to say with all four-letter words in place), all of *Dialogue Between a Priest and a Dying Man*, *Philosophy in the Bedroom*, *Eugénie de Franval*, and *Justine, or Good Conduct Well Chastised*.

These selections fill 558 of the book's 775 pages, the remaining 217 pages being devoted to a critical and bibliographical apparatus that includes a foreword by the editors, a publisher's preface, a critical treatise by Jean Paulhan and another by Maurice Blanchot, a detailed chronology of the life of Sade, seven of Sade's letters with annotations, a bibliography, and even Sade's last will and testament. The editors and the publisher have set out to make their offering as heavy as its price ($15), as if to make sure it comes into court wearing full academic regalia.

For make no mistake—it will come to court soon; and once there it promises to have a long career before the last appeal has been filed and the last ruling delivered. Sade, like it or not, is a perdurable figure of European literature. He will come to court because he was born to face the bench. And Grove has done well to see to it that it is no gaudy paperback but rather a scholar's tome that stands to judgment.

For *The Marquis de Sade* is, in one sense, the ultimate test case. If this book is not banned, then no book can be banned; if it is cleared all books are cleared.

When Judge Hudson ruled against William Burroughs's *Naked Lunch* he could only find it "obscene, indecent, and impure." In Sade's case one would have to add not only an endlessly detailed and sometimes fully four-lettered catalogue of sexual perversions and tortures, but a zealot's commitment to sacrilege, and an almost missionary desire to find ways of giving offense to every established principle of social respectability. Burroughs partakes of some desire to shock but he is, finally, absorbed in the needs of his addict's hallucination: he offends respectability simply by being himself, and within that nightmare of himself he is often too turgid to be decipherable. Unintelligibility, I am premising, is not the most effective means of communicating obscenity. Sade, on the other hand, works deliberately and ingeniously to stab at those points that will soonest revolt social respectability. And to compound his crime, his writing is never anything but clear in the fullest and sickest detail.

If the argument is entered on the grounds that Sade's writing is designed to generate lascivious desires in a man of average sensibility (I believe it was Justice Holmes who established *l'homme moyen sensuel* as the criterion), no reasonably able prosecutor should have trouble establishing that the writing is, in fact, so designed, though even the most atrocious of Sade's details become boring in their repetitiveness. There is significant literary import in Sade's work, but it is, I believe, only the man of fine, rather than average, literary sensitivity who will read him for that.

That man, however, should read him and must read him. Is it necessary to argue that there is a sick dislocation in our age and that our social platitudes and our committee-room reasons will not find it? Yet all good artists and all men of mind must seek it out, face it, scrutinize it, and learn its pose and nature. The man of insights must ponder the mark of the beast, and Sade's works are one of the documents he must ponder. Or shall we pretend that Buchenwald and Dachau did not happen, or that they were the hideous encampments of monsters who were not really human beings? Only man is un-man, and he must be known entire.

I am suggesting that the contest at law is, finally, a contest to determine who shall be served. Because another man may read this book leeringly, am I to be denied the legal right to read it toward some hopefully compassionate sense of what is sick in all of us? Yes, I am revolted by it at times, and, yes, I am bored by it more often than not—as I am, for example, when I read of the Nazis. Evil, like innocence, can be revolting and boring, but both evil and innocence must be accounted for in any man's psyche before he has faced himself fully. No man knows himself until he has been embarrassed by what he knows of himself. Sade is one of the documents of that embarrassing self-recognition. Face this sick man in your own nervous system and learn to account for him, and there may yet be a hope of mercy and self-mercy in you. Nor has the law any right to withhold such a test of himself from any man.

Sade is disturbing. Let me confess that he drives me from an earlier position I once defended too smugly, arguing that my children were free to read any book with my blessing so long as they would discuss it with me. I am bound to say I am not willing to have them read Sade this side of their adulthood. The details of sodomy, incest, orgies, homosexuality, coprophagy, and the tortures invented in the hallucinations of a demented philosopher are no diet I can endorse for those too young and too formless to have developed their own principle of selection and their own dispassion. I shall keep the book away from my children in about the same way I should vote against including any substantial treatise on abnormal psychology in the public school curriculum— though I grant I am not quite sure I have identified the markings that distinguish normal from abnormal psychology. Whatever confusion that may be, though it is a necessary part of the college curriculum, is better avoided at lower levels.

But if a parent is appropriately the censor of his own young, the law is not appropriately the censor of man's ideas—not at least until those ideas threaten a clearly impending social violence. The law, as it has demonstrated in one censorship case after another, is incompetent to judge literature. A camel is better able to write a book about a man than a judge is to determine the social value of a book. The works of the Marquis de Sade, whether in the present Grove Press edition or in any subsequent selection, should be permitted full legal freedom to circulate for the simple reason that every book should have that freedom.

October 2, 1965

The Right to Read

Is it a rule of public conduct that people of firm and narrow principle must always be better organized for civic action than are those of firm but broader principle? "I hate" seems ever to be a more effective organizing force than "Well, now, let's talk it over." So, at least, it seems to be in the contest between those who are moved to censor books and those who are moved to resent censorship.

Or so the case seemed to stand until I encountered the New Jersey Committee for the Right to Read, and long may it wave. The Committee raises funds, recruits members, holds seminars and panel sessions, collects information on book-banning cases, presents clear arguments in favor of the right to read, addresses protests to local officials who suppress books, and publishes a regular bulletin titled *The Readers' Rights*.

I am especially grateful to *The Readers' Rights* for bringing to my attention the report of the Kinsey Institute for Sex Research titled *Sex Offenders: An Analysis of Types*, a statistical study of 2,721 sex offenders, 1,356 of whom were interviewed in jail while serving sentences for sex crimes.

The book-banners like to argue that there is a direct connection between "sexy" literature and sex crime. And certainly, could such a connection be shown to exist, it would provide a powerful reason for censorship. The Kinsey Institute report, however, finds no

230

such connection. As summarized for the *Ladies' Home Journal* by Dr. Paul Gebhard, who took part in the report, and as reprinted in *The Readers' Rights,* the Kinsey researchers found that:

The stereotyped "sex criminal" of popular imagination turns out to be many different kinds of men. Contrary to general belief, few of them take dope, although many of them do commit their crimes under the influence of alcohol. And few are in any way inspired by pornography. As the Institute's previous reports have shown, pornography of all kinds is mostly read and enjoyed by men of more than average intelligence and with vivid imaginations. The men in prison for sexual offenses, on the other hand, turned out to be men of rather low intelligence and imagination. Their disinterested [Did Dr. Gebhard mean "uninterested?"] and indeed scornful attitude toward pornography was perhaps best summed up by one fairly typical prisoner who told me, "You can't do nothin' with a pitcher."

Many of the mothers of America should find reassurance in this fact. Boys, at puberty, often begin to take a surreptitious interest in risqué magazines, and sometimes wind up with collections of outright pornography. A mother who finds such possessions hidden in her son's room need not be unduly concerned, for this does not mean he will grow up into a fiend or a pervert. Not one of the men we interviewed seemed to have gone to prison as a result of exposure to pornography, either immediately before his crime or even at some distant time back in his adolescence.

I happen to know a smidgin-bit about the mothers of America. I had one of my own once and I ended up married to another. If they cannot find their reassurance in Dr. Gebhard's results, let me suggest they ask one of the fathers of America, perhaps the one they happen to be married to. If he is honest enough to confess to his own adolescence he will be able to tell them that Dr. Gebhard is describing something like the normal process of early puberty.

THE RIGHT TO REFUSE (OR VALOR AMONG THE GARBAGE CANS): It may seem frivolous to turn from so large an issue to the one that has set Mr. J. J. Kyker at odds with the Nashville garbage collectors, and it was in some sort of minor mood that I paused in the Nashville Airport to buy a copy of the Nashville *Tennessean* in which I read, in the act of killing time, about Mr. Kyker's stand among the garbage cans. By the time I had finished reading, however, I was beyond frivolity and firm to praise a man who knows his own mind.

Mr. Kyker has been informed by the local commissioner of garbage that he will have to buy a specified sort of galvanized garbage can "or face the consequence"—and what a lovely fossil specimen of an official fossil phrase that official fossil phrase is! Mr. Kyker for his part has refused to back down on the purest of American premises. "I don't like to be pushed around," he announced. And let me announce that I don't like to see him pushed around, either.

I have, moreover, read the garbage laws as quoted in the paper, and I have seen a clear photo of Mr. Kyker's garbage cans. They are obviously fine, upstanding American garbage cans and I am all for them. They have nothing to do with those galvanized frivolities that pass through our lives in a brief contest to see whether the bottoms will rust out before the collectors mash the sides flat, or whether the sides will be mashed flat before the bottoms rust out. Mr. Kyker has two sound metal drums, which are in themselves enough to dispose me in his favor. And in addition to a clear right, I find a fine accommodating patience on his side.

Garbage law in Nashville specifies thirty-gallon drums with tight-fitting lids, and Mr. Kyker has thirty-gallon drums with tight-fitting lids. His drums were originally used to ship yellow paint and, though the law is mute on the point, the garbage commissioner is afraid some of the paint still clings to the drums and that his collectors will get their hands dirty. Very well, Mr. Kyker has countered, he will scrub them out with turpentine. And if they want handles on the cans he is willing to have handles welded on—though on this point, too, the law is mute.

I should have thought that Mr. Kyker had met every objection that could be raised by the most garbagy of commissioners, but the garbage set had one more up its sleeve. The drums, it declared, are too heavy. It was at that point that I joined the local forces of rebellion.

Don't you believe them for a minute, Mr. Kyker. Their real objection is that the drums won't mash as easily as the galvanized

232

cans. They are madmen, Sir, and it is their fetish to crush every pseudo-metal shell they can lay hands on, nothing will drive them into a frenzy sooner than real and resistant metal. They will, to be sure, demolish even your fine drums given time enough, but meanwhile theirs is the rage of frustration.

I see from the papers, Sir, that you may be subject to a fine of no more than $50 and three months in jail and that you would sooner go to jail than be pushed around. I see, alternatively, that the commissioner may decide to deliver two galvanized cans to your door and to bill you for them. Refuse them, Mr. Kyker. Or use them to put the commissioner in, if he should come around. But don't let him push you around—I like the way you say that, Sir. I can't get three months off to go to jail for you, but it would be a pleasure to pay your fine if the garbage heads—I mean the heads of local garbage—insist on acting like themselves. I like a man who doesn't like to be pushed around. (Have you ever read Thoreau, Mr. Kyker? I think you would like the feel of his mind.)

Stand fast, Mr. Kyker, and let Nashville make the most of it. Caesar had his Brutus, Charles I had his Cromwell, and Nashville. . . .

November 6, 1965

Religion and Citizenship

I have formed the habit of tossing collections of newspaper clippings into a file for later browsing and second thinking, and so it is that I find myself poring over reports on the Supreme Court's school-prayer decision and on clerical reactions to it. I shall not pretend to disinterest, for certainly the first and the central question to arise from the court's decision and from the clerical response to it involves the right of the nonbeliever to full citizen-

233

ship, and on that issue I have all of my own confused world to defend.

The Supreme Court has taken the position that it is unconstitutional for an agency of the government to coerce religious expression, and it has held that for a public school to require the reading of a prayer as part of its standard procedure constitutes such coercion even when dissenting pupils are permitted to abstain from the reading.

Churchmen, by and large, have cried out against this decision. A scattering of Protestant ministers and relatively more rabbis have supported it, but what I take to be the essential position of most clergymen was baldly stated by *The Advocate*, a Catholic publication in New Jersey:

In the majority opinion there is the vote that by denying the use of this prayer in the schools of New York, the court is upholding what it claims to be a traditional wall of separation of Church and State. More truly could it be said that it is erecting a wall of separation of God and State. The impact of this decision can have lasting effects on the minds and hearts of every child attending a public school in the United States of America.

That the effect of such a decision will be far-reaching seems certain, but that the results will be bad, as *The Advocate*'s editorialist implies, is a conclusion I must oppose, and without intending any attack upon religion. A man's religion is his own business; his own, and that of any clergy whose guidance and discipline he voluntarily accepts. If he is given to prayer, there is nothing to keep him from praying silently at any time. Nor can I recall having read any churchman to the effect that God cannot hear a silent prayer as readily as one spoken aloud. It is, rather, an essence of every modern religion I know anything about that God need not be shouted at, and that the quiet heart may reach Him as readily as any.

But it is not religion I mean to argue. Reason may hope to speak to reason on many topics, but I have seldom found religion to be one of them. For years I had to forbid my freshman English students to take religion as the topic of their weekly themes. It was my duty, as part of a hoped-for conversation in reason, to demand

234

of them intelligent generalizations (sometimes called topic sentences) and to demand that those generalizations be supported by orderly, thoughtful, and coherent evidence or deduction, or both. But what happens when the instructor must criticize the reasoning process, only to have the student cry, "That's my religion!"? All hope of communication ends right there. Sooner or later the instructor learns to insist that his students avoid any topic that makes dispassionate comment unacceptable. What the instructor so learns, the instructor-turned-columnist is not likely to forget.

The issue, I repeat, is not religion but my right to make up my own mind—and to let my children make up theirs—on such matters as God, prayer, and the intent, if any, of the Universe. It is the right to reach a personal decision with no least trace of coercion from any branch of government. And it is the right to unimpaired citizenship no matter what final view one comes up with.

It would not be honest to pretend that I have not reached what I take to be a reasonably firm and final view. I do not pray, and I am not aware that a belief in supernatural forces motivates anything I do. I am not moved to be militant about my view. Our local Presbyterian Church has a good choir, my daughter likes to sing, and my wife happens to feel more comfortable when she can edge the kids to Sunday School. The kids seem to enjoy Sunday School there, and there they go. As far as I am concerned, they may stop going whenever they please, or they are free to stay with it all the way through ordination if that is the road they find for themselves. When they ask about my own views, I try to give them as fair an answer as I can form, but never a directive one. I mean to coerce no man's view of the Universe, and certainly not theirs.

If I did not believe my secularism to be as valid as any man's religion, I should, of course, change my view. Why take a second-class seat to mortality? I hold to the best I can see. And I may be wrong. But my tolerance ends at the point at which any man dares to rise to me in my error—if error is what it is—to say that I am required as a citizen to believe, and publically to avow, that the United States exists, as the Eisenhower pledge of allegiance would have it, "under God."

I do not so believe, nor will I accept such a belief as a condition of my citizenship. Yet, by insisting on the federal rightness of their own point of view, the sponsors of this religious insertion into a civil declaration have made it impossible for me to be quiet in my own conscience in pretending to pledge allegiance to the flag. For even if I omit the words "under God," I still seem to be endorsing them, and I will not permit such seeming. If there must be such an interpolation, let me suggest substituting for it the words "in this Universe." I am confident that the nation does exist somewhere in the Universe. I can say that much in good conscience. At the same time, any man who believes the Universe to be God-suffused, can read into this substitution his own affirmation of belief, and so, in good democratic principle, may we both be served.

The Advocate's editorialist argued that the Court's decision erected a wall between God and State. I, for one, insist upon that wall, for in practice God and State cannot be distinguished from Church and State. If it is entered as a public premise that God will speak to the State, it will certainly be the churchmen who will rise to say the words for Him, and forgive me for suspecting that *The Advocate*'s editorialist would be among the first volunteers.

I will insist with the minority of the clergy that the Court's decision is fundamental to the idea of the American democracy. It takes religion away from no man and forces it upon none. It declares again that though a man is free to worship as he sees fit, or not to worship at all, his citizenship is secular and in no way dependent upon his affirmation of religious belief, or upon his refusal to make such an affirmation. For what point can there be in defending the right of the individual conscience, if the individual is not free, in conscience, to come to the less popular conclusion as well as to the more popular one?

September 22, 1962

Ride a Hot Horse

The opening of the Seattle World's Fair was marred by an incident in which a disabled jet crashed into a row of houses, killing an elderly man and woman under their own roof while the pilot parachuted to safety miles away. A sad accident and one that is becoming sadly common as the jets fill the sky above and the housing developments fill the ground below.

But was it entirely an accident? It is possible, to be sure, that the plane was hopelessly out of control. But it is just as possible that the pilot, had he stayed with it all the way, could have managed to crash into an empty field rather than into those houses. I am asking if a pilot has the right to bail out of a disabled plane over thickly settled country, and I am moved to argue that he has not.

Nobody wants to splash the boys over the landscape. If a pilot runs into trouble and bails out over a desert, who could blame him for that, even if his jet happens by freak chance to come down on the one house within range or on a passing automobile? But to bail out over an urban or a suburban area is another case, and there, I must insist, the pilot clearly funks if he fails to ride it all the way down. There is always that chance that he can at the last instant avoid visiting his disaster on those below. And even if he cannot, even if his death goes for nothing, it is his job to try.

It is his job for the simple reason that he asked for it. No one gets drafted into flying jets. The boys have to want to, they have to fight for the chance to try, and they have to buck hard to get through their training. How can a would-be pilot ask for the job—and ask for it that hard—without understanding that he has a moral contract to spend everything, including his own life, to avoid dumping his disabled buzzer on the people below? Suppose, to select a horrendous example, that house with the elderly couple in it had been a school building. How does the pilot walk away from his parachute after that?

It may be that we have entered the age of the final moral funk, wherein sentiment can justify all. The government certainly went a long way toward justifying the funk of pilot Powers in the U-2 incident. Our government, to be sure, is now imitating the Communists in handing out only that information it wants the people to have, and perhaps, therefore, the whole truth will never be known. It is on record, however, that Powers was drawing $30,-000 a year for occasional flights over Russia, and that his equipment included a destruction button and a poisoned pin. What can one conclude but that the button and the pin were meant for use and that the $30,000 salary was jeopardy pay? And what can one then conclude but that Powers took the cash and then funked it?

The boys know what they are asking for when they buck for wings. They like the flying pay, they like the badges, and they like the glamour the badges bring. Perhaps, above all, they like the feel of the hot horse under them. The hottest horse of all is, of course, death, and so long as there are boys in this world, some of them will fall in love with the sensation of riding him. As Melville wrote, "All wars are boyish and are fought by boys." That love affair with the hot horse is of the boyhood of the race. But once a boy is on that horse, then it is his man's job to ride it all the way.

T. E. Shaw (Lawrence of Arabia) was such a boy-man. He lived with his itch to ride the hottest horse. He died, foolishly enough (if I recall correctly what I read years ago and have since forgotten where), of his passion for riding a motorcycle too fast. The motorcycle happened to be his hot horse of the moment. But if he was still boy enough to have to open it up all the way, he was man enough to know it was not a free ride. He died of a choice he had made within himself long before. Gunning his crazy machine down the road, he came to that instant when he must kill either an innocent pedestrian or himself. He swerved off the road and killed himself.

There is no need to grow romantic about the splendor of his choice. What was splendid about the man, finally, was his talent.

238

What sent the boy hightailing down the road was no splendor but a problem for the psychiatrist's couch. What remains is the fact that, between man and boy, Shaw made his choice clean.

The boys that fly the hot ones have the same choice to make. And like Shaw they have to make that choice in their own minds long before the moment of truth. It has to be made firmly beforehand, or their reflexes will make the wrong choice too late.

It may be a crazy choice to have forced upon oneself. Maybe they have to be a bit crazy to want to fly the hot ones. Maybe we are all crazy for having made a world in which we need a sky full of hot horses. But no boy—and he has to be a boy, whatever bar, leaf, eagle, or star he wears on his collar—can be allowed to go for crazy up to the time his buzzer runs into trouble, and then to dump his trouble on a row of houses while he floats sanely down in his parachute.

As the best, and least printable, of World War II's flying songs starts off:

> I wanted wings,
> Now I've got the goddamn things.
> Hell, I don't want them anymore.

A lot of the hotshot boys, who had a high stateside fling flashing their wings for the girls, discovered in combat that they didn't really want them anymore. But the fact remains that few of them broke and funked out. They had signed a contract with themselves. They had accepted the glamour, the flight pay, and the gravy-train freedom from all the nasty chores an ingrate army can dream up for noncrew members. They had asked for it and they had taken it. That adds up to a contract, and, like it or not, you keep that contract come flak, fighters, fire, or the heebie-jeebies. You may not want those wings anymore, but you've got them: they are tattooed on you. If you get killed flying, that's tough, buddy, but nobody wrote out any special dispensation for your special skin. The contract itself was written on skin, on skin that was always of the most special kind—the only kind there is.

If the boys in those jet cockpits do not have their contract clearly enough understood as a moral decision, it may be time to make it a court-martial decision. The gentle among us may cry

239

out in horror against such a decision. It is no way to treat our dear boys, they will cry; the boys risk enough just in flying those ships to protect us.

But what we have to realize is that we cannot be protected by boys who risk enough. Nothing will cover us sufficiently until they risk everything. And, remember, the boys have not been forced. They asked for it. Every one of those bright badges has a piece of skin under it, and if the civilians insist on funking that fact, the boys had better get it clear, or clear out and go back to being civilians.

October 6, 1962

The Trivial History of Our Times

All of us know by now that we are living in a time that spells HISTORY in upper case letters. How shall our age be known to the future, assuming there is to be one? Shall it be as the Age of Decision? As the Turning Point? As the Age of Seconal? Or perhaps the future will know us as the Age that Tried to Be Last.

No matter what the final caption, such history as we see moving about us looms large, and its very size stirs our anxiety. It is for the trivial that we shall yet learn to be grateful. If only we can manage to keep trivia going, we may yet find it possible to make it into some sort of habitable future.

"Hell," I was once moved to observe, "is the denial of the ordinary." I had been reading a book about concentration camps, wherein depraved men have certainly done their best to stage a production of hell on earth. The essence of that hell, I found myself thinking, was in the fact that the trivial had been swept away by a nightmare in which everything—a remark, a crust of

240

bread, the mood of a jailer, the irritations of a fellow sufferer—
became portentous and deadly.

Toward the dream of the ordinary kingdom, therefore, and in
the fear we must all feel at the stirring of the portentous, I offer
these randomly collected trivia of 1962 as some part of one man's
good, and in the momentous (but not, I hope, portentous) hope
that this world may be spared for its exercise of the trivial.

YOU, SIR, ARE A DAMNED FOOL: I have by now received just about
every conceivable communication from our readers, but let me
remember 1962, above all, as the year in which an Air Force captain stationed in Germany read my column on pilots bailing out
of disabled jets, and relieved himself, at cable rates, of a firm sentiment. The text read· YOU, SIR, ARE A DAMNED FOOL.

I am having the cable framed to hang over my desk at *SR*. For
my reply I borrowed happily from H. L. Mencken one of his
favorite form letters:

> Dear Sir or Madam:
> You may be right at that.
> Yours truly,

THE CHANGING WORLD AS CONVERSATION AT THE BAR: In the course of
various mixtures of bourbon and water over various bars, I had
long since caught on to the fact that Reno lies a bit west of Los
Angeles, and that if a line is extended due south from Detroit,
the first foreign country it will hit will be Canada, but it was in
1962 that, lounging in a Northwest Orient plane and browsing
through a polar map and an attached table of air mileages, I finally
caught on to the rudiments of the new geography, discovering that
New York, which is 1,100 miles north of Miami, is 445 miles
closer to Manila (8,948 nautical miles and 9,393 nautical miles,
respectively). Or so at least Northwest Orient computes the
distances, noting by the way that "Mileages shown are great circle
mileages, for general information only." New York, for general
information only, is also 463 miles closer than Miami to both Tokyo
and Seoul (the distances from the first being 7,066 and 7,529, and
from the second 7,800 and 8,263, all in nautical miles, and always
respectively).

I shall not pretend to be sure what these facts from the changing world import on any major scale, but in the measure of this world's trivia, I am willing to bet that such golden information can be worked for a free drink at any convivial bar. Convivial bars, moreover, must stand high in the orders of the ordinary on the simple assumption that so long as they are with us, hope still keeps one small clearing in the jungles of our days.

MANHATTAN MYTHOLOGY: Among the least trivia of 1962, I dabbled for a while in TV, and, in mid-dabble, picked up the story of a friend who had been working on a "Special" (a TV show not part of a regular series). In the course of things he had spent several days lining up an important lady as a guest for the show. The lady had other commitments, and in order to persuade her to change her plans, my friend poured out his soul on the importance of the show and, furthermore, pledged himself to the scrupulous performance of all sorts of promises. His soul firmly in hock, he returned to the office only to be told the show had been canceled.

"But I have been pitching sincerities at her for three days!" he cried to the man behind the executive desk. "What am I going to tell that woman after all the promises I made her?"

The man behind the desk proved his executive caliber with an instant pronouncement.

"Level with her!" he said. "Lie!"

January 19, 1963

Mailbag: The Children's Hour

A junior correspondent who read some of my children's poems wrote me the following letter which I pass on in full, though with the signature veiled in the hope of protecting any future reputation he may acquire as a speller:

Dear Mr. Giradi:
I have been nijoing your book about poems. And the one where the boy was not hurgry. It is very halaryes.

Your fiend,
John Do

THE HOT HORSE AGAIN: I recently raised the question of the moral responsibility of jet pilots who bail out of disabled ships over thickly settled areas. Any number of readers read my remarks as an attack upon the Air Force, and all sorts of experts lectured me on glide ratios and on the absolute unmaneuverability of jets that have lost power. The latest objection is filed by the irate wife of an F102 pilot. She encloses the following newspaper clipping (undated and with no reference to the name of the paper) but with a dedication that reads: "Lest we forget the stupid and biased article you wrote some weeks ago":

PILOT STAYS WITH PLANE

Malibu, Calif. (AP)—When his engine failed at 40,000 feet, an Air Force pilot pointed the nose of his F106 jet fighter into the clouds in a blind descent—and emerged from the overcast directly over the center of Los Angeles.

Maj. Keith D. Chrietzberg stayed at the controls, stretched his glide as far as possible, and headed for the sea, 20 miles away.

He crossed the coastline at Malibu only 1,000 feet up, fired his ejection seat, and parachuted to the sea as his plane crashed offshore. He was picked up uninjured by a fishing boat minutes later.

Let me say to all partisans that I am happy to salute Maj. Chrietzberg as an *hombre*. The point of my original remarks was exactly that none other should apply for those cockpits. I cannot, of course, speak for the Major, but I suspect he would agree with me that had he done any less than he did, he would belong in jail for extracting federal pay under false pretenses. The thing about an *hombre* is that he does what has to be done. Had a lesser man bailed out and let her crash on the town below, and had I written to question that way of doing things, I am sure another body of experts would have been reading me the lecture on glide ratios, on the fact that controls lock when a jet looses power, and even—as one self-important insect argued—that the pilot's life is more important than the life of any civilian because the government had invested so much money in his training. Tell it to Major Chrietzberg, boys. I never said it was easy: only that there is no other way.

Happy landings, Major—happier ones. And thank you from all of us.

CLEAR, CONCISE, AND DOWN-TO-EARTH: Mr. G.M.C. of Sheboygan, Wisconsin, is no man for ambiguities. He writes to say: "I feel sure I echo the desire of many readers of *SR* to have a clear, concise, and down-to-earth exposition of what is, and what is not poetry." And he wants to know what I think of that.

What does one say to such a question? It is, alas, one of the commonest, as well as perhaps the dreariest, out of the mailbag. Nothing is less useful to the life of the arts than this literal-minded insistence on clear, concise, down-to-earth definition. At the comic end of the scale such litter-heads equate their demands with horse sense. At the equally comic, but purportedly intellectual other end, the same demand is made by analogy to the sciences, wherein (if we may believe these champions of certainty) all things are precisely defined. I have even had it put to me that psychology is a science, that it deals with human behavior, that the arts are one sort of human behavior, and that, therefore, the arts are a subbranch of psychology. Or if any reader would rather keep the betrayal within the family, let me cite from Oscar Williams's introduction to his *A Little Treasury of Modern Poetry* the following absurdity:

Extraordinary advances in critical method make the inspection of a poem by a first-class critic as close and careful as a chemical analysis.

A dreadful sort of thinking: the same words might be used in discussing the inspection of a sewer pipe by a "first-class" civil

244

engineer. Let it at least be said in Oscar Williams's favor that absurd as his attempts at critical statement have always been, he keeps a human psyche inside himself when he is not trying to make all-embracing statements about it, and that he can therefore (and does) pick good poems for his anthologies. Better a bird that flies than a flight-engineer who cannot get off the ground.

But for the totally ground-bound: nothing. Art simply is not for them. The man who wants his life-concepts in terms as plain as dollars and cents had best turn bookkeeper. (And let him stay away, at that, from tax accounting, lest he find even his digits changing complexion on him.) If poetry is to become a clear, concise, and down-to-earth exercise it can only do so by losing contact with the unclear, unconcise, and up-in-the-dreamscape shadows of any man's consciousness once he has opened it to the uncertainties and ambiguities of his own introspection. Or, for that matter, whether or not he ever does open himself to incipient self-awareness. For we do not become less complex in our stupidities but only better armored against an awareness of them.

It is of the nature of mind to reach. And what it reaches to at its best is forever beyond definition. What can be put within the boundaries of definition is never more than the kindergarten of perception. A beginning student of chemistry may deal in certainties. A chemical researcher, on the other hand, is a man reaching beyond definition to a better understanding of phenomena. At their far reach, our best chemists cannot even manage to be clear, concise, and down-to-earth about the difference between some organic compounds and some elementary life forms.

What the chemist comes to at that forward end of his professional development, the arts begin with as their native idiom and substance. There is no hope for any cause in this sort of impatient oversimplification, as there is no peace to be made with it.

If G.M.C. can grasp that point, we are at a beginning of hope. If not, I attach the following alternate reply:

Dear Sir:

I am afraid I cannot really answer your question until you help me put it in an answerable context. As a suggestion, if you will submit to being psychoanalyzed by an IBM machine, I shall be happy, upon receipt of certification that your nervous system has been properly transistorized and push-buttoned, to provide you with a clear, concise, down-to-earth (and therefore inhuman) exposition of what is and is not poetry.

Yours truly,
JOHN CIARDI.

March 2, 1963

Burning the Files

I have been at my annual chore of burning the accumulated files of the finished year. Sufficient unto the year are the papers thereof. The archivists we shall always have with us, but let me yet believe that every desk and every man's psyche should be searched and thinned out from time to time toward the dream of starting afresh, the litter tidied, old sins forgiven, old identities canceled, and all the world new and possible again.

My last armful of notes, clippings, and letters has now made it into the fireplace, and though I cannot exactly claim that my psyche has been wiped clean, I can once more see my desk top, on which only these last few items remain, without my really knowing why, except that something stayed my hand from chucking them into the fire until I had looked at them again.

I HOPE HE MADE IT: From *Life* magazine I recently clipped toward the praise of possible man the story of Navy Lieutenant Frank Ellis and have saved it in admiration.

In July of 1962, Lieutenant Ellis found he was about to crash his jet fighter into a populated area and stayed with his damaged ship long enough to steer it into a patch of woods. By the time

246

he felt free to eject himself, however, he was down to sixty-five feet. Somehow he survived, but at a frightful cost. Along with other injuries, he lost both legs below the knee.

If there is any vocabulary left us in which to praise a man, let me hope for as much of it as may speak a praise of Lieutenant Ellis.

Praise him first for his hard-pressed decision and for knowing how and when to make it. Lieutenant Ellis reported that at the time he found himself in trouble, his thoughts went back to a session in which he and other pilots talked about what they would do in a squeeze between bailing out over settled country or staying with the ship in the hope of crashing it into an open space. Lieutenant Ellis, in trouble, found that he had made his decision during the talk. Let me suspect he had made it long before in the very act of being himself.

And praise him once again for being the unstoppable man. Despite his double amputation, he fought the Navy's request that he resign, trained himself to pass every physical test required of a pilot, and insisted on being returned to flying duty.

As matters stood in late summer of 1963, he had won the Navy's permission to fly on limited status and was about to appear before a special board of flight surgeons convened to pass on his request for full flying status.

And so stands my file at year's end, for I have been able to find no further news of him. I hope some *SR* reader will have information that I may pass on.

I hope he made it. It only takes the technology of a society to design and build a jet, but it takes all the character of a society to put such a man as Lieutenant Ellis at the controls; and never until they are in the hands of just such a man are they really controls.

UNIVERSAL LITERACY: In the decline from praise to the sort of rueful recognition that better describes the world we are all trying to make a sad peace with, I find I have set aside two memos on the school system. I am indebted to John Reimann of New York for the following excerpt from the newspaper of what he describes (without otherwise identifying) as "one of New York's better-known progressive schools."

247

We are often confronted in a test situation with a question which [sic] means nothing to us. If we are especially adept, we are able to make a glorious "something" out of this "nothing." The anonymous students (for our purposes X and Y) are truly artists in this field. Below are two chemistry test questions followed by X's and Y's responses. Spelling and grammatical errors have been left uneditted [sic].

Question: Metallic solids are good conductors of electricity while [sic] ionic solids are not. Explain briefly but completely.

Answer: It is true that metallic solids are good conductors of electricity while other ionic solids are not. However, lets not get carried away with this statement because even though these metallic solids are good conductors they do have other bad qualities and implications, where ionic solids really don't have any truly bad features excluding the one mentioned above. This just goes to say that solids are of many different types and species and have many good and bad qualities just as other things do. Therefore, there is really no reason in taking sides in this case; it shows definitely lack of personnel integrity and good judgement on the part of those involved in this prejudice and injustice to the fine character of both ionic and metallic solids. This kind of prejudice can start here in this more or less unserious tone but can go on and have much more serious implications, implications that even I would not mention.

Question: Explain briefly but completely—liquid hydrogen cloride [sic] does not conduct electricity, but hydrocloric [sic] acid does.

Answer: Liquid hydrogen cloride does not conduct electricity because it does not contain those substances which hydrocloric acid does not lack. However, though hydrocloric acid is a good conductor of electricity it too has its disadvantages.

In the same folder, for reasons that will, I hope, declare themselves, I had filed from the Los Angeles *Times* a report by Mary Ann Callan on Dorothy Parker, schoolteacher. Miss Parker, it seems, had put in a rueful session at Los Angeles State College, and she apparently found in her classrooms plenty of solids but no conductors of electricity. A college, she discovered, is "18,000 students and 150 parking spaces." Within it, she was appalled to find no real pleasure in reading, a bland predisposition to happy TV endings, and a central lust for "three units" with the only regret that her course did not count for six. Asked by Miss Callan if she could write a satire about education in our modern colleges, she answered "It's much too sad to do that."

To which let me add only Ugolino's words to Dante in the last pit of Hell: "And if you do not weep, at what *are* you used to weeping?"

THE AMERICAN LANGUAGE: PROGRESS NOTES: Nor, having lived through the year in which a hair remover leg-goo was plugged on TV as "fragrant odorless," can I consign my last scraps to the fire without quoting gratefully the following epitaph on the language by Mitchell P. Briggs of Fresno, California.

ANOTHER WORD ON WEBSTER'S THIRD

I imply and you infer,
But please take care and don't refer
To Webster's Third, which may imply
It's all the same to you and I.

February 8, 1964

Bureaucracy and Frank Ellis

These last weeks, as I traveled around the country on a lecture tour, I kept searching all the papers of fifty different cities for final word in the case of Lieutenant Frank Ellis versus Navy bureaucracy. I was all but certain that a man could never win against the paper-clippers. Yet Lieutenant Ellis's case was so powerful that I went on hoping. Now the word has finally come, and, I am sorry to say, the paper-clippers won and the man lost.

Lieutenant Frank Ellis was flying a Navy jet fighter in California on July 12, 1962, when it went out of control and seemed about to crash into a row of houses. Lieutenant Ellis could have bailed out and let his plane plow through those houses, but he stayed with it, fighting the controls until he had it safely aimed into a patch of open ground. Only then did he eject himself, but with so little altitude that he suffered injuries requiring the amputation of both legs below the knee.

Heaven knows what special fuel goes into the psychic power plant of such a man. Despite his double amputation, Lieutenant Ellis trained himself to use his wooden legs so well that he passed every Navy test for physical fitness and fought against all precedent to remain on flying status. Finally a special board of Navy flight surgeons was convened in Pensacola to pass on his fitness and Lieutenant Ellis had his triumph: despite his handicap, he was reinstated to full Goup I flying status.

But Washington's desk-bound corps had yet to be heard from, and so an end of triumph. Group I status, as I understand it, qualifies a Navy pilot for every sort of flying including carrier landings. Group II, if I have it right, qualifies a pilot for every sort of flying except carrier landings. In Washington, Navy Under Secretary Paul B. Fay, Jr., reviewed the findings of the special board and decided that Lieutenant Ellis could be reinstated only to Group III status, which is to say he could only fly as a copilot in the company of pilots with Group I or Group II status.

The desk-bound, you may be sure, have delicate antennae and various sets of them. One semisensitive set feels out the mood of those lower down in the table of organization. A second and supersensitive set feels out the mood of those higher up in the anthill. A third set, almost as sensitive as the second, feels out something called "public relations."

That third set could not fail to feel out the fact that Lieutenant Ellis had become an American hero. Obviously it is good public relations to let heroes have their glory. But the message that came down the second set of antennae was the one that carried the real signal. And what the signal said was the central message of all bureaucracy: "Take cover."

The Official Voice was full of solicitude. It praised Lieutenant Ellis's "motivation and drive." It pointed out, however, that a carrier landing requires "a very delicate touch on the brakes and rudder." And with avuncular sincerity it turned to Lieutenant Ellis himself. "Frank," it said, "you and your wife could never live it down if your flying killed someone."

Meaning "Group III."

The Official Voice even got Lieutenant Ellis to make the sounds of a good loser. What else can a junior officer do? He expressed his thanks, he knew he had been given every consideration, he was grateful that he was able to remain "a useful aviator in the Navy." It had all, no doubt, been a pleasure and a privilege, and all hearts were touched.

I think it is called "good sportsmanship," or something of the sort. But if Lieutenant Ellis has to play it out in the vocabulary of the game-of-life boys, I have easy talents as a rotten sport, and, in the most pertinent vocabulary to come to mind, I say it stinks.

It is, to be sure, a tricky business to land a modern jet fighter on a carrier deck; so tricky that one in every so many landings is bound to go wrong. Nevertheless, Lieutenant Ellis has demonstrated the delicacy of his touch to the satisfaction of an examining board, as he has demonstrated the firmness of his purpose to all the world. Nor has it been demonstrated that the Navy has anyone better qualified for carrier operations. Nor, I must believe, is qualification the point. The Official Voice is simply taking cover against the possibility that one of those bad landings might be made by Lieutenant Ellis.

For if that landing is made by any other pilot in the Navy, the brass will have nothing on its hands but a case of operational percentages. If, on the other hand, it is made by Lieutenant Frank Ellis, then the desk jockey responsible for giving him that clearance is immediately guilty of bad judgment.

In bureaucratic logic, bad judgment is any decision that can lead to embarrassing questions, even if the decision was itself right. Therefore take cover. No man with an eye on a career can afford to be right when he can manage to be safe. The desk jockey who

251

cut Lieutenant Ellis down to Group III knew what he was doing, all right. And he had his public relations vocabulary all primed for it. But in my vocabulary he was avoiding the only valorous decision he could have made in honor of a valorous man, whereby all of us have one less assurance overhead.

June 13, 1964

Still in Defense

Among the rebuttals I have since received in the mail, I was especially taken by one from a Navy pilot, a good man I once had the pleasure of meeting, but one, I am sure, who will prefer to remain anonymous.

I share—or perhaps surpass—your distaste for bureaucracy, and I am a past associate and admirer of Ellis. Nonetheless, I think you have a sticky wicket here when you suggest that a man with artificial limbs should be placed in the position of attempting to taxi a modern fighter airplane on the always treacherous and crowded deck of an aircraft carrier. As one who has done it, and as one who has been responsible for the flight-deck operations of a carrier, I would view with stark terror a situation in which a pilot was attempting to taxi with anything less than the ultimate possible capability. Artificial limbs could never provide the required "feel." I would, however, be perfectly happy with the situation anywhere but on a carrier; Douglas Bader proved that legs are not necessary for fighter pilots.

Here, obviously, is an authoritative voice, whereas mine is, just as obviously, distant and amateur in such matters. But has the last word been said?

252

Wing Air Commander Douglas Bader was certainly a case in point, a double amputee who continued to fly as one of the RAF's best. And the Luftwaffe had another such, as I understand, though with few details in hand, in Oberst Rudel. Lieutenant Ellis's case is unprecedented only among American pilots. There is precedent enough abroad to enforce the argument that where there is enough man, the legs are attached to him, not he to the legs.

Who, I must insist, really knows how much man Lieutenant Ellis's legs are attached to? My correspondent thinks those legs leave Lieutenant Ellis short of "ultimate possible capability." But can any man know that to be a firm fact?

It is firm fact that Lieutenant Ellis has passed his physical tests with room to spare. He has even taught himself to waterski on his wooden legs. I wonder if any man would have thought that possible until Lieutenant Ellis did it. We are dealing, sir, with an hombre. I submit that he may just be more hombre than can be guessed at in a general way.

And why leave it to any man's guess, however serious the guesser? All that is necessary is to let Lieutenant Ellis show what he can do in an actual test. The test can certainly be arranged so that no one else need be endangered. Let him try. Let him kill himself trying, if it must come to that. The man wants to try. And who has earned a better right to be judged by what he can do rather than by a guess about what he can do?

I am saying that I refuse to generalize about "ultimate possible capability." And I am saying to the Navy that it still has a chance to give a good man a fitting answer. Let the Navy's experts—my correspondent among them—set up any test of flying skill. Let them take Under Secretary Fay off the hook by establishing that any man who can pass that test is automatically qualified for full flying status. Then give Lieutenant Ellis a plane and let him supply his own answers. Let the Navy do that and I shall withdraw, with full apologies, every word I said about bureaucracy and playing it safe with the desk jockeys. It may just turn out that Lieutenant Ellis is his own authority on his own "ultimate possible capability."

I think he can do it. If the tricky part, as my correspondent assures me, is the business of shooting landings, of taxiing, and of taking off from the crowded deck of a carrier, and if the Navy will let Lieutenant Ellis try it in a two-seater, he can have my carcass in the back seat any time as a private vote of confidence. Not for acrobatics, thank you. It is an aging carcass I am pledging, and I do not care to find out how many gravities it can stand in a pull-out. Just the tricky part, please, without the heroics. I never set out to be an hombre in the first place. But I think I am ready to take Frank Ellis's word any time for what he can and cannot do.

July 11, 1964

War Surplus

I know nothing about the Army's way of taking inventory and of checking its accounts, but in the course of a recent conversation on something else I was reminded of a question I have long wanted to ask the officer in charge of the ammunition inventory at Mather Field, California, toward the end of 1945. Specifically, I should like to know what he did about approximately 12,000,000 rounds of belted fifty-caliber ammunition that was not supposed to be there but was.

I know both that it was there and that it was not supposed to be, a bit of information I came by as part of a long process that began in October of 1944. At that time the B-29 on which I was technically a gunner and actually a rather expensive piece of excess baggage left Walker Field, Kansas, for something called "staging" at Kearney, Nebraska. At Kearney, after a month-long fiddle-faddle, we were finally set to move on. As one part of the final preparations, our ammunition cans were filled with 12,000 rounds of machine-gun ammunition, one belt of 1,000 rounds to each gun. Our immediate destination was Mather Field, California, which was designated our Port of Aerial Embarkation for a top-secret Pacific destination—and certainly no more than 100 per cent of the people at Walker, Kearney, and Mather, and something less than 90 per cent of the people within fifty miles of those fields knew for sure that it was Saipan.

Within the technicalities of everything, as I dimly understood them, we were in the American Theater of War until our wheels left the ground at Mather, whereupon we were instantly in the Pacific Theater. The relevant point within the technicality was that in the American Theater we were accountable for a number of items of equipment, including ammunition, that became officially expendable the instant we were in the Pacific Theater. So at least the case was explained to me.

The legalist who did the explaining was an enterprising sergeant at Mather. His particular enterprise was whiskey, his system was flawless, and even his prices—as befitted his status as a large-scale jobber—were moderate.

What he proposed was a happy coordination. The final inspection would be finished at least an hour before takeoff. If, immediately after the inspection, we would strip the ammunition belts out of the cans and pile them by the aft hatch, he would arrive with a truck, haul off the ammunition to put back in the dump, and sell us, at $60 a case, enough whiskey to fill up our ammunition cans.

There were eleven men on a B-29 flight crew and we were flying our maintenance crew chief with us. Not everyone was interested, but it took the rest of us something like ten minutes to ante up $1,500 wherewith to stake a claim on twenty-five cases. For the word had also found its way back from our top-secret destination (maybe written on the back of the sealed orders?) that the going price for black market whiskey on Saipan was $35 a fifth.

The information, moreover, turned out to be exactly right, though we did not know then that the whiskey being black-marketed to G.I.'s at $35 was a back-flow from the monthly ration supplied to officers at something like $1.10 a fifth.

In any case our deal was made, the ammunition belts were stripped from the cans and dumped in the sergeant's truck, the twenty-five cases were lovingly stored in the ammunition cans. Off we went (our ammunition obviously expended the minute we

255

took off) for Oahu, and then to Kwajelein, and so to Saipan. We could not, of course, have fired our guns, but that was no problem since there was nothing to fire them at this side of Saipan, or, for that matter, this side of Japan.

We arrived on Saipan in time for the first Tokyo raid in November of 1944, and I flew back (with the same pilot but with an otherwise different crew) in late September of 1945. In the meantime, well over 1,000 B-29s had flown out from Mather to Saipan, Tinian, and Guam. And as best I could check into the fact of things, by observation and by exchange with other rumor-mongers, practically every incoming plane was armed with 90-proof ammunition cans. A thousand whiskey-specials out of the total arrivals seems in every way a conservative guess. Which is to say that at least 1,000 times in the course of that bit-less-than-a-year, the B-29s that left Mather had made a gift to the ammunition dump of twelve belts of fifty-caliber ammunition, each belt containing 1,000 rounds, whereby a total of 12,000,000 rounds must have free-enterprised its way back into the inventory.

For all I know, the Army may have a simple system for taking care of such matters. Though from where I sat, nothing in the Army turned out to be simple except the minds of most of the G.I.s and of all of the officers.

I don't really know how it would go, but I have mused at times over the mental picture of an ordnance officer checking and re-checking his accounts.

And then I have found myself imagining one of those decisive squareheads who would *make* it come out right. He is the one I think I am familiar with, the small-town Alexander with a Boy Scout knife with which to saw through any Gordian knot. Such a character would balance the books whether or not they liked being balanced. He is the one who would call out the local troops for a special fitness program, line them up on the firing range, and keep them there until the 12,000,000 rounds had been fired. At that point he would announce to the troops that they were fit, let them understand that they were lucky to have so farsighted an officer in command, send them off to make up the work they had been neglecting for their range practice, and himself return to a neatly balanced inventory—a place for every fiction and every fiction in its place.

256

As I say, I am only indulging my imagination. I haven't a firm fact in sight on which to hang anything like a conclusion. But, if only as an exercise in conjecture, it seems reasonable enough. It might have been that way. That, at least, would have been recognizably an Army way of doing things.

In any case, if you happened to be working at that ammunition dump, and if you ever had occasion to wonder about those 12,-000,000 rounds, this belated account will explain how they got there.

Or if you happened to G.I. at Mather in late 1945 or so, and if you found yourself doing a lot of range work with fifty calibers, this account may explain why.

And in case there are any left-over curiosities, let me say I had hit a crap game on my first arrival at Mather and was able to put in $480 for eight cases, which allowed me to set up housekeeping on Saipan with a whiskey cellar worth $3,360 at G.I. rates. Though as I figure it out at officer rates it only came to $105.60—which will once more illustrate the economic fallacy of being poor. It costs too much. At times, in fact, I think only the very rich can afford it.

November 9, 1963

An Open Letter to Twenty-Seven Irate Virtues

Dear Irate Virtues:
The belated memorandum I filed with the former United States Army Air Corps in this column, discussed a large quantity of fifty-caliber belted machinegun ammunition that accumulated at Mather Field in 1944–45, a surplus resulting from the custom prev-

257

alent among B-29 crews of stripping their ammunition cans in order to load them with bottles of whiskey before taking off for the Pacific. May I stress the point that I was discussing a custom of the tribe and not only my own arrangements within it.

As far as I know, the ammunition went back to the ammunition dump for whatever audit awaited it, the whiskey went to Saipan, Tinian, or Guam, the war went on, and no one aware of this change in the bill of lading found cause to think the aerial offensive against Japan had been damaged.

No one, that is, until my memorandum moved twenty-seven of you to thunder against my character, to charge me with sabotage, and even, some of you, to demand that I be tried for treason in time of war.

To the charge against my character, I plead lack of interest. To the charge of sabotage, I confess that my induction was an obvious blow at the war effort and I throw myself on the mercy of the court. To the charge of treason, I plead Patrick Henry—if this be treason, make the most of it.

I am not sure, as a matter of fact, of what I am charged, except that your indignations are involved. To clear the record, let me say that I did not take my supply of whiskey overseas in order to sell it. On that point I need not even plead honorable intention. In the first place, had I sold the stuff on the black market, I should only have had to buy it back later at the same prices—a transaction to no purpose. I did trade some of it for minor luxuries of the good life in the jungle. And I managed to get rid of surprising amounts of it in two memorable parties—one on Christmas Eve of 1944 and one on New Year's Eve of approaching 1945. Must a man give up a civil social life simply because the Army in its uncertainty decides to call him a soldier? I was under such powerful civilian compulsion to play host and did so in a civilian sport shirt and loved it. In any case, I had no notion of trading my snug whiskey for anything so random as money.

In the second place, it is a fact known to all informed citizens that the Army is a floating crap game followed around by a few sharks and swarms of minnows. The trick of staying clear of the sharks is probably beyond the reach of pure virtue, but no wary man need go broke and thirsty for long. The minnows will provide.

258

I did, as a matter of fact, run out of my original supply long before my almost-year on Saipan was up. In a squeeze, I suppose, I might have used my minnow-money to buy on the black market. But I was never squeezed that hard. In one way or another, I managed to lay hands on various amounts of officers' whiskey. (Remember, dear Virtues, that officers were getting whiskey at $1.10 a fifth and that GIs were buying the same stuff on the black market at $35 a fifth.)

Let me particularly thank General Emmett (Rosie) O'Donnell for several generous contributions, nor will I dishonor the spirit of a fighting man's generosity by suggesting that he was unaware of his own largess. And let me thank, too, various brass-bound specimens who regularly offered me bribes of whiskey when I was taken off my crew and put in charge of Awards and Decorations for the 73rd Wing. Since it was my job to write up all decorations, and since all brass was ribbon-happy, these senior guardians of virtue obviously felt that a well-oiled friend at court could do no harm, and they paid up hopefully. Let me assure them (and you) that they never got so much as an extra adjective for it, and that wherever possible they got nothing but the truth to sit blank beside their theater ribbons. In any case, as I hope I make clear, I kept myself supplied. Supply, as you may gather, is one of my hobbies.

Is that part of the charge you bring? I am, I confess, a man of fixed tendencies. I happen to like whiskey in holdable amounts. And at the end of any day on which I have been seriously shot at, I tend to crave it to the point of a relaxing fuzziness. If, that is, I have not been punctured—and I am happy to say I never was.

One of the troubles with trying to drink when you have been punctured is that the stuff might leak out. Conversely, one supreme reason for drinking when one has not been punctured is the simple and grateful celebration of the fact that one is still a non-leaky container. What a lovely skin it can be when it is still whiskey-tight!

There is even, I shall argue, a social contract involved, and that on the evening of any day in which my country asks me to get shot at for the public good, the country is left with a certain courteous responsibility to offer me a drink, circumstances permitting. On Saipan, circumstances always permitted the country to be generous in its dispensation to officers, whereas citizens in merely GI skins had to make do with one can of warm beer a night.

On that point, dear Virtues, I must hold the country to be in default. I was in the Army as a civilian-in-transit. It was my civilian sense, and still is, that I had paid off my end of the social contract, at least for that day, in putting my civilian hide on the line. My dues thus paid, I was under no moral compulsion to take officers, or the Army, at their own evaluation of the social order. What's whiskey for one is whiskey for all.

From where I sat (behind the wing at the right blister) it was clear that the Army had misread the social contract, and I, accordingly, took civilian precautions in defense of democratic principle. The terms of my contract are clear enough: a skin put up at auction entitles bearer to a partial skinful when off duty. These terms, I can report, made for a peaceful coexistence, left my efficiency unimpaired by thirst neuroses, and allowed me to leave the Army with no regrets on either side. A clear gain: by my own free-enterprise I made up for the Army's shortsightedness and so helped to maintain a working balance. The defeat of Japan, I submit, was inevitable.

So much for duty and the social contract, to whatever extent this much may answer your charges. If I have, in fact, located the root of your charges and indignations.

If on the other hand, you are suggesting that the United States Army is an intellectual principle of social justice to which it was my duty to bow without question, and that those brass-bound fruitheads at the Officers' Club Bar were a fatherhood to which I was obliged to respond with nothing but obedient devotion, then you, dear Virtues, must allow me to think of you as having all the social and intellectual acuity of a cereal-stuffed meatball, and I shall insist that you further permit me the pleasure of signing myself:

To your negligible damnation,

T/Sgt. J. Ciardi, 11069345 (ex).

January 18, 1964

Skin

Every major occasion of public ritual, I am now convinced, is a backward step in evolution. Show me a massive public observance and I will show you the patterns of the tribe below civilization.

Along with everyone I know, I recently watched the tribes of Albion perform the ritual of burying Winston Churchill. My own view, let me confess, has been limited. I don't own a TV set: ours quit working about a year ago and I chucked it out of the house. Nor, let me add, have I had any regrets: we even go so far as to read a book these days, sometimes we even talk to one another, and when we do, we turn and look at the person we are talking to instead of tossing the remark over one shoulder, our eyes riveted on the magic screen; and in general I find in us a better sense of house and family than I was able to feel in the days when the set was forever on and forever the center.

These are, of course, asides, and I make them primarily to explain that I have not watched the Churchill rites from start to finish, but only in glimpses, as I found myself near someone else's set for a while.

It is possible, therefore, that I missed the total cumulative impact of the ritual. Still, I am left with no doubt that wherever I sampled it, it gave off the same sense of parade, a sort of hypnosis of mass motion, an idea so ornately primitive that it never failed to leave me uneasy.

I have, let me say, no thought of dishonoring a great man. What word of mine could? The record of Winston Churchill's life is self-declaring and self-summing. I am simply recording—to one side of great occasion, and from half-known sources within myself —that parades dismay me. I find myself wondering if the idea of the human race can be expressed in any worse way than by columns of men marching.

I watch the wooden procession, and I am reminded of something Einstein once said, sharing some of my revulsion at the mechanism a man becomes when he takes his place in the ranks. "If the object of the individual is to march in a column"—I am approximating a remark I cannot quote exactly—"he need never have developed a brain: the spinal column would have been enough."

And I am reminded, with something of a shudder, of my own experience of hypnosis-in-ranks. Back in 1942 I signed on with the Aviation Cadets and was eventually delivered by slow freight to the Classification Center at Nashville, arriving with my fellow-cattle at about 2:00 A.M. of a full moon. In our various states of decay (we had been in our cattle cars for over forty hours) we were lined up and marched into camp, an officer calling off a quiet and insistent cadence.

And suddenly it happened. It was the moon, it was the release from confinement, it was the cadence, it was the terrible fact that we were all so young, it was the hush of the night, it was the beginning of whatever unknown life we had signed on for. It was all those things together. And suddenly we were marching.

I don't mean simply that we were moving down the road. We were marching. A rhythm rose and fell. The heads and shoulders before me became part of a regular undulation. The tramp of our feet became a heartbeat. A tide set in and carried us. And I was appalled to find the hypnosis of it was as savagely joyous as it was mindless.

We were no longer men. We were a powerful rhythmic Thing full of lethal possibility. Had the command been given, I felt sure the Thing would have turned in any direction and tramped over and through anything, without a thought. It would do so by the particular hypnosis that detached every man from his own will and his own idea of himself. I sensed instantly what the professional soldier is after in his drill and discipline, and I knew instantly that we were all in danger of ourselves. From that instant I became a hopelessly bad soldier, forever concerned to rescue myself from the hypnosis of the mindless. My one idea was to save my skin—no, not necessarily to avoid danger: being

262

young and a fool I was eager to see how I would react to it. I mean the skin of identity and idea.

For an idea has to be something with a skin around it. If you cannot accept the necessity for that binding, go read Emmanuel Kant. Then maybe when you are dead, your skinless ghost can sit around the hole in an atom and talk to its echo about Pure Reason.

In the meantime, however, you need to be inside a skin to make even that decision. And not only inside a skin, but in a given kind of skin. For there is no skin without intellectual characteristics. Suppose, for example, that your proto-grandfather half a million years ago had been a reptile instead of a monkey's cognate. Would a later cognate have had Oedipus to think about? That idea could never have made it through that kind of skin. He'd have had to write about something like yolk-fetishism instead. *Playboy* would be featuring tattoo patterns of the month. And Caligula would have gone down in history as a monster who organized egg-splattering orgies. These, of course, are only guesses. I don't have the right sort of skin to verify them in.

I have to go back—along with Confucius and Buddha and Aristotle—to the kind of skin we got from that monkey's cognate. Unless, of course, you live in Tennessee, in which case you got yours directly from the monkey.

Skin, of course, comes with various attachments. Ears are the attachment that finally imagined Mozart. Eyes have been imagining all sorts of things. Noses have been smelling them out. Lips have been mouthing them. The inside flap that became a tongue has been tasting them and rattling on about them. And the whole shebang has been feeling its way to such ideas as hot and cold, rough and smooth, sexy and blah. Many of these ideas are still not far from where the monkey's cognate left them, but others have come a long way.

And other ideas have cropped up inside the skin, all up and down the nervous system—which looks a little like a Portuguese man-of-war and which knows less about what ocean it is floating on.

But the most lost, I turn away thinking, is an hours-long processional of mechanical soldiers who have peeled off their skins and glued on uniforms in order to become part of a tribal cadence.

Mercifully, night and exhaustion will set in. They will fall out of ranks, loosen the uniform, and be men again, back in their own skins and concerned with the hollow inside and with the blisters outside. With self-measuring fact.

But keep them in those ranks and in that cadence for long, and they will certainly march all the way back to the tribal clearing behind civilization. I think the fear I feel in every parade is just the fear that the men and boys inside that rhythmic monster will never find their way back from that clearing, which is the darkest place under the skin. Every parade, alas, is toward it. The one hope is that all ranks will break soon enough to leave each man in his own skin again.

March 13, 1965

Dear Mr. President

Dear Mr. President:

I am not at all sure a private citizen should clutter your mailbox even to offer you his admiration. As a matter of fact, I am not sure I am a whole private citizen. Ever since my wife joined the League of Women Voters she has been using up 100 percent of her private citizenship and 50 percent of mine. When she gets back from meetings, I am free within my 50 percent to do as I am told. I don't really mind that sort of executive authority, especially since she knows she is always right. Yet, I find myself sympathizing with your feelings. I, too, would like to persuade someone that I am a truly peerless leader. Every now and then, therefore, I issue a wisely balanced declaration of authority along with a plea for a little basic 100 percent faith in my peerlessness. And every time I finish speaking, a self-appointed elite of local commentators goes on the air with immediate and querulous criticism.

264

Like you, I would hate to impose a gag law. In fairness, I prefer that they impose it on themselves—or else. It seems to me I have earned the right to be Big Daddy to a respectful and unquerulous family to which I freely grant the right of happy obedience. The trouble is that my family is too American for long-range comparison. It keeps insisting I put up or shut up.

I know I have tried everything I could think of to create the right image. Last New Year's Day I called them together and apologized openly for the cost-of-living cut in last Christmas. I begged them, however, to have faith in me, promising in return that I would lead them to a new Christmas before another New Year rolled around. All I got out of that was a disorderly demonstration by the kids. They staged an all-night Bronx cheer. I must say they certainly did sound like impudent intellectual snobs to me.

That's when I had a long talk with my wife and appointed her official Silent Majority in residence. She promised to go along with me, at least in front of the kids, but in no time at all I began to hear her alto Bronx cheer from the back of the choir.

Mr. President, you know the feeling of being in too deep to pull out. I hauled the dressmaker's dummy down from the attic, put three mirrors around it to create an instant multitude, and then set up the dummy as the new Silent Majority. I think you may be happy to know it worked, too. I don't think I have ever seen anything as silent as my Silent Majority.

Yet, I confess I woke up this morning feeling at least inadequate and probably fictitious, though that isn't entirely why I thought of you. I did have some idea of writing to offer my sympathy as a fellow sufferer, but I wasn't focused yet. Then, groping my way to breakfast, I stumbled over the dummy and smashed the mirrors, reducing my built-in Silent Majority to a multiple mess. It was then I really began to identify with you and to sense all you have gone through for us. Your house is so much larger than ours that you must have a miserable time groping around for something you can sink your teeth into, and stumbling over a lot more dummies than I have been able to invent out of my private sense of fantasy.

Like you, too, I leased my house from the Southside Mortgage Company and I had to put up with some nasty stipulations. I had,

265

for example, to take on a handy man picked out by Southside. I even had to promise on the q.t. to campaign for a judge that Southside wanted on the bench. He was nothing I wanted to meet in court, but it was a case of play ball or not get the lease, and I had to have the lease. Luckily, Southside's nominee flunked his final exam and I was off that hook, but I still have this handy man I got saddled with. We call him Spiral Ague, because he is forever dizzying around with chills and fevers due to a bad case of hoof-in-mouth disease.

Well, sir, I got my secretary to write up some phony speeches attacking everything that stood between me and my peerlessness, and she gave them to Ague and sent him out to deliver them in the local schools where the word was sure to reach my kids. I must say he spewed manfully, even if he couldn't pronounce all the words or manage to pause in all the right places. He just isn't much of a sight reader. Even at that it warmed my cockles to get back most of the favorable comments my wife and my secretary had planted for me.

I was, of course, careful to avoid Ague for weeks before he went off speechifying. My secretary took care of the whole business. When the kids started asking nasty questions, therefore, I was able to answer with a fine, clean-cut, high-minded, shoulders-back, chin-out air of busy hypocrisy that I hadn't seen or talked to Ague in weeks, and that whatever he had said, he was the only one who had said it.

Please don't think I admire you less if I suggest that maybe you have had enough practice on the domestic scene. Isn't it time for a little applied sneakiness on the international level? I know you have a whole mess of sneaky handy men that came with your lease. Couldn't you send one to out-sneak Hanoi, and maybe one to Greece and the Middle East, and some of the rest to Cuba, Biafra, Russia, Taiwan, Red China, and so forth? Bring that off, and I don't see how anyone could doubt your peerlessness.

Meanwhile I certainly would be grateful if you would send me some pamphlets on how to be peerless around the house, and on how to get all my querulous commentators to gag themselves.

I've tried, my secretary has tried, Spiral Ague has done as well as anyone could expect, and I even hid a tape player in the dummy

266

of my Silent Majority. The trouble is that dummies talk only when the button is pressed, and the button always makes a loud click. This generation of kids, alas, has a fantastic ear for the sound of a button-click. Drat their impudent snobbery, they have even memorized all the tapes, and they chant them at me in rock rhythm whenever I switch my dummy on.

That's why I keep dreaming of a dummy with a real voice in it. That would make those impudent snobs sit up and listen! Besides, if you put a real voice into it, there is always a good chance that it might stop being a dummy. I guess I really want to say that I hunger for a real voice. I know that if I once heard one I might stop waking up in the morning feeling at least inadequate and probably fictitious. I think I might even begin to feel real, even if I had to give up the dream of being peerless.

There must be a real voice somewhere inside one of your unused PR images. I write in the hope you might be persuaded to try it sometime. The man in the biggest house in the world should be able to say something real to the people in the little houses. I, for one, would like you to know that I will be waiting to hear what it might be, and that I will be more than eager to cheer for anything real.

In sympathy and admiration, sir, I remain,

Yours hopefully,

John Q. Citizen

December 13, 1969

Children's Corner

THE MAN WHO LIVED IN A HOUSE TOO BIG

for Dickie

There was a man who lived in a house,
  A big white house with a fence around it.
He lost his way from room to room
  And nobody ever found it.

He went to the phone and called the police:
  "Please come to my house and find me."
"Where are you?" they said. "I'm in one of my rooms
  With the rest before and behind me.

I'm in one of my rooms on one of my floors
  With the rest before and behind me,
Except for some above and below.
  If fifty men can't find me,

Send fifty more. I'll phone the cook
  To feed them pork and beans.
If you haven't found me by New Year's Day,
  I'll phone for the Horse Marines."

That was in January, I think,
  About three years ago.
A hundred-police and the Horse Marines
  Ate up ten tons or so

Of pork and beans, then ten tons more,
   And twenty of pancake pie.
The horses ate forty tons of oats.
   The cook began to cry.

The man kept phoning from room to room.
   The cook kept phoning the store.
Said the man on the phone, "Have you found me yet?"
   Said the cook, "Send ten tons more."

Said the hundred police and the Horse Marines
   Whenever they answered the phone,
"Can you look around and see where you are?"
   Said the man, "I am here and alone."

They finished the pork. They finished the beans.
   They finished the cook—she quit.
The phone keeps ringing in her room,
   But nobody answers it.

A hundred police and the Horse Marines
   Are running around and around
Looking for something else to eat,
   And there's nothing to be found.

Not pork and beans. Not pancake pie.
   Not a cup of dishwater tea.
Not even the man they came to find,
   Whoever he turns out to be

If he ever turns up from wherever he is
   In the big white house with the fence around it.
He is in there yet, but he lost his way
   And nobody ever found it.

February 6, 1971

Innocence and Other Drugs

Every beginning is an innocence. Nostalgia, I suspect, is the condition of thinking back to innocence as if one still wished for it and as if irony had never entered the world. Irony, of course, is the condition of recalling innocence wryly.

It is too late for me to reach for innocence, but I did find myself passing from nostalgia to irony as I read a recent newspaper article about bird watchers in the Jersey Meadows. There rose before me the ghostly images of a number of cheerful elderly ladies for whom I had run errands as a boy. They were graying maiden ladies, widows, or housewives who spent slow, easy days at home. All the most cheerful of them, as I recall, kept canaries. The canary, in fact, passed into my prop-room of associations as the bird of cheerfulness: I have never known a dour canary owner.

My ladies' canary cages were always lined with newspaper. One maiden lady for whom I used to run errands had a glassed-in porch she called a conservatory, and her cages swung above a wide bench of potted plants. All my other ladies kept their cages in a corner of the kitchen and spread newspapers under them to catch the seed the canaries scattered.

Canaries, when they feed, shake their heads, more than shake them—quiver them from side to side in that intensity of motion that marks all small birds. I recall them darting from an upper perch to the perch by their feeding trough; then they would jab their heads into the seed, hop back to the upper perch, and there quiver their heads, scattering as much seed as they swallowed and scattering it far.

There was generally a seedy mess under the cages, and my ladies would scold cheerfully as they swept it up, baby-talking that their fluffs were being bad that day. Then, dinner over for a while at that small but constant board, the fluffs would unreel astonishing trills and vibratos from their throats, cheered on by my ladies, who always explained that good fluff, dear fluff, sweet fluff was singing his thanks for the nice seed.

My ladies and their canaries kept happy houses, as I sensed things then: even a single canary in full throat could ring cheerfully; a chorus of six or eight, when fully turned on, could fill the house with rapture. "They are my sweet company all the day at home," my ladies would say in one form or another. And all of them would then add, always in the same words, "What would I do without them?"

Today's counterparts of my ladies of yesterday no longer think of doing without canaries. They have simply forgotten to think about them. I know one counterpart lady who dotes on two parakeets, coaxing them to fly to her fingers and to pick tidbits from her lips when she calls "Kiss me!" But I don't know any canary keepers. I know I haven't seen a canary in more than twenty years. The fact seems to be that canaries no longer sing—not at least as they used to, filling the house with rapturous fits of sound.

It was the newspaper article that called up these reflections of yesterday's ladies and their canaries. The bird watchers of the Jersey Meadows are not Sunday strollers but government men who scan the meadows with binoculars looking for flocks of excited birds. When they spot such a frenzied wheel—usually of blackbirds—they move a crew into those sodden flats and dig up the weeds the birds have been feeding on. The government men are a marijuana patrol.

The Jersey Meadows have long served as a dump for surrounding communities. In the days when rapturous canaries were strewing seeds around their cages and on the kitchen floors, those cage-lining and floor-covering newspapers were picked up at intervals, and those that were not burned went into the trash. When the trash reached the Jersey Meadows, some of the seed got into the soil, enough, in fact, to sow substantial patches of cannabis. It is this canary legacy the government bird watchers are after.

How shall I think, now, of those ghostly dear ladies who baby-talked their trilling fluffs among the joys of innocence? How shall I tell their memory that the canaries sang so sweetly because

271

they were potheads on a marijuana jag? Marijuana was all but un-known in those days, though someone must have noticed that canaries sang best on seed mixtures richly laced with it. It was only when government decree forbade the inclusion of marijuana in birdseed that canaries lost their voice and fell from popularity.

Did they, I wonder, suffer withdrawal fits and sicken? Think of that last lost generation of canaries suddenly switched from dream seed to bland, the pulse gone from their throats, the im-pulse from their hearts, while sad old ladies coaxed them in baby talk to rise from the mopes and flats of songless diet to the highs and raptures of their once well-potted days.

The collector of sad ironies might even wonder about, some of my ladies. It is impossible for me to imagine them as secret drink-ers—they were more likely to be members of the Temperance Union. Yet, I do recall that among my errands were almost daily trips to the drugstore for various tonics and female remedies; simultaneously I recall Stewart Holbrook telling me that he worked on New England lumber drives during Prohibition, and that whenever the crews bedded down near a town, they would send out for cases of a popular "female remedy" with a notably high alcoholic content.

To push irony a step further, I wonder what sweet lost old ladies my sweet lost old ladies recalled from their childhood with-out ever guessing that some of them must have been not only in-nocent tipplers but well-hooked and well-deceived junkies. Go back one long life's memories from the Twenties and ask why frugal old ladies (and gentlemen) would get up a dollar a bottle as soon as the medicine man had finished his spiel. A dollar was a big dollar in those days and the medicine man had no artistry in him-self for extracting that dollar. He had no need of artistry: that medicine man was Great-Aunt Agatha's connection, his nostrums free of government regulation and well laced with opium deriva-tives and laudanum (opium in an alcoholic solution).

Great-Aunt Agatha, of course, knew what sweet relief her dollar bought. Didn't she always feel better after taking Dr. Quack's Indian Herb Panacea? Don't junkies always feel better after they have a proper fix?

There, then, to dream on is the ghostly image of lost genteel ladies cooing to the rapturous canaries of a lost innocence. Some

272

of them, certainly, were at least minor tipplers, though they would have denounced alcohol as the devil's distillation. Some of them must have been children and grandchildren of proper matrons who suffered from obscure female maladies none of which could possibly have been diagnosed as a craving for opium. And so to learn that even the canaries of my childhood were potheads!

Such is the imagery of irony. But let irony be sad. Let it be anything but innocent. Innocence is the one condition irony must deny, and that wisdom, even in compassion, must not dare.

October 25, 1969

The Strangest Thing Happened
to a Friend of Mine

A friend with whom I was having lunch told me the story of a friend of his, a well-designed dress designer who liked to knit and to turn out stunning effects in sweaters in which she turned out stunning effects. He did not say, "Stop me if you've heard this one," or even "Have you heard the story about . . . ?" No, he launched his story as a straight acount of something that had happened to someone he knew. It occurred to me as he rambled on that "claiming kin" (as my Missouri-born wife still says at times) has all but become the official way of telling a story these days.

For all I knew the story he was telling me had been made up on somebody else's expense account at another bar and grill the day before and had been passed on at the office water cooler that morning. Or it had been around for twenty years. Or it may even have been, as he claimed, the story of what had really happened to

273

a friend of his, though with a few embellishments he was not inclined to label as such. All I am sure of is that storytellers have become oddly sneaky these days. They think nothing of claiming to know a person to whom the oddest thing happened to happen. Nor are these widely acquainted liars even mildly disturbed by the fact that the same thing happens to have been happening to Pat and Mike since before Joe Miller went to press.

A few months ago, for example, I had dinner with a judge who had just sent a man to jail for lying in court, and I'll be a perjuror's nominee for a back room at the county poorhouse if his honor didn't tell me numbers 17, 42, and 167 from the minutes of the 1778 convention of the Liar's International as things that had happened to his wife just the week before. Well, maybe it wasn't exactly perjury the man went to jail for, and maybe it hadn't been the week before, and maybe it was the 1804 convention, and, come to think of it, my friend was really a shoe salesman who had been in court not as the judge but as a member of the jury. But let me confess that I enter these qualifications timidly and, of course, in confidence. I am in no way eager to acquire a reputation for unvarnished honesty among my usually varnished friends.

Not, of course, that we ever believe one another. It would upset all conventions to detect anything like credulity taking place. House rules, however, seem to demand that we pretend to believe lightly what none of us would be caught believing seriously. Manners, after all, are one definition of a society.

All of which is a long way from the well-designed designer, though anyone who has come this far might just as well stay till taps is played over the body. The lady had visited Chinatown and had there spotted some Chinese writing so pleasing to her eye that she whipped out a Polaroid, photographed it, and went home to block out the characters on a larger scale as a decorative motif across the breast of an otherwise plain but definitely high-style sweater she then knitted.

The total effect of the sweater (pick your own color combinations) was described as "dramatic" until, at the party there always is, someone (the friend of a friend) who had been brought up in China as the son of a missionary and who had studied Chinese, took one look and let out the guffaw that always comes. The characters, in their well-designed row across the designer's well-

274

designed breast, read: "This dish cheap but unmistakably good."

Though, truth to tell, the man was not really the son of a missionary and could not really read Chinese. He was, as I happen to know, the lessee-operator of a gas station in Hoboken, he had come to New York for the weekend as a wetback, and he had overheard an immigration agent telling the story to another immigration agent as he was hiding from the two of them under Pier 16. Or it may not have been Pier 16. But he was obviously a quick-witted fellow despite an unfortunate background.

I suspect the whole concoction (except that it wasn't a gas station) of being related to a story told me by the late marvelous Fletcher Pratt, who swore that it had happened to the still marvelous Jeanne Vandervort, who even nodded in agreement during the telling—the fraud. Jeanne went to Japan on some assignment with just enough forewarning to get in a three-month course in Japanese. She arrived in Tokyo proud of having Berlitz-krieged the language and, knowledge being freedom, she made her way to a cab, got in, and said something on the order of "Take me to the seventh house of the street to which the locust does not come except by invitation."

The driver immediately got out of the cab, opened the back door, and spoke more Japanese than Jeanne could fathom, accompanied by more gestures than she could knit characters for. All she could think to do was to repeat the address, but that worked no better than before, and by now a crowd had gathered, all of it chattering and tittering in the throes of some mystery that was finally cleared up when a bilingual gentleman approached the cab.

"Madame," he said in whatever English you care to believe or to invent for yourself, "the driver is unclear and wishes to know why you wish him to throw you into the street and to command the birds to stamp upon you. He would be honored if you would be led to some other wish."

But to prove that fraud has no real standing, I can report a bilingual incident that did happen to happen to my good friend Silvio Senigallia, whom I recently saw in Rome. Silvio, now an American citizen but raised as an Italian-Italian, was staying on Second Avenue in an apartment house whose janitor was Italian-American. Honored at having the real article, and a lawyer and a

275

gentleman, in his apartment house, the janitor introduced himself one cold morning when the steam heat had failed. "*Io sono il genitore*," he said, "*e mi dispiace ma non c'è stima nelle pipe.*"

But in Italian "*genitore*" means not janitor but "father." "*Stima*" means not "steam" (which is, properly, "*vapore*") but "esteem." And "*pipe*" means always and only "pipes for smoking" and not "plumbing pipes" which is, properly, "*tube.*" What the janitor had said in cross-fertilizing his broken English and his fading Italian could only be translated by something on the order of "I am your father and I am sorry but there is no esteem in pipes" or, more pithily, "I am your father and I am sorry to say pipe smokers do not esteem one another."

Though maybe it wasn't Silvio Senigallia he said it to but Fiorello La Guardia. And maybe it wasn't the janitor who said it but a friend of Ogden Nash's called Al the Barber. Besides which, Silvio doesn't practice law any more. Though it *was* in Rome that I saw him this past summer. And Milton Hebald, too, who is working on a life-size bronze of James Joyce to go over the tomb in Zurich. Joyce's that is. Or did I hear him say it was for Keats's grave in the Protestant Cemetery?

Which reminds me of the oddest thing that happened to a friend of mine who ghostwrites for a friend of mine named William Lederer, who . . .

November 27, 1963

Subject Unknown

A friend of mine recently set me off on a still unidentified ramble into the nature of things, and though I am not at all sure what point I have reached, these are the windings I have wandered:

My friend began it all by remarking that archeologists have never excavated a settled place of human habitation without finding evidence of wine making and wine storage. Though I have no way of verifying his statement, I am inclined to accept in reason what I cannot demonstrate in fact—that fermentation and civilization are inseparable. One may find the rudiments of civilization in some early nomadic peoples, but it seems reasonable to argue that what we understand as the arts, crafts, and civil contracts of true civilization could not get underway until man settled down to live in one place.

But there had to be something to keep him there, and what would be a more likely reason than alcohol? Wandering herdsmen could, of course, ferment goat's milk in leather sacks, and almost certainly did. But for anything like satisfactory drinking, man had finally to get himself a vineyard. Thereupon, having his grapes and grape juice in civilizing quantities, he had to find something better than goatskins to put them in. So—or so at least this argument would run, unencumbered by anything so gross as facts—man's first clay jug of wine gave him his first, most enduring reason for staying home, as well as his best reason for building a safe, cool, and substantial cellar in which to keep his (now plural) jugs. For a man with a goatskin full of fermented milk is free to sling it over his shoulder and catch the next camel to anywhere, but a man with a cozy row of wine-filled amphorae is at once a man of property and of fixed residence.

Distillation is, of course, another, much later phenomenon. A knowledgeable friend, a professor of history, assures me that the Mohammedans had achieved distilled spirits of a sort and that the Irish had achieved usquebaugh, both by the ninth century. With grain in normally short supply, however, such spirits remained rare, he adds, and it was not until the eighteenth century, with the introduction into Europe of the potato, that a plentiful and cheap supply of distilled spirits became available. I join my friend in suspecting that modern civilization may be dated from the development of the distillery, as primitive civilization began at the grape press. On such a reading of history, no man has spoken the gospel more briskly than Bernard DeVoto (*The Hour*, Houghton-Mifflin 1948):

The American people achieved nationality and Old Monongahely in a single generation, which should surprise no one, since nations flower swiftly once their genius has budded.

DeVoto, I submit, makes out the best defense yet entered for taking the continent away from the Indians. What could they ever have done with it?

Concede that they had ingenuity and by means of it achieved a marvel: they took a couple of wild grasses and bred them up to corn. But what did they do with corn? Century succeeded century and, regarding it as a mere food, they could not meet the challenge on which, as Mr. Toynbee had pointed out, their hopes of civilization hung. Across the continent, every time the rains came some of the corn stored in their granaries began to rot. Would it be doom, the Age of Polished Stone forever, or toward the stars? The historian watches, his breathing suspended, and sees the pointer settle toward decline. They threw the spoiled stuff out for the birds, angrily reproaching their supernaturals, and never knew that the supernaturals had given them a mash.

If it is a fact (continues my ramble) that civilization and alcohol are truly twin manifestations, the civil objection to alcohol is, of course, that though one cup restores the spirit, another takes away reason. Since the law should be supreme in all matters touching upon the social contract, let Blackstone be heard (IV, 26):

It has been observed that the real use of strong liquors, and the abuse of them by drinking to excess, depend much upon the temperature of the climate in which we live. The same indulgence which may be necessary to make the blood move in Norway, would make an Italian mad. A German, therefore, says President Montesquieu, drinks through custom founded upon constitutional necessity; a Spaniard drinks through choice, or out of mere wantonness of luxury; and drunkenness, he adds, ought to be more severely punished where it makes men mischievous and mad, as in Spain and Italy, than where it only renders them stupid and heavy, as in Germany and more northern countries.

278

Blackstone's is a curiously climatological thesis, and one that perhaps gives special point to our phrase "cold sober." Something in the ethnic tradition of the Anglo-Saxon tends to equate coldness with virtue and warmth with vicious and libidinous inclination. Blackstone's Anglo-Saxon mystique on the matter of temperance and temperature is matched by his views on latitude and lechery when he comments on polygamy (IV, 164):

Polygamy can never be endured under any rational civil establishment, whatever specious reasons may be urged for it by the Eastern nations, the fallaciousness of which has been fully proved by many sensible writers: but in Northern countries the very nature of the climate seems to reclaim against it; it never having obtained in this part of the world, even from the time of our German ancestors, who, as Tacitus informs us, *"prope soli barbarorum singulis uxoribus contenti sunt"* (almost alone among the barbarians are satisfied by a single wife).

I wish Blackstone had been moved to carry a bit further the parallel between liquor and libido suggested by these two comments. What, in any case, emerges as the next loop of this present ramble is the ease with which men of any given civilization claim its virtues as their own while passing on its vices to their neighbors. For example, Englishmen call syphilis "the French disease," Frenchmen call it "the Italian disease," and Italians call it "the Spanish disease," each demonstrating the peculiar orthodoxy of Europeans in referring vice and its consequences not only to a neighbor, but to some more southerly latitude.

Perhaps prejudice, like alcohol, is also indispensable to civilization. Of the two, alcohol seems, by much, to be the clearer essence, and the less baneful, for at worst it ruins lives no more than one liver at a time, whereas the drunkenness of prejudice, when carried to excess, leads invariably to the binge of warfare.

And let that be the end of my ramble—hopefully at some tavern of all souls in which every man drinks moderately to the measure of his life's climate, allowing to every man his own climate and measure, and passing on to his neighbor no fault he does not recognize in himself.

June 1, 1963

Grant's Whom?

That neo-bulbous mound of stone pastry at Riverside Drive and 122d Street, once known to passing natives and visiting tourists as Grant's Tomb, is now in the ongoing, post-conceptual process of having its nomenclature contemporized in a restructuring toward a more maximal impact, prestige-wise.

The National Park Service, that is to say, has taken over, the objective has been concretized, a target date set, the destruct button wired, and the countdown begun toward blasting the obsoletized nomenclature into outer space. So, at least (I am once more clearing out my year-end Quirk & Kink File), I read in a story I clipped from *The New York Times* on November 22 last, under the by-line of McCandlish Phillips. Mr. Phillips, I am pleased to note, writes his piece with a good journalistic poker face. The National Park Service emerges from his typewriter fairly reported in its devotions. As I begin to read Mr. Phillips's article, I am even stirred to sympathy for these doughty rear-guardsmen of the National Park Service, valiant losers every one, heroes to the core in their official defense of nonlanguage.

For they are at war, these guardians. Nor let it be said of them (at least to begin with) that they underestimate the odds against them. Their valor, as I began to believe, is exactly in the fullness of the knowledge with which they foresee failure and still fight on. But let me quote Mr. Phillips's report of the mood and cause of our fighting men:

> Most people call it "Grant's Tomb." That makes members of the National Park Service wince. They prefer the official name, the General Grant National Memorial.

280

They are, I submit, dedicated men, these guardians of the National Park Service, firm in their purpose, yet easy wincers when the public good is at stake. There is, to be sure, not only the public good but the pride of the service at stake. It was the service that gave the building its new name when the service took custody in 1959.

Let me pause to imagine what stirring days those must have been in the National Park Service. In my mind's eye I see rows of "in" baskets in perfect alignment, each with its clerk standing by at attention as this new responsibility is laid upon the service. That ceremony concluded, I see the Summons to Nomenclature, the Trooping of the Jargon, the Echeloning of the Memoranda, the Closing of the Committeeroom Doors, then, triumphantly, the Installation of the Preposterous, the good men of the National Park Service rising to give three maximalized cheers for the "General Grant National Memorial."

Heady moments, those. But the way since then has been arduous though high the goal. "It has," Mr. Phillips reports for the service, "been hard to win even a small degree of public acceptance for the longer name."

Yet, surely men of so polysyllabic a purpose, their character untainted by idiom, every one a wincer for the common good, will fight on, finding at the bottom of every wince the courage of renewed resolve. Let it be said of them that wince they may, falter they will not, nor yet fall to the tongues of mankind while there is yet officialese to stay them in the oratorios of the purblind and the pure deaf. Is not life itself a folly? It is the valor with which men sustain the integrity of their error that moves us to admire them.

It was in this frame of mind that I found myself beginning to admire Mr. Phillips's spokesman for the National Park Service, a Mr. Jerry Wagers, who comes classified as Chief of Historical Interpretation for the National Park Service in New York. "A changeover like this is very slow in coming," said Jerry Wagers, "But all the guidebooks and the tour people are very careful to use our terminology now."

I read that far and I am moved to tell Mr. Wagers I admire his spirit. I can sympathize with you when you wince, sir. I can mourn with you the world's indifference to the good you insist on doing

281

for it in the name of the National Park Service. I can feel with you the dreary slow passage of ineffectual time when high cause hangs ignored. I confess to a sneaking admiration for the way you foxed those guidebook people and those tour people into saying (like it or not), "And now we come to the General Grant National Memorial."

There is a touch of the tragic Greek in a man who can feel the sealing of his own fate and still try to cajole the decree of the gods by cunning wiles. But the Greek, Mr. Wagers, was at his noblest only in the greatness of his failure. He was above the assertion of piddling optimisms. I don't mind your pushing your terminology, hopeless as it must be, onto those guidebook and tour people, but, alas, you blasted my last hope of moral grandeur when you added "We expect in a few more years, it [the new name] will gradually take over."

Piffle, Mr. Wagers. Piffle to the General Grant National Memorial, sir. Piffle to the thought of its taking over. It will not. Not now. Not in a few years. Not in eternity.

> To whom,
> When he means "Grant's Tomb,"
> Would anyone not bureaucratically conspiratorial
> Say "The General Grant National Memorial?"

And even if you had the cadence of it right, Mr. Wagers your oddly national Park Service has the quality of the American idea dead wrong. If it has to go into your misguided books as a national memorial, then at least set it down as the President Grant National Memorial. By American custom, we bury our variously honored dead at their highest rank, and it has long been a fixed idea among us that Presidents outrank generals, even when they were great generals first and bad Presidents later.

If the National Park Service has any doubts on the nature of that American principle, let it only think back to an Administration easily within the memory of a chief historical interpreter, when a National Memorial named Harry S Truman reestablished the order of precedence as it concerned a bit of the national service called MacArthur, Douglas, General, USA (retired).

Principle aside, I am reminded that never in all the times I have

282

driven by your mound of neo-nothing up there on the Drive have I stopped to go inside. I'll have to do that one of these days, just to see if there can possibly be an inside to match such an outside.

I'll see you at Grant's Tomb, Mr. Wagers. Ulysses S. Grant, that is—the President.

March 9, 1968

New York: Don't Say Hello

I have noted, first during the blackout, and again in the first days of the transportation strike, how many newspaper, radio, and TV commentators took occasion to sing the joys of a new-found friendliness among New Yorkers.

Perhaps all these commentators were expiating a common guilt for all those incidents in which New Yorkers had witnessed acts of violence and done nothing about them, not even phoned the police from the safety of their homes when they heard the screams of a woman being murdered outside their windows. None of them wanted to get involved. And then, of course, there are the dark incidents of those who did get involved in trying to stop trouble that was not their own and who were killed or injured for their pains, or who ran into trouble with the police, who do have a free-handed tendency to pick up all parties to a disturbance and to ask questions at their own later pleasure.

It is not hard to understand that reluctance to jump into someone else's fight, much as we may be shamed by such cowardice. New York can be savage. And certainly there are humanoid animals among us. Outside an opium den (as I imagine such dens to be), or the vistas of Asiatic poverty, or the atrocious memories of the Dachaus, I wonder if there can be a more depressing ex-

283

perience of the human race than to walk Forty-second Street from Broadway to Eighth Avenue. It is Scum Beach there these days, and not even the Bowery can offer so many inhuman faces.

Small towns have their humanoid animals, too, but not in such concentration and not hidden in the cloak of anonymity that is the natural gift of New York. It is anonymity that most emboldens the animals. Whatever the mood and method of their depravity, they find it easy to strike and disappear, leaving behind them nothing but the victim and the silence of the passers-by, or at best a series of conflicting descriptions.

The presence of these beasts is enough in itself to impose a restraint on New Yorkers. Nor do they always wear animal uniforms. Nor is their ruin always instantly apparent in their faces. That man at the bar with you, or waiting for the elevator, or lounging in your doorway may be all right, but you don't know him, there is no reason for trying to know him, and you have no way of guessing what he would turn out to be if you did get to know him. Better to leave him alone. There are, heaven knows, enough people in New York that you do know. Pass by in silence and call it luck when the silence remains unbroken.

Then something happens. The city is blacked out. Executive-looking types are sleeping on the benches in Penn Station. People are stranded on the streets or clustered around any radio. Traffic comes to a halt. It is Emergency Day and not only is everyone easily friendly, but even the normal working of crime comes to a halt.

Later New Yorkers think back to that easy friendliness of those strange days and even wish they might find it again. I am not at all sure, however, that they really would be made glad by it as a normal thing. I know I would not be.

For if the anonymity New York grants us is a problem, it is also a blessing. In small towns it is natural and easy to be passingly friendly with everyone nearby, and in small towns it works. But in New York there are too many people nearby. Just try to imagine walking down Madison Avenue and being friendly to everyone you meet there! Not only would you never get where you were going, but you would be making a nuisance of yourself to thousands of people with their own errands to run. The very

284

multitude of people makes it necessary for us to stare through and beyond one another.

Nor do I see anything wrong with that New York stare. If I read it correctly it speaks an implicit contract whose terms are: "Leave me the freedom of my anonymity and I will leave you the freedom of yours."

That may not be exactly folksy, but were I to get folksy with everyone riding the elevators at 380 Madison, or were the elevator-riders in general to get folksy with one another, it would take forever to get into and out of the building. People would be finishing friendly conversations with one foot in the elevator door, the buzzers would be buzzing an indignant Morse code, and every act of leaving or entering the building would be a lunatic rally.

Similarly, were I living in an apartment house, I would not care to know who lives above me, below me, or in the next apartment on either side. I want to choose my friends: I do not care to have them thrust upon me by the rental agency. And I do not want people dropping in to borrow whatever neighbors borrow, nor to chitchat whatever neighbors chitchat.

It isn't that I dislike you, neighbor, but I might if I got to know you, and if we had once played at being friendly, and if I do ever find you to be a bore, how do I then avoid you when you are living right there? One of the joys of New York is in the ease with which any man may avoid the people he chooses to avoid. And it is a joy, or at least a possibility toward joy, that I am not ready to surrender.

New Yorkers, I believe, are ready to be casually friendly exactly to the degree that the line of retreat to their necessary anonymity is covered. Strangers do talk at a bar, but they never identify themselves, and their chat is forever ended when one of them walks out the door.

Or—above all others—there is the cabbie. Get into the back seat, tell him where you want to go, and, the chances are, you will find yourself in instant, even possibly intimate conversation. Cabbies have told me their sex lives, their problems with their children, wives, and in-laws, their views on New York city-planning, their dreams of retiring to run a marina, their hatred of the police, their considered philosophy of life, and their predictions for the day's races, separately or in any combination, all within a five-minute ride plus fifteen minutes' standing-time in the traffic jam. And I have made up my own lies to pass the time. We aren't saying anything: we're just talking, and we are free to play any conversational game we choose exactly because we know it will be broken off in mid-sentence and that we will probably never meet again, or that if we do meet again we will not know we have met before. The cabbie does, of course, have his name, photo, and license displayed in the cab, but who ever pays any attention to that? We have our anonymity in common, and because we have a secure pact to respect it, we may be as casually friendly as we please.

Maybe New York needs a central exchange for just such casual friendliness; say a series of telephone numbers that plug into one another and that cannot be traced, but that are there to be called by anyone who wants to rattle on, baring his soul at random, but secure in the knowledge that he can hang up whenever he wants to and go back to being anonymous.

It *can* be lonely at times inside that anonymity, but let a small-town friendliness echo through those canyons and the future would be chaos forever, bumper to bumper and nose to nose from here to infinity.

February 12, 1966

Notes: The Big Idea

Not long ago in this column I muddied the springs of choice with a few thoughts about New York, about my neighbors there, and about why I do not want to know them.

Shortly before writing that column I had spent a few days in my wife's hometown, which is Frankford, Missouri, population (a guess) plus or minus 450. They are good, honest, friendly, hearty folk in Frankford, and taken in fractions of 450 or so, I like them and enjoy being with them. Though I confess to having been a bit stunned one summer when I drove the seven miles in from the farm to get a haircut at Roy Ruffin's, and drove back to be greeted by my mother-in-law with the day's news: "I hear you've been handing out twenty-five-cent tips!"

As I recall the transaction, the haircut had come to something like seventy-five cents and I had automatically waved away the change. I have always wanted to be the last of the big-time spenders, but I had hardly expected my magnanimous gesture to be flashed to all points on the party line!

The PLBS (Party Line Broadcasting System) served as a pleasant enough joke for that afternoon. Back in New York, however, I found myself thinking I did not really want my neighbors to know about me in that sort of detail. A small town is a friendly place to visit, but I just don't want to live there. Nor do I want to live in New York on small-town premises. Being entirely visible to a few hundred people is one thing: being entirely visible to eight and a half million nighttime New Yorkers and to another eight million or so commuters would be unbearable.

Had I thought of it at the time of the writing, I would certainly have added a further sentiment received from Louis Sherwin, writing from The Players (and thank you, sir, and agreed:)

You might have added that another point to the credit of the true New Yorker is that he is not a dropper-inner. A civilized man, before paying a visit without invitation, telephones to ascertain whether or not his visit will be (a) convenient (b) agreeable.

These views, I submit, are sufficiently self-evident. I want the anonymity granted me by the millions of New Yorkers around me, and I return them the grant of their own anonymity as part of a sound and necessary social contract. It occurs to me, as a matter of fact, that I never look at panhandlers when I give them money. I am ready enough to recognize their need. I just don't want to see their faces: why should the needy or even the conniving, not have the right to remain anonymous?

I violated that rule just once, and in Boston rather than New

287

York. I was staying at the old Copley-Plaza, now a Sheraton, and had strolled across the street to the liquor store, emerging with a wrapped bottle in my hand, to be met by a shuffling wino. "How about buying me a drink?" he said. I reached into my pocket and came up with the one coin I could find—a fifty-cent piece. He took it but stood firm. "That won't buy a bottle of wine," he said. He had me there. My own bottle was in my hand: why shouldn't he have his? I dug again and came up with a dollar bill. "Drink hearty," I said, and this time I looked at him, and I will swear to this day that I was looking at Albert Einstein, the face sunk a bit out of focus, the chin stubbly, and still the face. I do not know what thought this is. Nor will I do as the most delicate man in town. But I was sorry I had looked. Let all those who are lost and damned to their own thirst be given what they need to die of as they must and will. But let them pass without faces. Why should I offend the man with pity when all he wants of me is a drink?

I shall not pretend that I entirely understand this feeling about the self-damned. The preference for anonymity in the otherwise asphyxiating crowd, however, seems a matter of simple necessity, and such was the simple burden of my remarks.

But nothing is allowed to stay simple once the amateur intellectuals have found it. My remarks called forth an extraordinary number of letters, a few from ministers and most of the rest from college students, the gentler of the letters asking me if I was familiar with Harvey Cox's *The Secular City*, the harsher of them accusing me of having plagiarized my remarks from him. Harvey Cox, it seems, has had things to say about metropolitan mores.

To all letter writers let me say I am sorry I have not read Harvey Cox. My curiosity now piqued, I shall look forward to getting a copy of the book, though with a desk full of manuscripts that must be worked on I am in danger of contracting writer's illiteracy. But let me confess to a touch of astonishment—if astonishment may be said to come in touches; a brush of thunder, so to speak.

What astonishes me in this burst of correspondence is the assumption that the obvious cannot be arrived at except through a bibliography. Shucks, children, if you have to read socio-theological treatises in order to see the fetishistic noses on your totemistic faces, why then the tribe is in a bad way for improvisers of whatever magic it means to concoct. I am, believe me, delighted to know that you are reading, but let me suggest that no book is any good unless now and then you look up from it and take a good inquiring look at your roommate or at your own face in the mirror. We are all strange specimens when looked at by the right curiosity. And we are all capable of inciting to idea when looked at by eyes that are prepared to see idea. Books are great preparers of the right eyes to see with. But let me believe they are not the world itself but properly assistants to the world, indispensable and delightful servants that become mutinous only when you allow them the assumption that they are the world itself, and that things exist only in them. Be wary of compounding innocence with a pedantic solemnity.

Understand me, please—I am not against innocence, I must note, however, that the state of innocence provides the occupational grounds of both preachers and swindlers, though the preacher seeks to add to it whereas the swindler seeks to subtract from it. Has anyone said that in a book? I just read it from the world. And what a bibliography the world comes to!

It is always a mistake to misread it. Why fall into mere innocence when there is experience to die of? And what good is it to read ideas from books if one is not capable of going through any door to find he has walked smack into an idea, and that it is alive and moving its endless parts all around him, four hundred and fifty at a time, or fifteen or sixteen million at a time, and going its own way, which is hearty, or evasive, or shuffling, or striding, and with a cornfield in the background, or a traffic jam, and sometimes populated by one of those girls who pull the eyes right out of your face, or sometimes just oppressive in its too-many-ness, or sometimes countrified easy, but there, and to be read of itself, ready to be enlarged by any time you are willing to spend in the library, but still apart from the library, with itself to be, itself the thing that gives point to libraries and that checks the books, finally, for accuracy?

April 2, 1966

289

A Frenzy Without a Face

I walked up Seventh Avenue through Animal Square, the neons and Neanderthals blinking and signaling together. It was already Mugger's Dark in Fag Alley, ash cans and lidless winos knocked over, the Rat Pack sniffing, circling on pointed toes. Ma and Pa, carefully looking at nothing, headed for subway entrances. Proper Getters with attaché cases signaled for cabs that refused to stop, then strode on to the next light to signal again, trying from intersection to intersection for a sure, possessive, managerial stride, but unable to keep their heads from swiveling warily.

The Gland Patrols waddled under the neons in boots; stretch pants; shaggy, collarless, imitation fur jackets; and hairdos teased and lacquered into enormous puffs. Had they sewn on tails with pompon tips they would have looked like high cosmetic poodles tiptoeing on their hind legs: fuzzy on top and around the middle with long bare necks and legs that would have looked bare but for the fluorescent stripes that blinked on and off with the neons. Like trained poodles, they rode their hind legs on teetery balances, their heads high and swiveling from side to side, at least in their first patrol. Later, as they grew bored and tired, they would stop parading and merely trudge, letting their faces go blank, leaving their fuzz, their make-up, and their stripedy legs to advertise for them under the neons in which their colors kept changing.

Just north of the main stroboscope, one flight up from Madame Astra's Gypsy Fortunes, fuchsia tassels and glimpses of skin whirled in the windows of Swishland. From the sidewalk across the street, a few teeny-boppers and their dog-foxes panted puffs

290

of gray breath and stared up for knothole glimpses of a possible heaven.

A block farther north, outside the Sodom A Go-Go, a whole sidewalk zoo stared in at a glass cage. Young bucks from Jersey High Schools. Tenth Avenue moles forever in psychic holes of their own digging, forever driven to stick their heads out for a look at whatever world they were undermining. Pomade baboons from the wharves and deadends in jeans and leather jackets, sniffing the bad air for whatever eager evil the night might bring. Harlem gazelles in silk jackets with embroidered backs. Off-Village beards and hair-drapes on a low float in the blare of light and sound. Spoiled square brats from the three-car suburbs in Nehru jackets and medallions, dreaming orgies their parents were sometimes able to work up to but never to imagine, not at least in the vocabulary of Animal Square. Red-neck stallions up from bluegrass to where the action is.

A bull in police blue stood in the doorway facing them. A sub-manager, nervous as a spooked antelope, stood at his side. One by one, in couples or in small groups, animals from the zoo came up to the bull showing wallets with identity cards and with gray-green edges of paper money carefully fanned out as proof of solvency. The bull pretended to examine the identity cards, but always with one eye on the sub-manager. When the sign was right he let a few of the animals into heaven. Mostly, however, he denied their ages but, insisting only that they leave a passage in the middle of the sidewalk, he let them stand back and sniff sin through glass, as if it really were sin, as advertised, almost as if the animals, in the innocence of their depravity, could guess the difference between sin and tinsel, who, denied other pleasures, would yet bleed or let blood before dawn-stain, prowling to be what's happening.

Over the head of the bull and the sub-manager, speakers blasted tom-toms and wailers into the smog-mist on which the neons beat like strobe lights. The animals stood in the blare and flicker, twitching infinitesimally, but it was only incidentally to the music they turned their drugged, void faces.

It was to watch the goddesses of the animals that they had

291

stopped there. The Go-Go was fronted by a huge show window and through it three goddesses, the nearest almost in the window itself, timed in spasm to the music, performed inside three glitter-sprayed cages mounted on three pedestals. I had meant to walk by but the sight of the nearest goddess stopped me and I drew back among the animals to watch.

Had I ever seen such energy in convulsion? It was delirium she twitched, out-blaring the music in a high narcotic rage that beat its fists on all walls at once. A seizure twitching in a brass rave. Machine jigged legs, hips, torso, arms, stitching. Not energy but its madness. A withdrawal fit turned on. A jitter at the top of its smoky high like a monkey on a squeeze-stick. I lost track of time. Could it have been fifteen minutes she kept up that pace before she jumped down and was replaced by a copy of herself? Impossible. No body could put out such energy for more than a spasm at a time. Yet they went on and on, with the music but somehow trying to outclimb it, to reach some frenetic peak higher than all amplification.

But what gripped me was their faces, their lack of faces. From the neck down they were an orgy of motion. From the neck up —nothing, not a change of expression, not an opening of the mouth to suck in air, not so much as a focusing of the eyes. The eyes were turned in on themselves, away from their epileptic bodies. The faces were shut and locked away in some other place. It was a frenzy without a face. A violence without a presence. A bone jive. And when I stole a look at the animals on either side of me, I saw the same non-face, an inside-out and away, riding its own violent inwards, leaving nothing to show outside.

Yes, I had seen something like it before, I recalled, but never quite this. In Los Angeles at the Pickle and in Dallas at the Riviera it had been topless, its meat sacs tom-tomming clumsily, going through motions. In San Francisco at the Blank Mange it came sliding down brass poles, its eye sockets the two colors of litmus paper testing nothing, its armpits caked with a colloid of bone-dust talcum. In Athens in the Taberna it was the homosexual painted like a rag doll and preening for any taker, ready for anything but to change expression. In London, it was the girls who

292

posed motionless for the nude tableaux in the music halls, their bodies out and their faces in.

And I had seen bodily violence to equal that of the animal goddesses. The Fiji kootch dancers who shake it on Oahu are certainly as frenzied, but those girls laugh and roll their eyes in the joy of their abandonment. What I had not seen before was such delirium from the neck down and such stolidity—more than stolidity, such absence—from the neck up.

I moved on and finally got a cab, convinced I had seen a pictogram of our times. As surely as Hebrew characters hold their candelabra up to a history they are the basic pictures of, that faceless frenzy in its cage is the picture of a generation, perhaps of an age.

I found myself thinking of the storm trooper turned to the agonies he gave the signals for, the dying gyrating before him, his face creased and official as his uniform. I thought of Caligula dozing off before the torture was finished, of the face of the boredom of Caligula. But I could think of no instance in which the face of the zombie rode the neck of the dervish.

It took our children to create that monster, as it took us to be the parents of its creators; the face of the void frenzy, blank before, during, and after, as if bodily violence exists apart from the identity of the violent, as if the mind has no need to know what the arms are beating, the thumbs gouging, or the feet stomping. An assault ignoring itself. Us? Ours.

February 15, 1969

The Refugee Angel (*A, Perhaps, Allegory*)

Homesick for ourselves, we refugee angels inserted personals in the leading newspapers and became pen pals. It wasn't, of course, the same thing as going home, wherever that had been, whatever was left of it.

But just to have someone to talk to in our own language (which we are forever inventing) is almost the next thing to a reality, like phoning long distance from a combat zone: there's half a world and all its cables between saying and being; and still if you shouted you could be heard, and if you strained you could almost hear what was almost a voice of someone almost remembered saying Yes, the weather was fine, and wanting to know how you were. And when you said goodbye, to nothing, that was a month's pay shot.

As a matter of fact we phoned only in the beginning. In the long run the letters (with always the dim snapshots) were not only cheaper but more satisfactory. A letter is an evidence. It can be folded and carried in a pocket and reopened at night and read again. And, during the day, touched. It is the next thing to being almost real. It is a thing and, therefore, partly believable.

Even when you forgot who had written it, it was there with its dim snapshots of whoever it had been you had meant to remember.

Even when it was from no one you knew except as a name, the name was still vaguely of someone who knew what you knew about the towers and choir stalls and gold villages.

294

It was always from someone who had been there when you had been there and who spoke parts of the language you were forever inventing as the way all of you have of trying to remember how far back it is to never again.

Though, really, it wasn't so much that I wanted to be a pen pal as that I had nothing else to be.

Maybe it's like smoking cigarettes after you get the habit of it: you don't really want the cigarette, but what on earth do you do without it?

So I chain-smoked and pen-palled from all the endless world's ends I was forever being sent to, and I kept the letters that came to me, some of them from space, and some of them almost halfway to being nearly understandable. For after those first few times, I never again tried to reach back by cable.

And after the first few letters carried into combat and bloodied a bit, I never folded them into my pockets but mounted them in bound tomes and stored them in the squadron files to read again on furloughs.

When I was finally discharged with my two Band-Aids and my disability pay, I was sure I had all that was left of the libraries of Heaven.

I had to turn down Air Force transportation and make my way back by freighter just to get the crates of books back to the ranch-style abbey I had picked out in San Diego.

And here I am, and even now I can pass days just stroking the bindings, feeling the weight of all those words we were forever inventing, hefting the bulk of the great proofs I used to read when I could see.

Sometimes another angel passes through town and drops in and I bring out the wine and we toast the names we invent again as if we could really remember what we once knew.

In the end, of course, we have nothing to say.

The bottle is always empty too soon.

He is still on active duty and he has his orders and it is time to say goodbye.

It is always time, from the beginning, to say goodbye.

I cannot see him and I am sure he does not see me.

He came not to hear what I had to say but what he had to say.

He admires my library but he cannot read it either.

And still I know what it makes him feel just to stroke the bindings and to heft the bulk of all those proofs.

I know how much he wants to persuade himself that we were real once and that we might again become real.

I let him listen to himself and I pretend that I, too, am listening, and sometimes I am, but not to him.

What I am doing is listening through him.

I hear all the waters of all the oceans we have crossed from nothing to nothing.

I hear the express rush of space, the raging silence.

I remember when I had eyes in that dark too wide to see across.

I think how it was really the same as being blind.

Whatever we were looking for was farther across the dark than we could see to, except for those pinpricks of light at the opposite nothing.

Blind, I can imagine that much as clearly as I saw it then.

He ignores me and I ignore him and we stroke the bindings and heft the weight of the proofs and empty the bottle and it is always time to say goodbye.

Sometimes the letters still arrive, two or three at a time, dog-eared and limp, and I can guess how many times they have been forwarded from God-knows-where and the way stations between.

But even if I opened them and even if I could read them, what could they say that I don't know already?

Yes, I confess I can never quite bring myself to throw them out. I toss them into a drawer and forget about them.

The fact is I no longer care to invent what I never was in the first place—or what I can no longer remember having been, which is really the same thing.

I think sometimes of the blood I shed in combat and I wish it had been real.

I touch the sewed-on scars and think of unstitching them, but it's like throwing out the letters—some inner feeling stops me: what could I pretend to be without them?

I could even open my eyes and see the dark again, the uncrossable fact of it. But why?

If I think hard enough, shut here in my own willed dark, I
believe I could reinvent myself as a thing.

A mote would be enough: I have survived ambition, I tell
myself.

And then I know I have been gulped down into the same pride
I rose in once.

That insistence on being real.

Always that insistence.

Among other dreams.

Of nothing.

January 22, 1966

Reflections of a Square

For one hundred dollars plus the prerequisite amnesia of what
the human race has been dreaming about since the start of things,
you may buy a key to the Playboy Tower of Fun recently opened
in New York. Your key paid for, you may then buy your drinks
at $1.50 apiece on the promise that you will overtip everyone,
but especially the Bunny who is assigned to wink her assemblages
at you, with the understanding that it is *infra dig* to wink back
and utter social ruin to touch or even to think of touching. What
you pay for, plus tips, is the basic male freedom to have nothing
to do with sex when it is waved at you all over the place. A Play-
boynik is there to play it cool. No hot little hands, no hot little
thoughts. Mr. Hefner said cool, man, cool, and Mr. Hefner has
piled up something like fifteen million utterly detached but highly
communicative dollars in the course of showing you what he
means.

That Bunny-tailed Utopia Mr. Hefner has conjured into a
commercial empire is the land of the ultimate gadgetry and the

country of the arrested adolescent. The gadgets are clothes, bachelor apartments, sports cars, insignia, hi-fi, girls, bottle openers, sliding panels, swimming pools, and a vocabulary of unmanners. The two laws of this Utopia are Detachment and Aplomb. Thou shalt not commit Love, Mr. Hefner has announced. And thou shalt not commit Uncertainty.

Thou shalt not commit Uncertainty, for the way is known, your duty set. Your duty is, simply, to consume negligently and exquisitely but only to sip. Nothing requires a more excruciating certainty than your choice of sport cars, girls, wardrobe, or hi-fi; and, that each gadget may be perfect of its kind, Mr. Hefner has made available to all the faithful the exact specifications to which each item must answer, as well as the range of permissible latitudes.

But perfection is a sometime thing. It is your duty—if only to prove that you are no square but the splendidly conspicuous brat of affluence—to condescend to perfection. After all, next year's model will be better and you must be ready to dismiss all of this year's inventory with a bored wave of the hand.

A square, on the other hand, is one who commits affection, even to the point of attaching himself in love to some other notably non-cool and otherwise imperfect specimen or specimens of the human race. Thou shalt not be Square; neither shalt thou be a Beatnik.

The Beatniks, to be sure, have much in common with the Boyniks, but, as one major difference, Mr. Hefner's Boyniks are at least as commercial as Merrill, Lynch, Pierce, Fenner and, now, Smith. The proper Boynik was born with a gilt-edged certificate for a caul and a deceptive avarice for a heritage. He gives the easy impression of neglecting a job he is square enough to worship and shrewd enough to handle well. With his seemingly effortless income, he further distinguishes himself from the Beatnik by setting himself up in an apartment rather than a pad. And he buys and uses vastly more soap.

Both Boynik and Beatnik, however, are out to play it cool, the first with elaborate accessories, the second without. For both, however, the essential religion is detachment.

And for both, the cut-off age is about thirty. Both, after all, are cases of adolescent arrest in the affluent society, the Boynik making it on the Junior Executive credit card, the Beatnik on the allowance left him by the margin of affluence. A few from each party do, to be sure, make it into a state of permanent emotional arrest. But to most people in or related to the human family in its standing imperfections, there comes eventually a message from a pair of squares named Adam and Eve. They were squares, above all, because they could not exist except as they were paired—a shocking lack of detachment.

That message can take many forms. One of the Boyniks or Beatniks might, for example, be summoned from his negligent carouse to stand at his father's deathbed while his mother stands by—or the other way around. There it might even occur to him that the old man begot him in joy and hope and that the old woman begot him in pain and hope. It is even conceivable, despite their obvious imperfections, that they loved one another and grew together in need of one another, and that even in hag-ridden old age they were joined by a ray that encompasses even our Boynik, who, seen by the eyes of love, turns out to be someone's son and thereby a member of the human race after all, which is to say a member of the Adam and Eve Club.

Or the message might arrive in the happier form of an assemblage called a girl. Conceivably she might show up with all her clothes on, without even a cottontail to her Bunny-bump, without ever having taken off her clothes for a mass media camera, and even without any real knowledge of sports clubs, weskits, hi-fi components, key clubs, and other such philosophical concepts. God knows how she manages to convey her girlish message without any of the Hefner-endorsed props, but sooner or later even a Boynik tends to get the idea, and the idea begins to work on him not only to the point of a potentially non-cool attachment but even to the abyss of overt matrimony. And there's one more lost from the Key Club to the Adam and Eve Club.

Because finally the Adam and Eve Club is the only one that endures and because not even Hugh Hefner can invent a fourth sex that actually works, sooner or later his former Boyniks and Bunnies will let their subscriptions lapse and start reading Spock. Whereupon their gadget list will begin to include such non-cool items as diapers and strollers, and their budgets will develop departments labeled "Orthodontia" and "College Fund."

Much of that will still be under the management of the affluent society. There is precious little sweat of the brow that goes into it these days: the current investment is more likely to be the twinge of anxiety.

The point, however, is that you do it together. In joy, in pain, in hope, in love, in recognition of one another's imperfections, but together. And that, friends, means by the rules of the Adam and Eve Club, right back at Cube Corners in Squaresville, which, finally, turns out to be the only enduring address for whatever Garden there can be.

November 2, 1963

Is Everybody Happy?

The right to pursue happiness is issued to Americans with their birth certificates, but no one seems quite sure which way it ran. It may be we are issued a hunting license but offered no game. Jonathan Swift seemed to think so when he attacked the idea of happiness as "the possession of being well-deceived," the felicity of being "a fool among knaves." For Swift saw society as Vanity Fair, the land of false goals.

It is, of course, un-American to think in terms of fools and knaves. We do, however, seem to be dedicated to the idea of buying our way to happiness. We shall all have made it to Heaven when we possess enough.

And at the same time the forces of American commercialism are hugely dedicated to making us deliberately unhappy. Advertising is one of our major industries, and advertising exists not to satisfy desires but to create them—and to create them faster than any man's budget can satisfy them. For that matter, our whole economy is based on a dedicated insatiability. We are taught that to possess is to be happy, and then we are made to

300

want. We are even told it is our duty to want. It was only a few years ago, to cite a single example, that car dealers across the country were flying banners that read "You Auto Buy Now." They were calling upon Americans, as an act approaching patriotism, to buy at once, with money they did not have, automobiles they did not really need, and which they would be required to grow tired of by the time the next year's models were released.

Or look at any of the women's magazines. There, as Bernard DeVoto once pointed out, advertising begins as poetry in the front pages and ends as pharmacopoeia and therapy in the back pages. The poetry of the front matter is the dream of perfect beauty. This is the baby skin that must be hers. These, the flawless teeth. This, the perfumed breath she must exhale. This, the sixteen-year-old figure she must display at forty, at fifty, at sixty, and forever.

Once past the vaguely uplifting fiction and feature articles, the reader finds the other face of the dream in the back matter. This is the harness into which Mother must strap herself in order to display that perfect figure. These, the chin straps she must sleep in. This is the salve that restores all, this is her laxative, these are the tablets that melt away fat, these are the hormones of perpetual youth, these are the stockings that hide varicose veins.

Obviously no half-sane person can be completely persuaded either by such poetry or by such pharmacopoeia and orthopedics. Yet someone is obviously trying to buy the dream as offered and spending billions every year in the attempt. Clearly the happiness market is not running out of customers, but what are we trying to buy?

The idea "happiness," to be sure, will not sit still for easy definition: the best one can do is to try to set some extremes to the idea and then work in toward the middle. To think of happiness as acquisitive and competitive will do to set the materialistic extreme. To think of it as the idea one senses in, say, a holy man of India will do to set the spiritual extreme. That holy man's ideal of happiness is in needing nothing from outside himself. In wanting nothing, he lacks nothing. He sits immobile, rapt in contemplation, free even of his own body. Or nearly free of it. If devout admirers bring him food he eats it; if not, he starves indifferently.

Why be concerned? What is physical is an illusion to him. Contemplation is his joy and he achieves it through a fantastically demanding discipline, the accomplishment of which is itself a joy within him.

Is he a happy man? Perhaps his happiness is only another sort of illusion. But who can take it from him? And who will dare say it is more illusory than happiness on the installment plan?

But, perhaps because I am Western, I doubt such catatonic happiness, as I doubt the dreams of the happiness market. What is certain is that his way of happiness would be torture to almost any Western man. Yet these extremes will still serve to frame the area within which all of us must find some sort of balance. Thoreau—a creature of both Eastern and Western thought—had his own firm sense of that balance. His aim was to save on the low levels in order to spend on the high.

Possession for its own sake or in competition with the rest of the neighborhood would have been Thoreau's idea of the low levels. The active discipline of heightening one's perception of what is enduring in nature would have been his idea of the high. What he saved from the low was time and effort he could spend on the high. Thoreau certainly disapproved of starvation, but he would put into feeding himself only as much effort as would keep him functioning for more important efforts.

Effort is the gist of it. There is no happiness except as we take on life-engaging difficulties. Short of the impossible, as Yeats put it, the satisfactions we get from a lifetime depend on how high we choose our difficulties. Robert Frost was thinking in something like the same terms when he spoke of "the pleasure of taking pains." The mortal flaw in the advertised version of happiness is in the fact that it purports to be effortless.

We demand difficulty even in our games. We demand it because without difficulty there can be no game. A game is a way of making something hard for the fun of it. The rules of the game are an arbitrary imposition of difficulty. When the spoilsport ruins the fun, he always does so by refusing to play by the rules. It is easier to win at chess if you are free, at your pleasure, to change the wholly arbitrary rules, but the fun is in winning within the rules. No difficulty, no fun.

The buyers and sellers at the happiness market seem too often

302

to have lost their sense of the pleasure of difficulty. Heaven knows what they are playing, but it seems a dull game. The Indian holy man seems dull to us, I suppose, because he seems to be refusing to play anything at all. The Western weakness may be in the illusion that happiness can be bought. Perhaps the Eastern weakness is in the idea that there is such a thing as perfect (and therefore static) happiness.

Happiness is never more than partial. There are no pure states of mankind. Whatever else happiness may be, it is neither in having nor in being, but in becoming. What the Founding Fathers declared for us as an inherent right, we should do well to remember, was not happiness but the *pursuit* of happiness. What they might have underlined, could they have foreseen the happiness market, is the cardinal fact that happiness is in the pursuit itself, in the meaningful pursuit of what is life-engaging and life-revealing, which is to say, in the idea of *becoming*. A nation is not measured by what it possesses or wants to possess, but by what it wants to become.

By all means let the happiness market sell us minor satisfactions and even minor follies so long as we keep them in scale and buy them out of spiritual change. I am no customer for either puritanism or asceticism. But drop any real spiritual capital at those bazaars, and what you come home to will be your own poorhouse.

March 14, 1964

Love Laughs (and Cries) at Obstacles

A few months ago I flew to Indiana to lecture at Valparaiso University, and there I met Professor Richard Scheimann of the

303

Philosophy Department, from whom I have a tale to retell, the gist of which is that Professor Scheimann married Mrs. Scheimann but that it wasn't easy. At the tale's beginning, both he and Mrs. Scheimann-to-be were graduate students at the University of Chicago. I don't know whether he was a philosopher before his intricate experience or became one as a result of it, but I must certainly believe that only a man with a lover's purpose and with a firm sense of this world's ironies could have kept his mind whole and his perspective hopeful as he fought his way to the altar over the obstacle course that fate and its bureaucracy had contrived for him.

Let me say at once that the bride was willing, that the groom was eager, that a June date had been set, that a clergyman had agreed to perform the ceremony, and that City Hall had issued the license. All roads seemed to run smooth and straight. It was then Mr. Scheimann began his crooked mile.

The clergyman, as the first kink of fate would have it, was an army reservist and ten days before the wedding he was called up to take part in maneuvers, leaving Mr. Scheimann to scout around for a replacement. As it happened, one of Mr. Scheimann's former roommates was a clergyman, though in another state. What could be better than to have the ceremony performed by an old friend? Over the telephone the old friend immediately agreed, but pointed out that he was not legally empowered to execute a marriage certificate in Illinois. If, however, Mr. Scheimann would have his local clergyman fill out, sign, and predate the marriage certificate before leaving for the Army, friend-clergyman number two would be delighted to fly into Chicago and perform the ceremony.

Mr. Scheimann immediately raced over to his local clergyman to explain the new arrangement, and at this point everyone in our small but many-angled tale seems to have fallen into confusion. Mr. Scheimann's out-of-state friend seemed willing to perform a ceremony for which he lacked legal authority if Mr. Scheimann's local clergyman would illegally fill out and sign the marriage certificate before the fact and at one remove. And in whatever confusion the packing of his Army gear had left him, the local clergyman agreed. Mr. Scheimann, of course, had every right to be confused: he was about to be married.

So matters stood until three days before the wedding, at which

304

point Mr. Scheimann's out-of-state friend wired: "Cannot come. Get someone else."

With time running out, Mr. Scheimann turned to a third clergyman, also an old friend, but one who happened to be legal in Illinois. Clergyman number three, however, would have nothing to do with a marriage certificate illegally filled out, signed, and predated by someone else. Mr. Scheimann would have to go back to City Hall and get a duplicate.

City Hall, as any man knows, is its own sort of crooked mile, though it is one that does not necessarily lead anywhere and is forever ready to collapse into a chuckhole, if not a washout, at the touch of an undotted *i* or an uncrossed *t*. And Mr. Scheimann in love, in haste, and in innocence, blurted out no less a clerical irregularity than the whole truth. "I need a duplicate marriage license," he explained, "because this one has already been filled out, signed, and predated by the wrong clergyman."

That, I gather, was the point at which the earth opened and all roads buckled into the abyss. It was illegal, the man would have to be prosecuted, and Mr. Scheimann would have to produce him and testify against him.

As best he could, Mr. Scheimann explained that the clergyman had been called into the Army and parts unknown, that the second clergyman was from out of state but that he couldn't come, that a third clergyman stood ready to perform the ceremony, that he, Mr. Scheimann, would still like very much to get married, and might he be given a duplicate license, please?

The clerk, in his turn, made it clear that whether or not Mr. Scheimann managed to get married was irrelevant. What mattered was the irregularity of the thing and that the clerk had no authority to issue duplicate licenses. Mr. Scheimann would have to apply at office number two in building number two.

It was a simple bureaucratic route then from office number two to office number three from which Mr. Scheimann, still having avoided arrest, was routed back to office number one. There, after waiting out the line, Mr. Scheimann once more found himself facing clerk number one, who obviously was in no public mood for love and announced loudly a) that Mr. Scheimann was making a nuisance of himself, b) that there was nothing to be done, and c) that he had best clear out before a cop happened by. To which he immediately added in a whisper, "Look, buddy. Quit making trouble. Just go over to the other wicket, say you lost your damned license, and ask for a duplicate."

So, one more turning and one line later, Mr. Scheimann found himself facing a motherly looking lady who turned out to have her own sense of indignation. "Lost your marriage license," she said in a voice that called all men to witness her trials on this earth and in that city. "How can anyone lose his marriage license? What's the matter with you? Don't you want to get married? Where did you lose it?"

Mr. Scheimann, now committed to his bureaucratic fiction, tried to explain, in reverse order, that if he knew where he had lost it he would know where to find it, that yes he did want to get married and very much, that his very eagerness to get married might best explain what was the matter with him those days, and that anyone can lose a marriage license with the amount of help he had been given.

Well, friends, it did finally work out, as you already know. The motherly lady conquered her indignation long enough to produce a duplicate license, the marriage was both solemnized and legalized, and I am ready to guess that Professor and Mrs. Scheimann are living happily ever after. All that remains now is to find the moral that will properly describe, or at least decorate, whatever world this is in any finder's eye. For which purpose, from my eye to yours and toward a vision of the found world, I offer this thought: "Love conquers all, but it would be easier with fewer friends and without clerks."

July 25, 1964

Confessions of a Crackpot

Americans are still born free but their freedom neither lasts as long nor goes as far as it used to. Once the infant is smacked on the bottom and lets out his first taxable howl, he is immediately tagged, footprinted, blood-tested, classified, certificated, and generally taken in census. By the time that squawler has drawn the breath of adulthood he must have some clerk's permission to go to school or stay away, ride a bike, drive a car, collect his salary, carry a gun, fish, get married, go into the army or stay out, leave or re-enter the country, fly a plane, operate a power boat or a ham radio, buy a piece of land, build a house or knock one down, add a room to the house he has bought, burn his trash, park his car, keep a dog, run his business, go bankrupt, practice a profession, pick the wildflowers, bury the garbage, beg in the streets, sell whiskey in his store, peddle magazines from house to house, walk across a turnpike from one of his fields to another now that the state has divided him—the list is endless. Even in death his corpse must be certificated and licensed before the earth may swallow him legally. Freedom is no longer free but licensed.

To be sure there are reasons for all those licenses; even good reasons for some of them. We have long since bred ourselves out of Daniel Boone's kind of freedom. He needed a whole unpopulated horizon for his gestures. But if we throw our arms around that way we end up with a thumb in a neighbor's eye. Regulation is the price of congestion.

Licensing, moreover, invariably begets license. This world's clerks are always shortsighted men and never reluctant to compromise great principle if they can thereby regulate some trifling issue. The view of things from those wickets can be taken for

307

granted. But what shall ever save us when the citizen-licensees of these dark hallways begin to accept their endless licensing meekly?

Within my own neurosis, nothing has rankled in me quite as much as the fact that I had to apply for a license before I could get married. I even argued with the then Miss Hostetter for a common-law marriage. Why go looking for the clerks? Let them find us. What is more private than a marriage? Who has a right to license it?

A few years ago, as I recall it, I appeared on one of those talky TV panels, this one on the subject of freedom. Almost automatically I uncorked my rancor at the idea of a marriage license. Almost inevitably there was a Man of Reason present. "But surely you see the point," he said in an infuriatingly soothing tone, "—if only for the Wassermann test . . ."

And there is the true sound of the license-habituated mind. Let freedom risk its germs, I told him, I would sooner be syphilitic and free than sanitary and licensed. That, of course, made me a crackpot. So be it, but I will still believe that clerks are a creeping paralysis to which any plague may be preferred.

As for Miss Hostetter, she won, of course, and bless her. Whatever a man can deny his wife, he can deny his bride nothing. I paid the fee, gave my drop of blood, and accepted the permission of a clerk's signature like a good puppy.

But let it be noted on my tombstone that I did bark once, and might even have bit. I had moved hastily into New Jersey and since I did not have time to buy a house, I drove past a new development, looked at the model, and signed on for a split-level—total buying time about forty-five minutes, taxes payable to Bridgewater Township. Two years and one child later the house we wanted turned up in another town and we bought it, turning in the split-level like an old car (except—such is the world—with a slight profit)—total selling time, about fifteen minutes.

Off I went to Township Hall for my G.I. papers. And there the first thing I was asked by a dried pod of a female clerk was, "Have you a moving permit?" I asked what that might be and was informed that I could not move out of the township without a permit. Back came that neurosis: no, I did not have a moving permit nor did I want one; I had moved into her township without anyone's permission and I planned to move out the same way, thank you. She didn't call the FBI at once. In fact, she was painfully patient—to start with. "It doesn't *cost* anything," she said as if she had located the nucleus of the disease, "all you have to do is ask for it."

With various rhetorical flourishes I announced to her that it cost most of the remaining difference between me and a Russian, and that to ask for it was precisely what I refused to do. Three hours and several clerks later, the head man at that skim-milk distillery handed over my G.I. papers without the moving permit but warned me that I would be arrested if I tried to move without it. By then, however, I was smashing tea casks in Boston Harbor, crouching behind stone walls on the road to Lexington, and waiting for the whites of their eyes on Bunker Hill. I announced that I was moving the morning after next and that move I would, and without permission. I even had visions of poking out the picture window with a shotgun and shooting it out with George III, Geronimo, and J. Edgar Hoover.

I did, as I say, bark that once. And who knows?—I might even have bit, had I had a shotgun, and had majesty, maverick Indians, and the federal arm attacked. But these days a man can't win even in fantasy. On the appointed morning as I paced uneasily, preparing myself for jail, and blocking out the points of my appeal to the Supreme Court, the mover arrived and his men began calmly to stack our stuff in the van. As part of his normal procedure, he had taken out the permit for me. Worse, he not only had a permit for me to move out of the township, he had another permit allowing me to move into the new town.

As a dedicated crackpot—at least in my fantasy life—I wasn't quite through. I took time to call on my lawyer and from him I gathered that the law establishing moving permits was put on the books by landlords as a protection against rent skips, and by the municipalities to protect their claims to personal property taxes. Good enough reasons, to be sure, but measly ones in contrast to the principle of free movement that law brushed aside as a matter of no consequence. Could such a law be constitutional? My lawyer was certain it was not. He even pledged himself to fight it all the way to the top without fee, if I would pledge the court costs. It would take, he estimated, plus or minus three thousand dollars.

That was where I lost the last teeth from my bite. A toothless and a sadder man writes this, but a crackpot yet. If I must forego the steak of the spirit and gum the mush of clerks, let me yet raise the sticky bowl in a toast to their total damnation before all of us are reduced to inky digits in ledgers as musty as the minds that certificate and alphabetize us in the name of good—and measly—reason.

February 24, 1962

Parents and Proverbs

A child is an act of faith about which one grows increasingly uncertain. An adult, it might follow, is a gambler in the process of losing. Still the perpetual motion is love, and within that motion every generation has tried to save what it has already lost by teaching the losing game to its children. This state of confusion is called, by general agreement, parenthood.

I wonder if there is any such thing as a great parent. The more I hear my more heavily parented friends praise the stature of their parents, the more I distrust. For myself, I am moved to hope that I shall never ask of my children more than the right to be seen through their own mistakes. I shall hope for love, wistfully if need be, but the day love runs aground on respect, I shall know I have been a stuffed shirt.

Heaven knows, it is easy enough in our damp-souled culture for the young to fall into inane mother-love—with lyrics by Hallmark. Personally, I should find motherhood easier to respect as a generic thing were the prerequisites higher. It can, after all, happen to almost any girl. As for dad—still speaking generically—he is a simple enough accessory to the simple prerequisites. If he and she were foolish to start with, the act of procreation may make them sadder, but certainly not much wiser.

Once established as lords-of-the-hearth, it is easy enough for willful parents to impress themselves upon their children. Young twigs are easily bent. But parents become impressive at their own risk.

What generation has ever failed to give its children more than enough grounds for an indictment as hypocrites? How many questions is it possible to answer fully and honestly, in open confusion openly confessed? Too many parents prefer to pose in the certainties of gnomic wisdom. Let a fathead enter into parenthood with a stock of ten proverbs and a pompous air of adulthood; little big-eyes will have a blown-up balloon of a legend to quote from for the rest of his life.

All these thoughts spring from my observation of specific parents—two of them, married to each other, both of them very impressive, very self-assured, and very proverbial parents indeed. Not long ago, in the course of a cross-country lecture jaunt, I had the unpleasure of watching them through an entire Sunday of bending their little twigs. Never have I been made so aware of the fact that the world has changed out from under its proverbial guidelines.

These particular parents, as part of their prostration before their own images, had fallen into the habit of making many of their remarks to the children in proverbs importantly uttered. On the plane that took me on to the next stop, I found myself testing as many as I could recall.

In the hope that the children, now defenseless, may grow firmer of mind and learn to read and ask questions that will in turn lead them to see their parents as something less than monuments—and in the further hope that they not starve to death in the act of following their present instruction—I make this effort to rewrite part of their day's maxims. May they come upon these revisions in time:

Penny wise is inflation foolish.
Waste not and there will be no work.
A dollar saved is a quarter earned.

Honesty is the best policy without general coverage.

What goes up must come down—if it can solve the re-entry problem.

If Detroit had meant people to walk it would have manu-factured shoes.

Eyesight is only skin-deep.

Why start at the bottom of the ladder? Take the escalator.

A rolling stone gathers no pension.

Early to bed and early to rise probably indicates unskilled em-ployment.

A taxpayer and his money are soon parted.

Luckily the hostess brought one of those cardboard airline dinners at this point and I had to put up my pad, else the fit might have run on. But let me yet ask for all bemused and fumbling parents honest enough to live outside the monuments of gnomic sell-assurance—what *does* one tell the kids that will stay firm to any world they must live in on their own?

All I can quote by way of reply is the prescription of an old friend: "Have 'em, love 'em, and leave 'em be." Leaving 'em be is precisely that act of heroism that only the best parents—which is to say the least monumental and self-assured—learn to aspire to.

The trouble is, of course, that loving 'em can raise hob with leaving 'em be. But you have to try. The more you learn about not trusting yourself too complacently, the more able you be-come to trust them to their own mistakes. One thing remains certain for the gnomic to note—that the world and its proverbs are soon parted.

SONG OF THE SHORT AXE: I have this story from Nancy Hale, my heart's candidate for the title of World's Most Elegant Grand-mother. A lady (a well-known author), who is a friend of lovely Nancy's, had her childhood confused not only by having parents but by living across the street from Lizzie Borden, the same Lizzie who is metrically reputed to have taken an axe and to have done some felonious counting. After that mathematical unpleasantness and the following inquest, when Lizzie was back home, the child and author-to-be took to crossing the street to sit on the front steps with Lizzie. After a number of such visits, the then-child's mother suggested that she should not spend so much time "over there"—a remark that, as even gnomic parents know, leads inevitably to "Why, Mommy?"

I submit that Mommy committed a classic by way of reply, and may all the great white houses of the genteel find their sweet if slightly musty justification in it.

"Well," said Mommy, "she wasn't very nice to her parents."

May 26, 1962

A Cadillac Full of Diamonds

One day I did pull the right lever at the right time and I was rich!

I filled the car with diamonds as fast as they poured down the chute. I threw away the spare tire and the jack and crammed the trunk full. Then I yanked out the back seat. Then the right front seat. Then even the driver's seat. Then I crammed my pockets, throwing my money away to make room. Then I tied the bottoms of my pants and stuffed my pants legs. Then my shirt.

That about did it, but I still had to get into the car, and I couldn't open the door without starting an avalanche. Luckily I had left the left front window open, though I don't suppose I can take credit for that: I had had to pour them into the car through *some* opening.

But stuffed as I was, I could never wriggle through the window. There was no help for it: I had to unbutton my shirt, untie my pants legs, and let them spill. Then I had to empty my pockets. I was excited—who wouldn't be?—but I kept my head and took the time to bury them carefully. Waste not, want not.

And even then I couldn't make it through the window. I had, finally, to take my clothes off. Naked, I was just able to scrape through—and "scrape" is exactly the word: I was half way in, my hips ripped and raw, when I realized I had no driver's seat. It was an agony, but I forced my way out, retrieved the money I had thrown away, and made a padding out of it, pushing the stones around to make a little shelf. It was, to be sure, an improvisation, but it looked reasonably comfortable with the money smoothed out flat. Thank God I had just cashed a check!

So, finally, I managed to wriggle in and be seated. I was naked, scraped raw, and panting with exertion, but not seriously injured. Inevitably, some of the diamonds spilled out as I wiggled about to make room behind the wheel. I even thought for a fraction of an instant of getting out and burying them with the others, but that thought was immediately supplanted by the realization that in my excitement I had already forgotten where I had buried them.

I began to see I should have to develop a new attitude. Forcing myself to be calm, I concentrated on how to work the controls. Thank God I had an automatic shift: I could never have worked a stick shift in all that gravel. Even so, some of the rocks were jamming the brake and the accelerator. I had to keep poking around with my feet until I felt a little play in the pedals. It was going to be tricky—no doubt about that—but I could make it with a little luck. It wasn't much of a drive to my house.

But when I had made it at last—at what seemed to be a mile a week—there was no way to get out. A truck was blocking my driveway and when I looked closer, I saw it was bedded down in the macadam right to the axles. Don't ask me to explain. It's the sort of thing that just seems to keep happening. The truck had become a monument to all the world's past deliveries and was now no more movable than Grant's Tomb.

So the driveway was out. And every place at the curb was taken by cars that seemed to be made of girders pile-driven into the pavement and rusted together. Don't ask me to explain that either: every monument needs some sort of approach to it. I drove around the block twenty times, then around the next block and the next. There wasn't a place to park short of the last few farms, up there on the ridges.

And suppose I did get a farmer to rent me a field: could I just crawl out the window and ask it to crank itself shut from the inside? I had to unload. Sooner or later, too, I had to pick up some clothes. It was cold and some of these diamonds had sharp edges.

I drove back home and circled and circled until I honked my wife up. "Whatta ya want?" she yelled from the bedroom window. "Bring a bucket!" I shouted. But there were cars honking behind me, backed up for half a mile. I moved on and circled the block twelve times before she made it to the curb.

Without the bucket.

And another line of cars honking behind me.

"Here!" I said and tossed her a handful as I went by. I had to reach up and throw them over the top of the car from the left, and naturally they scattered all over the place.

I'll say this for her: she seemed to know the stuff was real even while it was still in the air. "Lemme get in!" she shrieked the next time around. "In where?" I shrieked back, tossing out another handful. "Stop it!" she shrieked, "I haven't any pockets!" Now, wasn't that just like her! "Get the damn bucket!" I bellowed back.

It went on that way all night and all day, and all the next night and the next day, too. By the third night we were both worn out, but she let me snatch some sandwiches as I went by, and then my service .45, and on the last lap, as I crawled along, she managed to get some gas into the tank by running behind me. She still hadn't focused enough to get the bucket, but I passed out a double handful of gravel, waved her off, and drove out to the country to get some sleep, the .45 on my lap.

I had hardly dozed off, of course, before the farmer was tapping at my window and shining his light in. But he wasn't any trouble. For half a million from my padding and a look at my .45, he sold me the field and threw in some boards to box in the gas pedal and the brake and even drilled holes in the two top boards for me. By pushing a stick through the holes in each box I could work the pedals fine, except that I hadn't room for two sticks,

315

so I had to keep fishing for the right knot hole as occasion demanded, and there was every chance that occasion might keep demanding it a bit faster than I could fish.

But he fixed me up as well as he could and he even brought me some coffee. He really turned out to be a pleasant sort. "I've tried those levers myself," he said. "It gives me heart to know someone has made it."

That was a long time ago.

We have it pretty well worked out by now, except that she has some sort of block about the bucket and never remembers to bring it out. I drive around more-or-less on schedule, depending on the traffic, and she's out there waiting. She holds the kid up so I can wave, and I toss them another handful of marbles. She has box lunches ready and a thermos and the receipted bills. We're trying to buy the house next door so we can tear it down for me to park there, if the dynamiters ever clear the cars parked in front of it. But the old buzzard won't sell, and none of the crews we have working has been able to budge the truck in front of my driveway.

It's no way to live. Many a time I've thought that if I had to make just one more circle, I'd just put the .45 to my head and pull the trigger. But I've got to hold on for my wife's sake and for the kids. It's even possible the buzzard next door will finally croak, though his kind never does. *Something* has to give. I almost wish it could be me, but I'm in no position to think just of myself. I have responsibilities. I've *got* to hold on.

March 7, 1964

316

In and Out of the Attic

I see I am fated to spend the rest of my life in the attic. There is, of course, a romantic power and presence in the idea of souls in garrets. I know of poets who have had their chance to move out and who turned it down. True to tradition, they stayed on in the garret and simply had it remodeled into an attic study. I even know one poet who turned his garret into a penthouse.

Toward such distinctions as are possible, I understand a garret to become an attic study when it is heated and air-conditioned. It becomes a penthouse when one reaches it by elevator and/or when it acquires something called décor, and especially when the décor spills out onto a terrace. Penthouses tend to such optional features as paneling, built-in hi-fi, modest but exquisite collections of paintings, or at least of etchings, and (though only for the frivolous) bars made of old barn siding.

Other possibly useful distinctions come to mind. In a garret there is likely to be no line between what one hopes is a wall and what one knows is a ceiling. In an attic study the ceiling slope stops at some point and drops a vertical that may sometimes be called a wall. In a penthouse, of course, the ceilings are parallel to the floor.

I do not come by these distinctions lightly. For twelve years, I tried to work in what was technically an attic study. At least it was partially heated and partially air-conditioned. Its slopes, however, were definitely garretish, and, in consequence, most of my books ended up on the floor. The trouble with such a book arrangement is that it turns a man into a four-legged hunter huffling about with a flashlight in his teeth (it can be done with one of those pocket-size Gulton rechargeables) as he tries to track

317

a title from one illegible book spine to another. In a lost golden age, my stacks had all turned their bindings in one direction and were in approximate alphabetical order. But in twelve years of yanking out the second-book-from-the-bottom, I had started too many avalanches, destroying thereby the order of alphabets. Toward the end I was down to playing beater in some sort of seriously taken snipe hunt: if I could not drive a quotation from Augustine into the bag, I would settle for one from Zola, and no matter. The word is the word and in it Alpha and Omega are one.

Nevertheless, and though I had a habituated fondness for attics, that fall from grace to all fours was more than I was willing to tolerate as a permanent condition. Though the avalanche destroy all first gardens, are there never to be book-lined rooms a man can walk upright, aligned to the alphabets of creation, where he is able to lay his hand on a title at will?

Attached to the house was a two-car garage we used for storing a tangle of bikes and power mowers, and as a private dump for junk too good to throw all the way out. I can testify that no car had ever been in it. Why bother? Come turn-in time no dealer ever asked me if I had loved and sheltered my car. He wanted to know its year of birth: all else was written in his book.

I decided to move from the attic to the garage, and, to make the move in proper style, I called in an architect. "These are interesting ideas," he said as I explained my scrawl sketches and my itemized dream specifications. "How far do you want to go?" he added, a bit warily, I thought.

But I ignored his wariness. This was dream stuff, and heady. "Beyond," I said.

Some weeks later he was back with plans strewn all over the dining room table. "I would estimate $3,500," he said. "Maybe $4,000."

They were elegant plans. I pinned them to a sloping ceiling in my soul and dreamed on them. "It's a deal," I breathed.

The contractors, too, were ready for deals. I called in something like the full local series offered by helpful friends and the Yellow Pages. And the lowest bid I got ran only a shade under $10,000. Nor were any of the contractors impressed when I pointed out that the room—basic ceiling, basic walls, and basic floor—was

318

already there. Had they thought I meant, perhaps, to build a house? It turned out they *had* understood. I seemed to be the only one who was out of touch with contractual reality, though I still had sense enough to say "no deal."

"I'll buy another house first," I told the last man in with a five-figure bid. "It will be cheaper."

It turned out to be not exactly cheaper but not much more expensive, either. The house we found turned out to have seven bedrooms. Surely a man with seven bedrooms has left the attic slopes forever. The "gray room," I decided, was it. It opened onto a great second-story porch it shared with the master bedroom (there were even dreams of glassing in the porch to make an elegant upstairs lounge of it). It was large enough. And it would require nothing but bookshelves I could run up myself in a week. We signed agreement A, then paper B, then form C, then document X, then a series of large checks, and in we moved.

As it happened I had to put off the bookshelves. Pressed by deadlines, I left the books in boxes and simply camped in the gray room till I could fight clear. It took me about seven minutes to discover that the gray room would not do as a study and that it was not even a desirable campsite. The children's rooms form an "L" around the gray room, and it, in turn, serves them as an echo chamber for three transistors, two record players, guitar practice, clarinet practice, and all the yowls and snarls of glad family living.

Nor were the third-floor rooms much better. I had moved into a poor man's version of Tennyson's pleasure house only to have to share it with the Beatles, the Mamas and the Papas, the Lovin' Spoonful, and whatever other groups of warm bodies happened to be raging their turns.

On the third floor, however, and closed off from the rest of the house, there was a lofty storage attic that reminded me, perhaps hopefully, of a neglected house in the pines, the pines nodding in through three windows in the far wall. The ceilings did slope, but if I dropped six-foot verticles from either slope, I would have a room about 20 x 20, up to the nine-foot wall of the cedar closet (ready and waiting for shelves), and the airspace above it.

Could it be soundproofed? My carpenter thought so, and after ten days of insulating, tar-papering, plasterboarding, lining, chinking in, and making tight, we were ready to test. By prearranged signal all transistors and record players were turned on full, all instruments were tortured, and all mouths not otherwise occupied were set to yowling.

Then the door was closed.

Silence.

My wife smiled.

My carpenter smiled—the smile of my inheritor.

I smiled, ready to bleed for him now, but secretly determined to cut him out of my will—assuming he left me an estate.

"Go ahead with it," I said.

With seven bedrooms on my hands, I was going back to the attic. Nor was I surprised to find I was happy in the thought. The only real garden is the first one again, with the landscaping expanded and improved.

September 16, 1967

On Making Sense

I don't trust people who are busy making sense. Their motives may be good enough, as motives go among low-order nervous systems, but they suffer from atrophy of the imagination. May they find fair weather in whatever universe they enter to constrict, but I don't want them at my house, and I won't go to theirs if I can help it. When we meet on the street, I look at my watch, pant a bit, and explain that I am late for an appointment. I am not even lying about that appointment, not even socially: Let one of these makers of sense appear and I am always instantly overdue for a group therapy session with my fantasy life.

"What are you doing these days?" they want to know, ignoring my watch, my panting, and my appointment.

320

Well, I am in for it. "I am memorizing the leaves of my lilac bush," I tell them. The bush is ancient and gnarled as a cypress root and needs fish oil to kill its scales (I think that's what the man told me), and I think no two of its leaves are exactly the same size, though I may be wrong. I have thought of picking each leaf and tracing it on thin paper and then of seeing if I could match any two of the tracings by putting a light under a glass-top table and candling the tracings, so to speak. Or perhaps it might be more accurate if I pinned them to paper and then sprayed their outlines. But either way I should first have to de-foliate—an ominous Vietnamish, Barry Goldwaterish, Pentagonal sort of idea. My blue jays would then have no green place to come to at window level when I am at breakfast. And who wants his blue jays suffering from defoliation, even if they would stay for it? So rather than pick my lilac to sticks in the name of scientific measurement, I have been memorizing the bush leaf by leaf and trying to match the leaves in memory. Always, of course, I lose track and have to start over. No matter: I like what I do and I am happy when it remains unmarred by progress.

But the makers of sense refuse me such green. Even when I have not told them the whole truth—simply on the basis of what little it is possible to say to them, they insist that I change my ways.

They remind me of the tribe of uncles who worried my way through college for me. I never told them I was heading for law school. They simply assumed it. What else is college for when you don't take pre-med? But they had heard of the poems I was publishing in the undergraduate magazine and they worried about me, honestly, one by one and as a group, and when they came to my house, or when we met on the street, they would take me aside. "John," they would say, "it's nice to know about all those poetry things, but"—always a big, sincere, and heartfelt "but," with one arm on my shoulder and a straight manly look eye to eye—"but you've got to be practical."

They were good enough men, all dead now, and I have left them an honest enough tear at graveside, a sadness for the men of my tribe. But I did not know then and I do not know now what practicality ever did for them. Does it make sense to go to your grave worried that you might not be making sense?

321

And still the makers of sense act as if I am pulling their legs. They want me to stop clowning. "Come on, now, what *are* you doing these days?"

"I am compiling neologisms for a lunch talk on Bloomsday. An early afternoon epithetary. I have slangonamous, vapilagic, bourgewalletarian, miscoitusion, and whole notebooks full of Eisenhower quotations, but no subject yet. And the days counted, mind you—a terrifictive pressure."

"Come, really—what are you doing these days?"—the voice of my fearfathers faring.

"I'm making money."

"Well, that's more like it!"

I have won approval.

"I am to be paid 7,000,000 zlotys plus expenses for delivering my Bloomsday lunch talk in Warsaw."

"How much is that in American money?"

"I don't know. There are currency restrictions. It can't be converted."

"Then why bother?"

I am being disapproved of.

"Well, I get the trip free, and the lunch, and I could buy 7,000,000 zlotys' worth of poles for people to vault over the Iron Curtain with, or 7,000,000 zlotys' worth of people for Poles to vault over the Iron Curtain to, or—"

"What sense is there in that?"

I am being further disapproved of.

"I have a contract for my book on lilac leaves," I say. "The working title is *Shiver in the Wind*, and I have an advance of $38,000."

"Now *that* makes sense."

I am in solid now.

"The book clubs have indicated interest," I say.

"When will it be published?"

"I don't know. I only have the title so far."

"But you have the advance."

"It's in escrow until I deliver the manuscript."

"Then get busy and deliver the manuscript."

"I am already busy memorizing the leaves."

"And when will you get *that* done?"

"I don't know. It takes more than one growing season. The leaves keep falling off before I have finished, and I have to start over in the spring."

"And how long has this been going on?"

I decide I might as well be honest. "All my life," I say.

At this point they throw their hands up and stop talking to me entirely. They talk to one another, even when they are alone, changing me into a third person. "He just doesn't make sense," they say. Or: "What's he talking about?"

It is, of course, the world I am talking about, but if I say so, they will accuse me of interrupting.

"A nut," they conclude. "I give him up."

A note of hope at last! I am not worth saying good-by to. I am being abandoned. And because they have come to expect nothing of me, they can no longer see me. I have the same permission as the Invisible Man. I can do as I please and go where I please, and I must be careful only about such things as staying hidden until my food has digested, about seeing that doors do not creak, and about not leaving footprints in the snow. I must also watch out for dogs—sniffing, suspicious brutes. And people who make sense are always surrounded by leashes and packs and kennels of the dogs they are going to. There is no escaping them. I can only hope to make friends with them—with the dogs, that is—and to make myself so familiar they will ignore me.

Then I shall be able to walk in and out observing how sense is made. I can watch husbands and wives killing everything they married for by demanding of one another that they make sense when they might better be making love. I can study parents as they box in their children by making sense in a drudging daily way when they might be making common cause in a sympathetic lifelong way. I can haunt cabinet meetings, and staff sessions, and committee rooms, and faculty meetings, and caucuses to watch all the deadly sense of the world being made.

What a book it would make! But I would never publish it. I would write it page by page every season from seed to rot, and when the leaves fell off my lilac, I would burn that season's pages and wait to start over in the spring—as long as I can stay for the spring, as long as there remains a spring to stay for, if the idea of spring manages to survive the cloud-domed gasp of a final sense being made by the nations.

February 18, 1967

A May Diary

A three-day drizzle and mist with only an hour or two of sun between clouds has made a tropic of the yard. There never was such green. Or if there always was, we forget it our winter through and need the fact of it to remind us, finding gratefully again that the fact is itself unbelievable. The ground in the flower beds is a conflagration of woody and mossy rot. Put a finger into it and a baby will take root. Nothing can *not* grow in such weather.

What was it Frost said in "Home Burial"?

> Three foggy mornings and one rainy day
> Will rot the best birch fence a man can build.

Rot weather is growing weather.

The first green this year was the lawn. The boys set the blades too low on the tractor-mower and scalped the grass where it now shows brown, but in such weather as this three days is already more than an inch of growth and the scalped places are healing. I put in 150 pounds of grass seed to thicken it and endless sacks of turf builder to boost it, plus a crick in the back to make it mine. I traveled last spring and had to neglect it, but it's coming back. Another boost next year should bring it around if it doesn't summer-burn.

Everything else is overdoing joyously. The flowering trees are

324

past. I finally had time with my wild apple tree. The tree is round and spreads sidewise at the base in a tropical-looking gnarl and makes a tent twenty feet high and thirty-five feet across. There's a place where you can duck inside it, and when it's in flower you can sit on the gnarl of the lower limbs with your feet on the ground and be in the father of all flower shows. For the last three years I had to be away when the tree was at its best, but this year I could stay home, and I had it all, including the blisters I got pulling out Virginia creeper to give the buds full sun in which to open.

The elm, too, has come through. With what I've paid for sprays and tending, I am ready to claim that tree as a tax dependent. Who could deny that the nation is richer for it—for as long as I can keep it alive? So far it has had only its dormant spray, but the leaves have come glossy and full with only one here and there eaten lacy by the leaf borers.

The first limb takes off from the trunk just at the window of my third floor landing, which is on the way to the study. I stopped there today to look at it, and there was a squirrel hunched in the curve of that first limb chewing at a moldy looking acorn. Its tail was wet and looked like a small-scale peacock feather daubed with mud and then run backwards through a piece of pipe—a sad excuse for any Bushy Tail—but the squirrel didn't seem to mind, and the nut must have tasted better than it looked, for the squirrel chomped it down, gave a swish of its bedraggled tail, and disappeared into green in a single leap.

I couldn't stand the study, puttered, gave it up, and went outside to mess a bit with the tomato plants that didn't need messing with. I only wanted to be out in the green mist. It's azalea time out there in huge red splashes. We'll have peonies in three days—perhaps even in one if the sun comes out full. With or without sun there will be roses tomorrow.

Only the rhododendrons are skimpy. Knowing friends tell me it's because they are under the elm, which sets up an alkaline condition. I must give them an acid treatment for a quick boost and cottonseed mash for the long run. By next year, I'll know if it works.

Nothing bothers the mountain laurel. Under elm, pine, spruce, hemlock, rotting old apple tree, dogwood, or red maple it comes on full, ready to open in a week.

The tomatoes are an experiment. I may yet put in a vegetable garden some year, but I haven't yet. I want to see if I can make ornamental bushes of these by keeping them wired. They can be attractive plants when gardeners don't let them draggle and get dusty.

I was late in getting in seed for the annuals, but they should be popping through in another few days and ready to transplant soon after that.

A week ago the fern was no more than fiddlehead sprouts among the lilies of the valley. Now it's a green comber rolling out of the hemlocks, and the lilies of the valley are drowned in it, though I can part the wave and find the white bells sparkling under it on a green reef.

Every green is another color. I look up at the spruces, and they are fifty-foot green waterfalls, the light green of the new growth like spray on the dark shaft of the fall.

I should have come back to the study earlier, but Dippy began yapping and begging in the garage with his eye on the Frisbee. Dippy is German shepherd and decided three years ago when the boys and I were tossing a Frisbee on the lawn that only he had the right to snatch the thing out of the air. I was without a fingernail for three months after I made the mistake of reaching for it just as he leaped. Since then his right has been unquestioned. We have it down to a routine now. He sits in front of me as I hold the Frisbee, circles behind me on signal, and goes sprinting off across the lawn while I flip the thing just over his head. If the throw is right, he will lunge like a tarpon four feet into the air, twist, and come down with the thing in his mouth.

On wet days his claws tear the grass when he leaps, and all four paws tear it when he comes down. The last thing on such days, therefore, is to replace the divots. At that they are not as bad as the rips Benn made when he decided to practice-drive the VW on the lawn, blast him. But let the divots fly and energy tear. So long as there is green enough everything can be put back.

I wait for Dippy to bring back the Frisbee—he has to worry it a while first—and I watch the green explode. No, you can't see it all at once. But you can see it from last week, and, so seen, it is nothing less than an explosion. I could prune for weeks and the place would still be a tangle. Let it tangle—within reason, to be sure, but let it tangle. Whatever tangle will let it grow without choking is within reason.

I'm glad of that crick in the back, and of the blisters I've had of it. It was the former owner who put in these plantings and loved them up to this riot of green. It's the blisters and the cricks that will finally, really make it mine.

May every man inherit green and then—if only partly—earn it. My one dark mood when it comes on me is that there is not green enough to keep enough people connected to a first sense of themselves—and that green may not last at the rate we are poisoning the root. We are a torn and fearful society without green enough to our thinking. Give every man his green acre, help him to keep it green and his, and the race will suffer nothing it can't live in to good enough ends.

June 20, 1970

Dawn Watch

Unless a man is up for the dawn and for the half hour or so of first light, he has missed the best of the day.

The traffic has just started, not yet a roar and a stink. One car at a time goes by, the tires humming almost like the sound of a brook a half mile down in the crease of a mountain I know—a sound that carries not because it is loud but because everything else is still.

It isn't exactly a mist that hangs in the thickets but more nearly the ghost of a mist—a phenomenon like side vision. Look hard and it isn't there, but glance without focusing and something

327

registers, an exhalation that will be gone three minutes after the sun comes over the treetops.

The lawns shine with a dew not exactly dew. There is a rabbit bobbing about on the lawn and then freezing. If it were truly a dew, his tracks would shine black on the grass, and he leaves no visible track. Yet, there is something on the grass that makes it glow a depth of green it will not show again all day. Or is that something in the dawn air?

Our cardinals know what time it is. They drop pure tones from the hemlock tops. The black gang of grackles that makes a slum of the pin oak also knows the time but can only grate at it. They sound like a convention of broken universal joints grating uphill. The grackles creak and squeak, and the cardinals form tones that only occasionally sound through the noise. I scatter sunflower seeds by the birdbath for the cardinals and hope the grackles won't find them.

My neighbor's tomcat comes across the lawn, probably on his way home from passion, or only acting as if he had had a big night. I suspect him of being one of those poolroom braggarts who can't get next to a girl but who likes to let on that he is a hot stud. This one is too can-fed and too lazy to hunt for anything. Here he comes now, ignoring the rabbit. And there he goes.

As soon as he has hopped the fence, I let my dog out. The dog charges the rabbit, watches it jump the fence, shakes himself in a self-satisfied way, then trots dutifully into the thicket for his morning service, stopping to sniff everything on the way back.

There is an old mountain laurel on the island of the driveway turn-around. From somewhere on the wind a white morning-glory rooted next to it and has climbed it. Now the laurel is woven full of white bells tinged pink by the first rays through the not quite mist. Only in earliest morning can they be seen. Come out two hours from now and there will be no morning-glories.

Dawn, too, is the hour of a weed I know only as day flower—a bright blue button that closes in full sunlight. I have weeded bales of it out of my flower beds, its one daytime virtue being the shallowness of its root system that allows it to be pulled out effortlessly in great handfuls. Yet, now it shines. Had it a few more hours of such shining in its cycle, I would cultivate it as a ground cover, but dawn is its one hour, and a garden is for whole days.

There is another blue morning weed whose name I do not know. This one grows from a bulb to pulpy stems and a bedraggled daytime sprawl. Only a shovel will dig it out. Try weeding it by hand and the stems will break off to be replaced by new ones and to sprawl over the chosen plants in the flower bed. Yet, now and for another hour it outshines its betters, its flowers about the size of a quarter and paler than those of the day flower but somehow more brilliant, perhaps because of the contrast of its paler foliage.

And now the sun is slanting in full. It is bright enough to make the leaves of the Japanese red maple seem a transparent red bronze when the tree is between me and the light. There must be others, but this is the only tree I know whose leaves let the sun through in this way—except, that is, when the fall colors start. Aspen leaves, when they first yellow and before they dry, are transparent in this way. I tell myself it must have something to do with the red-yellow range of the spectrum. Green takes sunlight and holds it, but red and yellow let it through.

The damned crabgrass is wrestling with the zinnias, and I stop to weed it out. The stuff weaves too close to the zinnias to make the iron claw usable. And it won't do to pull at the stalks. Crabgrass (at least in a mulched bed) can be weeded only with dirty fingers. Thumb and forefinger have to pincer into the dirt and grab the root-center. Weeding, of course, is an illusion of hope. Pulling out the root only stirs the soil and brings new crabgrass seeds into germinating position. Take a walk around the block and a new clump will have sprouted by the time you get back. But I am not ready to walk around the block. I fill a small basket with the plucked clumps, and for the instant I look at them, the zinnias are weedless.

Don't look back. I dump the weeds in the thicket where they will be smothered by the grass clippings I will pile on at the next cutting. On the way back I see the cardinals come down for the sunflower seeds, and the jays join them, and then the grackles

329

start ganging in, gate-crashing the buffet and clattering all over it. The dog stops chewing his rawhide and makes a dash into the puddle of birds, which splashes away from him.

I hear a brake-squeak I have been waiting for and know the paper has arrived. As usual, the news turns out to be another disaster count. The function of the wire services is to bring us tragedies faster than we can pity. In the end we shall all be inured, numb, and ready for emotionless programing. I sit on the patio and read until the sun grows too bright on the page. The cardinals have stopped singing, and the grackles have flown off. It's the end of birdsong again.

Then suddenly—better than song for its instant—a humming-bird the color of green crushed velvet hovers in the throat of my favorite lily, a lovely high-bloomer I got the bulbs for but not the name. The lily is a crest of white horns with red dots and red velvet tongues along the insides of the petals and with an odor that drowns the patio. The hummingbird darts in and out of each horn in turn, then hovers an instant, and disappears.

Even without the sun, I have had enough of the paper. I'll take that hummingbird as my news for this dawn. It is over now. I smoke one more cigarette too many and decide that, if I go to bed now, no one in the family need know I have stayed up for it again. Why do they insist on shaking their heads when they find me still up for breakfast, after having scribbled through the dark hours? They always do. They seem compelled to express pity for an old loony who can't find his own way to bed. Why won't they understand that this is the one hour of any day that must not be missed, as it is the one hour I couldn't imagine getting up for, though I can still get to it by staying up? It makes sense to me. There comes a time when the windows lighten and the twittering starts. I look up and know it's time to leave the papers in their mess. I could slip quietly into bed and avoid the family's headshakes, but this stroll-around first hour is too good to miss. Even my dog, still sniffing and circling, knows what hour this is.

Come on, boy. It's time to go in. The rabbit won't come back till tomorrow, and the birds have work to do. The dawn's over. It's time to call it a day.

November 6, 1971

Chrysanthemums

I have just come in from planting chrysanthemums, fourteen full-blooming plants of them. The edges of my porches are covered with their colors, my mood is still full of the tart, sweet odor of chrysanthemums, and there is still a smudge of dirt on my fingers, but let no man mistake me for an honest gardener, for I raise nothing from seed. These are the days of instant flowering. I bought my plants grown and blossomed from a mild-eyed and loam-knuckled man who lives near us and who spends his serene retirement in raising for his neighbors what they are too lazy to raise for themselves. These days my kind of gardening comes to little more than just-add-tap-water-and-set. It is to the flowering world what instant powder is to coffee, with the minor difference that the flower water should not be boiling, and with the major difference that the flowering result is as authentic as if the process were real.

Perhaps we no longer have time for the full process of a green reality. Yet there was a time when I knew my garden up from seed. My mother and aunt used to set out a huge kitchen garden when I was growing up and I was automatically its chore boy, even to the point of suffering the ridicule of my fellow hoodlums when we managed to corner a load of manure. At such times, I was appointed as the local substitute for the McCormick spreader while the boys stood by the fence and let me know how suitably I was occupied.

Nevertheless, we ate out of that garden and we ate well all summer and through the winter, too, out of the rows of Mason jars that crowded the cellar shelves. And when the last clacking stalks of the corn stood autumn-blown and the last apples were in, it was the chrysanthemums opening around the house foundations that announced the end of the season.

Whether home-grown or store-boughten, they are still the memorial flower, forever tuned to all the last colors of fruit and leaf. And if, these days, I am no more gardener than it takes to turn a shovelful of soft loam, fill the hole with water, and set in a plant someone else raised for me, there is still memory enough in the flowers themselves. They tell me summer is trailing off into the right colors, and they turn me back to thinking of the fruit of this summer and that of summers past.

I have it in mind, the odor of chrysanthemums still with me, that the peaches and grapes were bad this year and that they seem to be getting worse annually. I have about given up on grapes. Concords picked fresh from the vine are still what they were, but the California imports are dead on the taste by the time they arrive to market. They look good in their crates, but the sun is not in them. They were picked before the sun and were left to refrigerate to a tasteless nothing.

A pity. But it is the peaches I most regret. We had two peach trees behind the house, one early and one late, and my uncle had grafted onto each of them a few branches from some of his friends' trees. They were, consequently, several kinds of peaches on each tree. And barring a bad blow, few of them ended up as windfalls.

The trees were small and willowy. Even standing on the ground, I could reach halfway into them. Or with a stepladder I could pick them clean. But we were in no hurry to pick them clean. A few bushel baskets of the fruit were picked for canning, but the real ritual was to walk around the trees in their season, studying the boughs until the perfect peach announced itself to the eye. And that was the one to reach for. It came fuzzy and warm into the hand and had to be rubbed in the palms to get the fuzz off. Then, if the choice had been right, it would split open into two yellow halves, the inner hollow of each veined red by the pit, and the juice ready to burst on the tongue when the flesh was bitten.

My lazy-man's chrysanthemums reminded me that such a peach is the perfect fruit, the one fruit above all others. As it happened, I made a quick trip around the world this summer. President Carlos P. Romulo invited me to lecture at the University of the

Philippines and while I was there I feasted on mangos, papayas, fresh pineapples, endless kinds of bananas, and a whole series of tropic fruits I had never before tasted. All of them were delicious and all of them had been picked sun-ripe and brought to market without refrigeration. Yet none of them was a peach. The one perfect peach I came on all summer was from a bagful I bought in East Middlebury, Vermont, on August 16, the day I arrived at Bread Loaf. The grocer in East Middlebury had the remnants of one basket of local peaches on his counter and I bought him out. Arrived at Bread Loaf, I spread the fruit in the sun and instantly spotted the one I could put my hope in. It was large, firm, and exactly colored. I washed it, split it open, removed the pit, and bit into it, and it burst on my tongue as nothing had since I last balanced one of my own peaches out of my own trees.

It was the perfect fruit, and nothing in all the steamy jungles could come near it. And it was also the only perfect one of the lot. The others were good enough, but only good enough, and what good is that? A man thinking back from chrysanthemums is in no mode for adequacy. He needs to remember perfect things, if he can find them to remember. And so it is that I am reminded by chrysanthemums that this was the summer of a single perfect peach.

The apples have been good this year. Every roadside stand in New Jersey has had treasures to offer. I hope they have done well in upper New England. And in my autumn mood, I hope some farmer with the right memories has a barrel of cider left to harden and to set out in the field to freeze once winter sets in. For my chrysanthemums also remind me of field applejack. Not the distilled stuff, though it's good enough, but the field-frozen. Field-frozen applejack is another pure chrysanthemum taste. When a barrel of cider is left out to the winter, the water content freezes while the alcohol, along with all the marvelously unboiled apple-fleck impurities of pure taste draw to the center. When the barrel is frozen hard and has split its hoops, a man may run a hot iron through the ice to tap the liquid core. And nothing in the world is like it.

It is over twenty years since I had a taste of the real thing, but what else are chrysanthemums for? They are not only the flowers of memory but its sharpener. Their tang brings back the hope of

333

tang. To smell them is inevitably to remember what was perfect once. And what may be again, though we may have to wander through rare markets before we find it. Or perhaps I should say through small and backward markets. Certainly the supermarkets have little to offer that a man can eat and be satisfied with. Not if he has the odor and mood of chrysanthemums about him.

For the thing about chrysanthemums is that they are final and that they will have nothing to do with what is only good enough. They are the year's last perfect opening. They are not the harvest flower, but the flower after harvest. The memorial flower. The tank of the real year's end. And they make the mood that will settle only for what is perfect in memory, letting even instant gardeners in on the longest of what they remember best.

November 20, 1965

Years End When Leaves Fall

The calendar to the contrary, all our emotions know that autumn is the true memorial season and the true year's end, as they know that spring is its beginning. Primitive men—at least those whose tribes had wandered away from the steady equatorial mainlands and the climeless islands—had their seasons by heart rather than by mathematics. That heart's year starts with new leafage and the returning migrations. It ends with departures in the sky, with the flaming of green, and with apple fall, or perhaps with a dried and wizened last apple still stuck to its bough.

We still know that year by heart when we are not persuaded away from our own first sense of ourselves by that immemorial confusion the Romans began for us, partly by borrowing earlier errors and partly by adding their own. The ancient Romans tried to keep track of the year by some vaguely understood measure of ten variable months. It was a clumsy measure, as nearly as scholars have been able to decipher it, but it did answer to the original instinct to set spring as the beginning, the Ides of March having been clearly intended to coincide with the vernal equinox.

December is still "the tenth month" of that March-begun year, as September, October, and November are the seventh, eighth, and ninth. For most of a millennium, moreover, those months we now call July for Julius Caesar and August for Augustus were named simply the fifth and sixth months.

The first Roman calendar reform was decreed into being around 700 B.C. in the shadowy reign of Numa, who had obviously been having some royal bull sessions with his court mathematicians. Kings seldom listen to their mathematicians without leaving the world a moral. Let the moral in this case read: Kings and equations forget the sun. Numa ordered that a month to be named January be put in front of March and that another named February be put after December. So the spring-born year of all first understanding was lost to us.

Numa and his astrologist-priest-oracle-mathematicians had thought to put us on a twelve-month year, in answer to the moon's cycle. With one error and another, however, their year ran a disastrous ten and a quarter days short of the sun. Such an error would have compounded into more than a month in three years. In nine years it would have shifted the seasons by a whole quarter. And in eighteen years it would have rotated January's weather into June, and June's to January. Numa and his bookkeepers, therefore, were forced to insert an extra month of alternately twenty-two and twenty-three days into every second year. These additions did not, however, work out to sun-time, and other corrections had to be inserted into the calendar from time to time until it seems reasonable to doubt that even Rubius Goldbergensis could have figured out his mother-in-law's birthday among those fluttering kalends.

In 452 B.C. the Roman timekeepers got around to reversing the positions of February and January to establish approximately the sequence of months we now know, but by the time Julius Caesar got his mathematicians to work on the Julian calendar, the year had drifted off the vernal equinox by sixty-seven days. Authority

335

being what it is, Caesar decreed into the calendar of the last un-reformed year two nonrecurring months of thirty-three and thirty-four days respectively, and on the assumption that the world had caught up with the sun began the era of the Julian calendar on January 1, 46 B.C.

No one seemed entirely sure of how to take the new calendar and Augustus had to take on additional reforms in an effort to work out a year of 365 days with a leap year of 366, in spite of which the vernal equinox (Caesar had started it out on March 25) kept sliding back roughly one day each century. The sun, that is to say, remained unimpressed by the Roman timekeepers and con-tinued to make and take its own time.

My own arithmetic rests as an annual mystery between me and the internal revenuers and is not much assisted by a dim memory of having gone through Navigation School as an Aviation Cadet in, as I recall, the War of 1812. Accordingly, I gave the problem to a local slide rule whose oracle gave me back, as a round figure result, the information that the Julian calendar was set to run 44 minutes and 46 seconds ahead of the sun every four years, or 18 hours, 39 minutes, and 10 seconds a century—a divination I pass along on the assumption that the slide rule was a sound gauge and the oracle sober.

In a millennium, therefore, the Julian Calendar had drifted roughly eight days off the sun, and by the time Pope Gregory XIII got around to his calendar reform in A.D. 1582 (1628 of the Julian calendar) the vernal equinox had slipped back fourteen days toward the beginning of the year. The same rate of error projected to the present year would have put the calendar about sixteen days ahead of the sun.

To combat that drift, Gregory's mathematicians sharpened their styluses and added a provision that the double-zero year of any century would not be a leap year unless the number assigned to that century could be evenly divided by four hundred.

The Gregorian reform produced a year that is only twenty-six seconds too long but it still left an eccentric rotation of days and dates, thereby leaving room and reason for reformers who ad-vocate a calendar of thirteen equal months of twenty-eight days (a total of 364 days) plus a special holiday each year, plus another on the Gregorian leap years. Such a reformed calendar would

336

freeze the rotation of days and dates, for every month would begin on a Sunday or a Monday (depending on the denomination of the reformer) with the result that any given dates would always fall on the same day of each week.

Such tidiness must surely win the souls of all bookkeepers. For moneylenders it would raise, like a dream of the Golden Fleece, a vision of thirteen annual payments instead of twelve. For market analysts and economic statisticians it would do away with the need to adjust indices to allow for differences in the length of months. None of us, I suppose, need ever again worry about how many shopping days there are until Christmas. And IBM computers might make do with at least a mile or two less wire; or that mileage might be diverted to some other act of tidiness; or, conceivably, it might even be set aside to listen for signals from the sun or beyond.

I doubt, however, that any significant transmission will be coming in at IBM frequencies. All that can really be counted on is a humming and clicking efficiency that can have nothing to say to emotions whose atavisms reach beyond the Roman error back to sun time and to what the primitive knew of green beginnings and sere endings.

The Jews, with more time than the Romans in which to learn themselves by heart, had the only other possible good sense to choose September as their year's end and beginning again. And if their calendar still drifts off the sun a bit untidily, it drifts, nevertheless, toward a more fertile sense of what years are, and of what men are in their years: a total—so may the years teach us all—beyond the tidy enclosures of any bookkeeping. Let the mathematicians only keep the sun in place and what follows will be a year a man can know by heart.

October 30, 1965

Long Water Going

There is a man at a ship's rail looking down, and one by a water-
fall looking up, and another on one bank of a long water looking
out. They will not stay there forever, though someone will always
take the places they leave. No matter how many times man leaves
his place by running water, it will be there again and fresh and
first for any man's return to it. A man is deeper to himself when
he stands there, partly lost when he leaves, and always closer to
his own first of things when he comes again.

Always there is something about the unchanging changefulness
and about the changing constancy of water that lures him. Water,
perhaps, was the first timekeeper. Or, perhaps, it was the first
real metaphor for time. Or, perhaps, it is the most endless reminder (along with the stars) that time is longer than anything
that enters time.

This talk of the long waters is toward magic, of course, for we
do live, in part, by magic, though we have lost most of the vocabulary for it. We have been taught unreasonable vocabularies of
reason—unreasonable because they are not languages our feelings
can live by even when our proprieties try to. Watching water go,
we touch magic again, and are left dumb by it.

I know a stream in one seam of Bread Loaf Mountain in Vermont. In that stream there is a boulder I have been watching for
twenty-five Augusts now, and for twenty-five years the same
roil of water, about the size of a lock of hair in a curler, has been
standing off the east lip of the boulder.

A statistician could study the gradient of the streambed, the
stream's drainage area, the mean annual precipitation, and the
angle at which the boulder meets the flow. He could compute

338

then—perhaps, he could—how many millions or billions of gallons of mountain water go annually into keeping that one roil in constant position. I shouldn't be surprised to have a statistician tell me that all of Lake Champlain (which is to say, as much water as there is in all of Lake Champlain) has gone into and through that one roil since the glacier dumped my boulder and the stream shifted it into place.

But why should I care? Statisticians are dull fantasizers. They make a busy profession of gathering fact, but only to change it into something irrelevant or unreal. I prefer to take that one unchanging roil of the long waters as its own mystery of fact, equal entirely to itself, and therefore equal to nothing else. It waits for me there—which is to say I wait for it—year after year, a constancy beyond all else.

I am, of course, fantasizing as recklessly as any statistician. When I say I have been watching one unchanging roil for twenty-five years, I mean only that for twenty-five years, always in the same two weeks of August, the roil has been in place exactly as I remember having left it. For all I know, my roil may be drowned in spring, or it may sink away from the rock during a drought, or be frozen shut in winter. I must go there sometime in winter to see if the water freezes in the shape of my roil. I doubt that it does, but it would please me to learn that it did.

As water flows, twenty-five years is not, of course, any measure of constancy. Mark Twain returning to the Mississippi after something like twenty-five years was almost ready to think he had found a new river. And perhaps he had. But not a new water and not a new force and principle. The flow still came from a first of things, changing what tried to contain it, but never itself. A man had only to look over the rail to see the long principle going, always the same and forever shifting.

Even Niagara Falls has lost much of its edge, the rim rocks of the American Falls slanting to talus and threatening to change the falls into a chute and the chute into rapids, unless the engineers get titanically busy and restore the sheer drop the explorers discovered there. But even as a gat-toothed and stone-choked thing the cataract keeps its power over the tourist. His reasons for going there may be as tawdry as his jokes about not having (thank God) to pay the water bill, but no one can stand there unstirred. A man may resist the mood of such water; he cannot escape it.

There is a gypsy song whose English version, as I recall it, begins, "The world is old tonight, the world is old." That song, in its own florid and overtrilled way, tries to say what the long waters say to all of us with something like the first and last simplicity. Standing by those waters, a man cannot help being deepened to a sense of how long everything has been going on.

Somehow that deepening serenes him, though simply to be reminded that we are ephemera is hardly an experience in serenity. The serenity, I think, grows out of a sense of unchanging principle. Small we may be, but the long waters tell us we are attuned to something like a permanence, and somehow that sense of attunement is one our emotions can rest in, even when we notice how the waters are eating away the bounds that keep us.

And however much the inland waters may change banks and slopes, there is always the sea, always constant to its changeless changes. A man watching the sea from anything that floats is forever at his own first again.

In a small way I was playing this watch-the-sea game not long ago as I rode the Newport-Jamestown Ferry across Naragansett Bay. It was a raw and a rainy day, however, and I was doing my watching through a window of the upper-deck cabin. It is only a twenty-minute crossing there, but this mood comes at once. I watched, instantly hypnotized by the same restlessness of green water men have known from their first day's sailing.

Then a piece of sodden cardboard drifted by, then a bottle, then another piece of cardboard, then some sort of paper wrapper. I began to look for any stretch of clean water and could find none. Failing, I tried a game. Holding my head still, I kept my eyes on just that flow of water that came and went within the frame of one windowpane. I would win my game if at any time in the entire passage, my windowpane framed a piece of sea in which there was no floating refuse.

I lost my game. We all lost it. As we are all losing our game with the first of things.

What can any man, or all of mankind, do with a dirty sea? By the time we have finished poisoning every first thing, and thereby ourselves, all games will be over. Will it be any solace then to know that in time the waters will purify themselves again? The waters can only lose for a while. But we can lose forever, damned by our own flow of refuse.

Were you to go look at your own chosen water flowing, what would you see there? Will it be the first of things again, or the last coming? Will it be elements or slops?

I know that if the day comes when I walk my stream down Bread Loaf Mountain and find my chosen roil frothing detergents or clotted by the junk of someone's picnic, on that day I shall swear a damnation on the human race as unfit to occupy any planet.

Not that my damnation will matter except as it gives me a release of feeling. The race will have damned itself. As it may already have done.

March 18, 1967

Us Smiths

I was dog-walking my briefcase from *SR*'s offices to Penn Station in the standard New York pedestrian daze, my feet taking care of travel arrangements and my head in a daydream, when I found myself face to face with a red-faced cherub in pork-pie hat, bow tie, and sharp checked coat—a combination unmistakably from the $2 window at Aqueduct, and no winner.

"Joe!" he said. "Long time no see!"

"Longer than that," I said. "You've got the wrong man."

"Not a chance, Joe! I used to work upstairs, too."

We were in front of an office building, and he waved in the direction of "upstairs."

"Bill Morrissy's department," he elaborated.

"Believe me," I said. "I am a motherless child wayfaring through the valley, and I have never been upstairs."

"Well, whattaya know!" he said. "You got a twin. I mean you two look more like one another than you do like yourself. Hey, that's a good one, huh? Joe?"

"John," I told him.

"It's a pleasure," he said, shaking my hand. "John . . . uh . . . ?"

"Smith," I said.

"Harry," he said. "And how about that? I am also one of the Smiths."

"One of the Panhandle Smiths?"

He spread both arms and looked at the sky. "John," he said, "you're psychic. You got that extrasensory whatchamacallit—"

"Perception," I said.

"See! See what I mean? A mind reader!"

"How much?" I asked.

He lowered his voice. "I could use a few green ones, pal."

"For tomorrow's double?"

"For eating money," he said.

There was a bar just ahead. "Let me buy you a beer and break the bad news," I said.

"Bad news?" he said over the beer and a pastrami on rye that had got attached to the order.

"You are about to be gainfully employed," I said.

"A job!"

"No offense," I said. "You are the dressiest panhandler I've met since Tuesday."

He looked hurt.

"Tuesday, six years ago," I said.

He shook his head. "You got class, pal."

"It's your class I'm interested in. I write a column. Subject matter is where you find it. You tell me about the art of classy panhandling and I'll pay you five dollars."

"Ten," he said.

"That's what I meant," I said and ordered two more beers.

"John," he said after a good pull at the stein, "how much you get for writing this column?"

342

"Eleven dollars and fifty cents a month."

"Is that all they pay a writer guy?"

"It's a cruel world."

"Hey, pal, you putting me on?"

"Not really. But remember I am the one that's paying to ask the questions."

"You got a point," he said. "So ask."

"For a start, how did you get to the top of your profession?"

"You want the scene, huh? Okay, I'll earn the ten. I like the hosses, and I don't like work. I handicap 'em pretty good. When form pays off, I'm flush. Then the long shots start coming home, and I'm bust and on the street for a stake. You want I should go bumming? No class to it. You knock yourself out mumbling, 'Hey, Mac, help a fella,' and you knock down maybe fifteen bucks at two bits a shot. And then you have to square yourself with the cop because he has you marked lousy. Me, I dress nice, give a mark the old college glad hand. No arm. Just two pals on the street. And I score a hundred, hundred twenty. In a week I'm back at the Big A. In two weeks I get staked all the way to Hialeah." He finished the beer, and I ordered a new round. "That's it," he said.

"You want to go for five more?"

"Ten?"

"If it's worth it."

"Like what?"

"Tricks of the trade. How did you happen to pick me out of a sidewalkful?"

He smiled. "You want it straight, John?"

"From Smith to Smith."

"Well, to start with, I figure that sport coat goes for maybe two hundred and should have a wallet in the inside pocket. That's a nice easy-breezy slim-line briefcase, and new. It ain't for no slob buried in work, but just for a few papers that count. And you're daydreaming as you come along. And you look like a nice guy."

"Smith family flattery?"

"Article one. Only a nice guy will shell out."

"And the daydreaming?"

"That gives me surprise. I do what I call my cocktail-party

routine—like we're all standing around holding martinis and somebody comes up and says, 'Hi, pal,' and you talk right back, right? You gotta get the mark to talk. By the time he makes out he don't know you, you're into him."

I nodded. "Harry," I said, "you're a philosopher, and you get the full twenty."

"John," he said, "between us Smiths, I'll grab the check if you tell me one thing."

"It's a deal," I said.

"Back there," he said. "I do catch you by surprise, right?"

"Right."

"And still you had me made right off, right?"

"Had you made?"

"Identified. You knew I was panhandling you."

"Yes, I did."

"So why do you go on talking?"

"I told you. I write a column, and subject matter is where you find it."

"Where do I see this column?"

"In *Saturday Review*."

"And you get paid for it?"

"Meagerly."

"More than, say, twenty bucks?"

"A little."

"More than, say, a coupla hundred?"

"A little."

"So what I wanna know is—who's conning who?"

"Harry," I said, handing him two tens, "there has been no con. We Smiths are one another's profit. Good luck at Hialeah."

"John," he said, signaling for the check, "good luck to you everywhere. Us Smiths got it coming."

January 15, 1972

344

Goodbye

The following column was written to be the last in the Manner of Speaking series and was turned in as such to the editors of the new-and-revised Saturday Review, *who decided, for reasonable cause, not to publish it. For reasonable cause, it is published here.*

A three day storm had churned the Gulf. I rented a car, had the hotel pack a box lunch, and drove across the causeway to the Island, where I parked by the picnic tables and walked south, leaning into the wind that had been a gale yesterday and a near-hurricane before that.

Thousands of miles behind me, in the direction the wind was blowing, lay something called a world. Worlds are made up of memos to be misfiled, of walls to keep the wind out of the memos, and of committees that meet to consider the condition of the walls and of the memos the wind will get into in its own time despite all the committees in the world.

I was not of the world but of the earth. On earth the wind blew, the surf huffed and spumed, millions of seabirds—perhaps not literally millions, but emotionally millions of seabirds—screamed. The earth must have felt and smelled and sounded just so on opening day after the storm of creation.

Just above the surf line a strip about ten feet wide and forever long was strewn with dead fish half-buried in the sand. In places they lay so close together that they looked like the cobblestones of some ruined Roman road being taken back by the desert.

I walked its leeward side where the sand had been blown smooth. There hadn't been time yet for that pavement to stink. The birds would probably not give it time. They swarmed the whole length of that road, picking at the half-buried feast. Down

345

the whole length of the beach they fizzed like gas in the ravening of their energy. By squinting a little as I looked down the road—and the wind and salt grit made me squint—I could believe I was seeing heat waves quivering above a hot surface.

Not all the fish were buried flat. Here and there one seemed to be leaping out of the sand as if it were breaking water. About a mile north I came on a huge one I guessed to be a grouper. It curled up on the water (and windward) side of that road, curled just as a taxidermist might have mounted it except that its eyes had been picked out, that there were small crabs in its open mouth, and that gulls were picking at it, and sometimes at the crabs. It rose more than two feet out of the sand, all of its dorsal fin free and raised. Whatever road that was, the fish was an exactly right crazy milepost. The birds were eating well but they had not yet eaten into the essential shape of the fish. By the next day or the next, the birds and the sea would have shredded everything, but this was the earth, and, for a while yet, all shapes were eternal.

When I made it back to the car and opened my box lunch at a picnic table, my back to the wind, a triple row of terns took position in front of me, about ten feet in the air, and began to scream for scraps. In the box I found deviled eggs, chicken, slaw, and a lot of syrup-topped buns. When I tossed a pinch of bun into the air, the nearest tern would dart forward to snatch it and then fall back in line. It cost the birds only an occasional flicker of a wing to stretch out on the wind and to rest in place there. Were I God, I thought, I would keep heaven stocked with just such birds to play with at every meal.

The island was not only a fair imitation of heaven but twice heaven for being deserted. Lost in the world behind me were two hundred million people and not one of them had been willing to swallow a little salty grit in exchange for god-games.

I made it my game to pick one bird out of the twenty or so, and to toss my offering to it and no other. It wasn't easy. They were ranked about seven across and three deep. I pretended that the rows were A, B, and C in descending order and that the birds were numbered from left to right. It was easy to fire a scrap directly to C-3 or C-4. If I tossed my scrap to A-1 or to B-7, however, it had to pass diagonally in front of several other birds,

346

any one of which might snatch it. To hit the outside birds I had to throw my scrap across the wind and let it be vectored in.

I became so absorbed in the game that I ended by throwing my whole lunch to the wind without having tasted it. How often can a man sit and command such world-birds with a flick of the wrist? And they were world-birds. What boundaries had they? The minute I released them they could be off for Tunisia, Samoa, Labrador, Bombay. For creatures that easy on the wind only the world—the earth-world, not that walled one where the memos are—is home, and any place in it only a pause.

The last thing in the box was a slab of cherry pie, a red gelatinous mess that only my children and other barbarians could manage to swallow. I broke it into pieces, held the box in both hands, and heaved upward letting the pieces of sweet glop fly out. As best I could see, not one of them fell to the ground.

"That's it," I told the birds. "Goodbye. And tomorrow the world."

I drove back across the causeway blown and gritty. There was a shabby roadhouse on the way back to town and I got a shabby and birdless lunch there along with a good dry manhattan.

At the hotel, the bell captain handed me a message to call New York. I was sure I knew who was calling and what the message would be. I was in no hurry to say goodbye to nothing.

Nor had I any need to. I had already instructed one of my birds—one that would be headed for Labrador—to fly by with my answer. I had appointed B-7, the one with the most graceful nascelle marking starting just behind his mouth and flaring up and back to make a skull cap. And I had given him the best I had. I had aimed my buns, my bits of egg, and hunks of slaw at the other birds. At B-7 I had aimed most of the meat, though nearly half of it had been intercepted.

Yes, I suspect bribery is wasted on the world-bird. It comes for what you toss it, but it remembers nothing and it does not keep what promises it seems to make. Yet I sensed that B-7 and I had some sort of understanding. If he happened to be heading for Labrador, he certainly had no reason not to pass over New York. Once there, what could be more natural for him than to drop my message for me? He might, of course, be headed for Bombay first. Yet I felt that he had the look of Labrador to him

347

and would eventually head that way. Let him go by any detour. I didn't mind the delay. Time is time enough and why let a telephone hurry it?

In whatever time and by whatever bird or none, it is always time soon enough and nothing a telephone can enter into. Let it ring its fool head off. Given my choice, I will play my own games and make up my own rules for them, and by the rules of my game this message is for the birds to say through whatever walls there are and into the misfiled memos.

Goodbye.

ABOUT THE AUTHOR

John Ciardi, born in Boston, graduated from Tufts College in 1938 and received his A.M. from the University of Michigan in 1939. He joined the Army Air Corps in 1942 and saw service as an aerial gunner in the Pacific Theater.

After the war Mr. Ciardi taught for a number of years in various posts at Harvard and at Rutgers before becoming poetry editor and columnist at the *Saturday Review*. From 1955 to 1972 he was Director of the Bread Loaf Writers' Conference. Mr. Ciardi's most recent volume of poetry is the autobiographical *Lives of X*. His books of children's verse have won numerous awards, his incorruptibility speaking with happy directness to the incorruptibility of the very young.

The text of this book was set in Janson Linotype. Composed, printed and bound by Quinn & Boden Company, Inc., Rahway, New Jersey